THE MAKING OF INDIA

THE MAKING OF INDIA

GAMECHANGING TRANSITIONS

AKHILESH TILOTIA

RUPA

Published by
Rupa Publications India Pvt. Ltd 2015
7/16, Ansari Road, Daryaganj
New Delhi 110002

Sales Centres:

Allahabad Bengaluru Chennai
Hyderabad Jaipur Kathmandu
Kolkata Mumbai

ISBN: 978-81-291-3542-1

First impression 2015

10 9 8 7 6 5 4 3 2 1

The moral right of the author has been asserted.

Printed at Replika Press Pvt. Ltd, India

To my parents,
my wife Nikita,
and my daughter Kanak

CONTENTS

PREFACE

Over the last five years that I have had the opportunity of observing India's social, political and economic change, the country's mood (or at least, the mood of those who invest in India's capital markets) has moved from the depths of despair on a 'policy paralysis' to the excitement of *achche din*. Such descriptors are good indicators of how the market participants feel but rarely do justice to describing the complex process of change and tumult that India is going through. As we will see in this book, India is going through a multitude of transitions each connected with the other and influencing each other, as they proceed apace.

The ebb and flow of sentiments guides human actions and hence, make no mistake, the positivity that surrounds the 'can-do' approach is important. What, however, will make India actually achieve its goal of uplifting itself and its people into a more materially wealthy place with ease of living and doing business are hard-nosed decisions based on thought-through debates and discussions.

When we at Kotak started the GameChanger series half a decade ago, it focused on the institutional investor community to give it an idea of the various long-term macro changes taking place in society, economics and politics of India. For us the audience was the institutional investor who invested in the Indian equity market and our objective of highlighting these trends and themes was to help him take an informed call on the longer-term picture in India. We hoped this would help them in making a more convincing buy or sell argument about their holdings.

Over time, we realized that we were getting requests for our data-oriented and analytical reports from various parts of the group, whether the corporate banking channel or the wealth team servicing some of India's richest families. What worked, it seems, was that these reports would piece together data and analysis from varied sources and made out a coherent story about a big theme sweeping across India. This book is hence a natural culmination of putting together the various themes that we have worked on over the last many years and is a narrative of the changes taking place.

This book draws on the various reports that we have written over the last many years and hence seeks to be both a diary of what we are witnessing today in India and also a report on our prognosis of where we will potentially head. In cataloguing where we stand today, I have, using my training and background as an analyst, looked at the issue by deep-diving into data. In developing my prognosis I have attempted to bring together the inter-linkages between the various transitions.

This is of course easier said than done in India. There are limited high-quality or high-frequency data points that can be relied on to make assessments, judgements and eventually decisions. For example, in a country that expects to harvest a demographic dividend, the criticality of the information embedded in the labour market cannot be over-emphasized. In India, however, we survey our labour market only once in five years. An element which has not ceased to amaze me over the years is that opinions, ideologies and paths of actions remain steadfastly defined and hardly have any linkages with data. Maybe that is the defence mechanism that we have developed given our lack of working with data! Continuing with the theme on labour, the impact that NREGA has had on the availability of farm labour misses the point about how frequently it is used and the purpose the scheme serves. However, if one were to hear the two sides talk about it, the opinions and ideologies help define the path of action rather than any allusion to data.

In the need for a here-and-now analysis, changes taking place slowly seem to get missed out or not commented on in detail. For example, there is an amorphous understanding on why women have dropped out in such large numbers from the workforce in rural India and the implications that this can have on the lives of such women and for society as a whole in India. These issues will suddenly acquire an appeal when they surface even though their significance cannot be bottled into a short article, debate or discussion.

Across the various themes that we have explored in this book, I have put together the changes that are taking place in each and identified them with as high quality a data point as is available. Many of these data points not surprisingly emerge from the government. To measure social, political and economic changes, the government has traditionally been in the best position to collect and disseminate data both because it had the ability to spend on collecting data and because it would invariably be the repository of the data. As things currently stand, the quality of data is both poor and dated.

As the digital revolution starts percolating down, data will leave the preserve of the government and will start becoming available more broadly. For example, in developing the story on transportation in urban India, I struggled to get any recent good quality data on how frequently or fast people commute within cities. The best I could source was a report done in 2007. As crowd-sourced data starts to become available, transport design can immensely change using it. Data scientists, who are highly sought after in the tech industry will, hopefully soon, find a place of importance in matters of public policy.

One of the challenges of writing a book which seeks to encapsulate and document the changes that are permeating through India is that some of the changes can come by very quickly. In situations where change is brought on due to the correction of the imbalances that have built-up, situations change quickly if the price and information flow is fast and unfettered. For example, skilling the youth was considered to be a large challenge with a broken business model. However, as the futility of college education dawned on the people, vocational training courses which are connected with industry have started seeing a large number of registrations and placements. We will see similar changes taking place in urbanization (expansion of cities), agriculture (change in the composition of output), governance (freedom of information) and in consumption (premiumization).

One of the joys of writing this book is that these are changes that one is not only observing but is also an active part of. All the themes that I have encapsulated here are themes that I have seen actively play out in my own life. A question that I always get asked whenever we release a new report is how I chose this particular theme. My answer invariably is that whenever I see and feel a change around myself, I prompt myself to deep-dive into it.

All the themes that we will encounter in this book are those that I can—and I am sure a lot of the readers can—identify as our own: we are after all a part of the making of India. I am part of the demographic dividend that India is seeing: one of the many millions who are less than thirty-five years of age and hence form almost two-thirds of its population. As with many of my peers, the number of years that I spent educating myself is significantly higher than the education of the earlier generation. More importantly, this is true for the women in my family many of who are now a part of India's workforce. Not surprisingly, given that massive growth has taken place in the services sector over the last two decades, my wife and I are employed at an IT company and a banking/ securities company respectively. We do help in bringing in the dollars for the country: one by exporting her services, the other by advising foreign and domestic portfolio investors on their investments in India. We have both been drawn from smaller cities or suburban areas into Mumbai and are a part of the urbanization theme. My wife's office in Airoli is outside the conventional limits of Mumbai—we will see this point about the development of new business hubs in the urbanization story. Our food palate and also where we have our food has changed meaningfully over the last decade, as have our choices of clothes, housing, education and transport. We interact seamlessly with the government, the various businesses and fellow citizens on the digital network that India is now creating. Having said this, there are two observations that are in order here: (1) this is not a seamless transition and the various changes bring with them their own challenges and joys and (2) many of our fellow co-travellers from the demographic dividend cohort are in various phases of making all or many of these transitions.

Many of the changes that I have described in this book have already started taking place. They are and will be long-term secular themes which will continue to play out over multiple years. However, change comes unexpectedly and also from unexpected directions. I believe that many of the challenges that India now faces will almost similarly be resolved by the development and changes that are taking place quite far away. For example, India will see (and is seeing) an e-commerce revolution before the brick-and-mortar organized retail comes in or it will see the advent of mobile banks even as only a quarter of its population is currently served by traditional banks. The spread of communication technologies and collaborative tools is redesigning the shape of Indian cities which suffer from poor transport infrastructure.

In an exceptional paper, 'From Horse Power to Horsepower', Eric Morris (2007), then a PhD student at the University of California, identified the challenges that urban centres were facing in the late-nineteenth century: horse manure. This was because horses were the key mode of transport of both goods and people. The many thousands of horses that each city required were also helping generate significant horse manure: so much that there were public health concerns around the same. What changed the situation dramatically for the cities—and made the cities expand out dramatically from a small downtown core—was the invention of the internal combustion engine and the development of the car industry in the early part of the twentieth century.

Today personal transportation has again become a nightmare as cities struggle to create enough infrastructures to move their citizens around. Urban planners now worry about the falling proportion of public transport across the world as people move to personal vehicles. This also leads to loss-of-air-quality and increases commute time in cities. What could change this? It is hard to call: (1) Will communications technology become so strong that transportation needs fall—people will tele-commute rather than actually commute? (2) Smart cities which have far better information on the traffic situation at any given point in time (coupled with driverless cars) will lead to better traffic management? or (3) Something completely new and different will come up.

Looking at the problem from only one perspective tends to blinker us from potential GameChangers and hence it is important that we look at each problem in a composite manner. The ability to identify the inter-connectedness and tipping-points eludes the best of us but that should not stop us from trying. Such changes when they take place can be very meaningful and can quickly upend old ways of doing things and create some very interesting new opportunities. Recognizing such changes as they take place can create phenomenal wealth and precipitate meaningful social change. Such changes require cautious but pro-active handling from a governance point of view.

Let us look at two examples in India—one which has played out and the other which could possibly play out: in both the cases, the solution to the 'crisis' comes in from completely unexpected sources. The foreign exchange crisis of early 1990s made India open up its trading and manufacturing market: the idea was that if India is a more open country, foreign direct investment would come in which would help stabilize India's precarious foreign exchange position. At that time there was hardly any expectation that the industry that will bring in the much required dollars would be the IT industry and the remittances sent in by the diaspora. Especially over the last decade when the oil prices rose significantly, it is the inflow of dollars from the IT industry and remittances that helped keep India's foreign exchange reserves in place. If we look around today and wonder where the employment opportunities will emerge, I believe, the sudden emergence of new sectors will surprise us. The current expectations are that traditional industries like automobiles, textiles, retail and construction will create employment opportunities. However, it would not be surprising to see significant numbers of jobs being created in the industries associated with e-commerce: companies catering to the delivery and warehousing of the goods could become some of India's largest employers.

As we set out to make India, we should celebrate and nurture this change. Change that will come may be unexpected and in many cases, will not be painless. However, a vibrant economy which grows as it embraces change will create opportunities for those who are willing to take them. I hope what I am able to bring to you is a balanced perspective of where things stand and what will make them move. We will try and identify how, when and where the changes will emerge and we will outline them as GameChangers in each chapter. From a governance perspective, these trends need to be identified and nurtured, from an investor's perspective, there will be significant money to be made by investing in these themes and from a citizen's perspective, these transitions will make life easier to live so that we can pursue our dreams and happiness. I do hope this book provides food for thought to all these three audiences.

THE MAKING OF INDIA

Thousands of transitions

INDIA IS IN the throes of many simultaneous transitions: a young demographic is preparing to launch itself into the rapidly evolving economic structure. Their ability to skill themselves for the opportunities thrown open by a changing India can lead to a savings and consumption boom. The opportunities for such advancement that India has thrown up over the last quarter of a century have been primarily in the services sector: it is now hoping to turn into a manufacturing powerhouse. In any case, India is no longer dependent on agriculture for its output and this means that cities are taking centre stage in driving growth. Among all these transitions, the relationship of the Indian citizen with its government, its society, its businesses and its money is changing fast and is led and abetted by a communication and digital revolution. Each of these aspects presents many practically unbounded opportunities but which also requires the effective channelization of energies.

The idea of this book is to give you a big picture view of where things presently stand in the making of India and where they could reasonably head. We will substantiate our analysis with data, facts and a reasonable line of thinking. India will need to undertake many different types of changes as it deals with a new and rapidly changing reality. Some will require that the efficiency enhancing nature of markets be allowed to come in (for example, in the case of land and labour laws) and some will require that the government itself becomes a credible player in its own right, especially in the case of 'public goods' like *bijli, sadak, paani, shiksha, swasthya* and *suraksha* (power, roads, water, education, health and security). Connecting its vast young population to productive employment opportunities will set the tone for India's social cohesion and material upliftment. Despite its impressive progress, India remains a place where people still do not have access to basic goods and services, or in many cases, access to even their identity and title to their properties. In cases where people are left behind, identifying such people and making sure government interventions reach them will require a large scale use of technology.

An overview of change—but not of its inevitability

India's success (though admittedly, this comparison is relative to India's own earlier abysmal records and not with the best in the world) in the field of maternal healthcare and infant mortality has meant that kids now stand a much better chance of making it into adulthood. As this realization swept through various parts of the country in different periods of time (starting from South India and then heading onwards to the North), people have started having lesser number of children. Indeed, the cohort of kids born in India between the census years 1991–2001 was the largest—the cohort born between 2001 and 2011 was almost exactly equal in size to this cohort and all future cohorts are expected to be smaller. The implication of this is clear: India's demographic dividend has already been born and over the next few decades will be powering the rise in its workforce. India's workforce of 484 million people (in 2012) has the potential to increase to 850 million by 2025. This compares with the peak workforce of 830 million that China is expected to have in 2016. As China loses numbers in its workforce, potentially 366 million people can join the workforce in India over a decade and a half. However, women have hardly been a part of India's workforce. Whether they finally join in and become partners in India's progress will determine the power of India's demographic transition.

As the youth of India has started coming into the workforce, the structure of India's economy is changing fast. India has miserably failed in moving people out of agriculture with still half the workforce stuck in an activity that contributes progressively lesser and lesser to its economic output. Agriculture's share of output as a proportion to the overall output has fallen from a third to a sixth over the course of the last two decades. If half the population produces only a sixth of the output, it is no wonder that it is impoverished. The next generation of farmers are increasingly keen on moving away from agriculture not just out of desperation but they are also motivated by the desire to join the bandwagon of growth unleashed by the manufacturing and services sector. This points us to the challenge of skilling these people for the various jobs that they will want to look out for.

India's efforts at educating its youth to power this transition have been a mixed bag. Government schemes have brought around 97 per cent of the young children to schools. However, the quality of schooling is so obviously poor that parents have increasingly shifted their kids to private schools. According to the Annual Status of Education Report (ASER), 2013, in rural India, 29 per cent of the children went to private schools in 2013; up from 15 per cent in 2005. The poor quality of education in India, as further noted in the said report, means that a vast majority of children are not prepared at the foundational level to pick up skills that will eventually be required in the job market. What India lacks is a parallel track of education where children (say in their early to mid-teens) can move to finding the vocations that they find interesting or remunerative. India is still stuck with the model of primary, secondary and tertiary education. As we will explore in more detail later, this system now over-produces graduates who have gone through their tertiary education but significantly under-produces qualified people with vocational skills. No wonder we shake our heads in dismay when we find that the starting salaries being offered to engineers is similar to what cab drivers make.

It is obvious that when the rate of growth of the economy is as fast as it has been over the last quarter of a century, old work profiles quickly change. Newer and more varied skills come to be in demand as the nature of the work and output itself changes. A simple way to think about the quickness of the rate of change is this: if an economy grows at 7 per cent every year in real terms, it doubles in output over a decade and quadruples over two. A generation is typically defined as a period of 20–25 years and hence in less than a generation, the size of the economy (and hence, also incomes) grow four times. As the economy grows four times in size, the nature of jobs in the economy undoubtedly changes. This has two important implications: (1) the next generation cannot do what the previous generation was doing—this is what is encouraging people out of agriculture and rural India and more radically, is making caste system less relevant, at least in urban India and (2) the mode of skill development has to take into account the fact that there will be a dearth of teachers—those who can make money in the new economy will do so rather than become teachers.

One common lament about India's growth story is that it has not latched on to manufacturing led growth. The idea that India should be a hub of manufacture is a romantic one but beset with the reality of poor infrastructure both in hard terms like availability of power or last mile roads and also softer issues like enabling regulations and the availability and commitment of labour. India has, over the last decade, invested significantly in hard infrastructure of power and transport (roads, rails, ports, etc.) even as it struggles to figure out the right prices to charge for them to make these assets economically viable and propel further investments. The focus is now increasingly shifting to softer issues like skilled labour law reforms. Corporate India and small and medium enterprises (SME) have found a way out of rigid labour laws by employing contract labour. However, this *jugaad* solution is suboptimal for all: the employers do not have any commitment to the labour and hence do not upgrade their skills and the labourers do not have a certainty of getting their pay checks. India needs to recognize the reality of poor labour productivity and update its laws to reflect the current reality. Mercifully, India realized that manufacturing requires scale and hence over the last decade or two has progressively done away with small scale reservations.

India's lack of prowess in manufacturing is partly to blame for its poor foreign exchange position. Even though India had around US$ 300 billion in reserves in 2013, it suffered a big run on its currency as its trade deficit ballooned. India imported around US$ 500 billion worth of goods and exported only US$ 300 billion leading to a trade deficit of US$ 200 billion. This prompted the reiteration of calls for India to step up its exports or reduce its imports bill by manufacturing goods here. This will no doubt be an important component of India's strategy to employ its millions and to create its foreign exchange buffers. However, one must not lose sight of the fact that India's services economy, especially the IT industry brought in ~US$ 67 billion in revenues and the Indian diaspora sent in another US$ 65 billion in remittances to India in FY2014. Our external balance too reflects the strength of the Indian services industry.

The services sector remained somewhat less intruded by rules and laws framed by the government. This happened broadly because the boom in service sectors (like IT, telecom, pharma, banking and financial services) came in from new sectors or from sectors where the government behemoths could not compete effectively as their monopoly was taken away. As the services sector has come to dominate India's economy, it is easy to visualize how the sons and daughters of farmers and agricultural labourers will knock at the doors of companies in these sectors looking for jobs.

The corollary of a growing and dominating services economy is that most of the employment creation will take place in cities that are already established. India's urbanization will be the expanding out of the current cities and will not be in the creation of new cities. In the era when manufacturing led the growth of an economy, new cities came up around manufacturing hubs. In a services–dominated economy, older cities expand out. India is also witnessing a trend in what the government still recognizes as rural India: around a quarter of India's rural population lives in villages that have more than 5,000 people. Such large villages would be classified as urban in most countries in the world and no wonder they too are demanding service quality levels for their utilities (roads, power, water) that match urban standards. Unfortunately, the urban standards themselves are nothing to write home about. India has run down many of its urban utilities under the garb of hypocrisy: pricing the services of the utilities low so that the poor can afford them. However, it so impoverishes the utilities that the poor can hardly be served by them. Two sectors that will be the largest beneficiaries of urbanization will be the real estate and transport sectors. However, the nature of these sectors will radically alter.

In our chapter on consumption, we will see that even if we extend out our analysis to 2025, Indians across various economic classes will still spend, on average, 65 per cent of their wallet on basics like food, housing, health, education and transport; that leaves them with little to spend on leisure and a better quality of life. Unfortunately, for the lowest economic strata of society, the proportion will be as high as 71 per cent and for the highest strata the proportion will be 56 per cent. An effective public service delivery will be key to giving millions of households' access to a better quality of life where they can move beyond spending on the basics.

We have taken it as a given in our above discussion that India's economic growth will continue. The last few years have shown us that such an assumption is questionable and it requires focussed and diligent work to make growth happen. Most of these transitions are happening by the sheer force of the economic and social energies unleashed by successive actions and decisions that India has taken or indeed, in some cases, not taken. India cannot expect economic growth to be its birth-right simply because it will be enjoying a demographic dividend. In many economic and social aspects, India is perched rather precariously: we found that when India went through a foreign-exchange-flutter in 2013 or when its women feel unsafe to step out to work and hence don't join the workforce. The biggest agenda for Indian policy makers should be to connect its youth to productive jobs which can bring home the dollars. All the transitions will be obvious corollaries if India achieves success in this.

Private cost of public failure—making it easier to live and to do business

This brings us to the complex relationship that the Indian citizenry shares with the markets and businesses in general. Markets and prices, whether hidden or visible, have shaped our society, economy, demography and urbanization. India's difficult relationship with them has meant that it has tried to muzzle them sometimes, paid heed many a times but mostly, it has been flummoxed and surprised by the discovery of prices and the impact that they have on economic or social outcomes.

The function of markets is to produce two important prices of information: (1) the quantum of demand and supply that will clear and (2) the price at which it will clear. As practitioners of the art of planning, Indians are able to create reasonable estimates of the demand and supply sides of the equations in most cases (whether it is for agriculture, industries or utilities). However, given the historical narrative of socialism, Indians have had a troubled relationship with markets and prices. There has been an instinctive urge that Indian governments have had to use their rather visible hand to throttle markets and adjust prices in the economy, making it difficult to do business in the country.

In many instances, where the response required is either increasing supply or managing demand or creating a better infrastructure to link the two, Indian authorities have ended up distorting the market. Think, for example, of water and sewage or public transport in urban India. In both cases, as in the case of many other utilities like power, the pricing of the service of the utility is kept very low. The outcome is that city utilities do not generate enough resources to invest in creating the required infrastructure. People then get either completely excluded from the services of the utilities or get the outputs rationed. The rich (or the relatively better off) are able to create a parallel infrastructure for themselves at a significant private cost to themselves (think of water tankers or two- and four-wheelers) while the poor remain dependent on poor quality services that the utilities provide (water available only for a few hours a day or over-crowded buses and trains) and the hand-outs that politicians can arrange for them or end up paying a heavy 'black-market' premium.

This story plays out in sector after sector and we look at three examples: education (costly private schools for those who can afford and a right to education for those who cannot), food (private grain market for those can buy; a poor quality public distribution system for those who cannot) and health (pricey hospitals and doctor care for those who can afford it; a less-than-optimum healthcare for those who cannot). The point of discussion here is not whether the utilities of water, education, power, food, etc. should be in private hands or public: India has had a troubled experience in trying to make public-private partnerships work. The point here is that utilities (like any economic participants) require a reasonable inflow of funds and effective governance to offer good quality services.

The private cost that this public failure imposes on private citizens is detrimental to India on two counts: (1) the cost being high (as the creation of parallel infrastructure denies it scale benefits to reduce costs) forces the spending of a large part of India's wallet on basic necessities keeping Indians tethered to a lower quality life and (2) public failure hits the poor and the vulnerable the hardest. The failure of public utilities is hence not an option for India. Public utilities (that is, utilities run for general public purposes and not necessarily run by the public sector) have to be effective and efficient competitors to private alternatives. For example, a metro train can be run by either the public or the private sector. The critical thing is that it can and should be an effective competitor to the purchase of two- or four-wheelers.

The need for government to be a credible player is especially true in the case of public goods like *bijli, sadak, paani, shiksha, swasthya* and *suraksha* (power, roads, water, education, health and security). One aspect that we will continue to see is that of public failure and the cost of it being borne by private individuals. We call this the private cost of public failure. We see that in the (1) gensets that Indians buy since power availability and quality is uncertain (this means that they are reconciled to making their own power at Rs 15 per unit while the utilities shy away from raising prices to say Rs 5–7 a unit to make the many idling power plants viable); (2) the two-wheelers and four-wheelers that they buy since they cannot rely on public transport (which means that citizens will individually spend between Rs 2 and Rs 10 per km on their two wheelers and four wheelers without counting depreciation but city buses will still run at Re 1 or so per km); (3) the flourishing businesses of water purifiers and bottled water (where we pay anywhere between Re 1 and Rs 20 per litre of water but grudge paying our utilities Rs 0.10 per litre); (4) the mushrooming of private schools (where the concept of fees exists as opposed to 'free' education in public schools); (5) the wide disparity in services and access to health services between the rich and the poor; and (6) gated communities and private security agencies that have started protecting Indians individually.

What is a cost for one is revenue for another and as our models and discussions will show these will indeed be areas of business growth. It is hence important not to lose sight of the vast entrepreneurial and investment opportunities that this will throw up. In all these cases, the answer is not simply resorting to privatization but increasing the accountability and efficiency of the services being provided. One way to improve accountability and efficiency is to price the services being offered at economic rates. This incentivizes users (citizens) to demand better outcomes. What is given away free is many-a-time not valued. India remains a poor country; it needs to evolve a model where access to public goods is not blocked because a citizen is unable to pay for them. However, bringing in efficiency into the delivery of public goods will require a focus on governing them well and pricing them fairly rather than letting them be 'privatized' by stealth.

The interesting aspect is that India has had positive experiences to report as prices moved around either due to the invisible hand of the market or the iron hand of the government. Let us look at a few examples:

(1) The large increases in minimum support prices (MSPs) in cereals over the last decade have led to a sharp rise in their output. Between 2005 and 2013, the minimum support prices of wheat and paddy more than doubled. Wheat MSPs went up to Rs 13.5 per kg from Rs 6.5 per kg while paddy MSPs went up to Rs 12.8 per kg from Rs 5.9 per kg. Over the same period, wheat output grew to 94 million tons from 69 million tons and paddy went up to 104 million tons from 83 million tons.

(2) A similar story plays out in the dairy sector over the same period. Prices of milk at the farm level rose to Rs 30 a litre from Rs 12 a litre; the production jumped to 128 million tons from 95 million tons.

(3) Fruits and vegetables, the prices of which routinely feature as the cause of high inflation in India, have seen their output almost double in less than a decade. The total output of fruits and vegetables in India over the same period went up to 243 million tons from 152 million tons.

(4) The wages of engineering students rose so quickly and so much that millions wanted to becomes engineers. India will now graduate 1.5 million engineers in 2016 which is more than China (1.1 million) and the US (0.1 million) combined! As supply has increased and demand has slowed, Indian engineering colleges are now witnessing a sharp drop in enrolments.

(5) The price of agricultural labour rose so quickly and so fast (in part due to MG-NREGA), that it priced out labour from agriculture and

replaced it with tractors. The average rural wage rose to Rs 178 per day in 2013 from Rs 70 in 2007. Tractor prices also went up but the increase was proportionately was significantly lesser. An average tractor sold for Rs 450,000 in 2013, up from Rs 313,000 in 2007. In this transition, women were hard hit as we will see.

There is of course hope that the price mechanism—and a general ease of doing business—will find its roots in India. One of the most ambitious projects in India is delivering the benefits to the poor via cash transfers. There has been significant focus and debate on the ability of the system to deliver cash and for the participants to benefit from such cash (there is a paternalistic fear that the cash transferred will be blown away, for example, in alcohol). However, the process is carrying forward with more than 700 million people now enrolling for Aadhar (even as the Supreme Court has made Aadhar non-mandatory for direct benefits transfers).

The more important aspect to focus on is the corollary of giving cash to the poor instead of sending them, for example, grains or fuel. The amount that needs to be paid will need to be determined with reference to a market price. For example, let us say that it is decided that those below poverty line are entitled to 10 kg of rice every month at, say, Re 1 per kg. Now in order to calculate the sum of money to be transferred into the account of the beneficiary, we will need to know the market price for rice. Assuming that rice costs Rs 20 per kg in the market, the government will need to transfer Rs 190 into the account of the beneficiary this month. The corollary is hence this: if the beneficiaries are being given cash that means market prices will prevail for the goods so that the value of the transfer can be calculated.

Let us see why this is important and we will stick with the example of food. Indian diets, at the bottom of the pyramid, are caught in a cereal trap. Historically, governments have found it easy to procure and distribute food grains (there is a related point here: as the Indian farms have fragmented, the marginalized farmers have increasingly turned to cereal cultivation; the richer landowners have steadily moved into or diversified into cash crops and horticulture). The government hence finds it politically wise to keep the support price of cereals high, which makes it remunerative for marginal farmers to produce the cereals which, as we noted earlier, have seen a spectacular supply response. Similarly, India's subsidized public distribution system (PDS) recycles these cereals to those below the poverty line, perforce making cereals the default choice of food for the lower economic strata. India will need to move out of this cereals trap. Just as Indians who can afford to have their own transport and water as they grow richer, they also abandon PDS when they can do so and clamour for more protein in their diet.

The government can still choose to pay a high price to farmers (globally, especially in the US, there have been instances of idle payments also: governments paying farmers to just keep their lands fallow). Government can also determine the compensation to beneficiaries of the public distribution system. However, in all of this, the price of the cereals itself will be determined by the demand–supply dynamics in the country and not by government intervention. A few years of this mechanism working will rid the country of its excess food grains inventory better than any intervention.

This is of course no idle idealism or starry-eyed dream. Indian agriculture responded almost in a textbook fashion when prices of pulses shot up dramatically to Rs 100 per kg from around Rs 40 a kg in 2009. Since the government could not and did not materially influence these prices (its procurement machinery is limited primarily to wheat and rice), Indian farmers quickly turned their attention to pulses. India's production increased to 19 million tons from 14 million tons in a couple of years between 2009 and 2011 and pulses no longer dominate the headlines on inflation.

If the idea of direct benefit transfers takes off, we should expect to see prices being freed across a wide variety of sectors, for example, in fuels and fertilizers. Pump-sets, which guzzle low priced diesel, created irrigation potential but also distorted the water tables. Similarly, the low prices of urea have vitiated the ratio in which fertilizers should be used in India. Many of these aspects of Indian agriculture will change. The changes will lead to a different way of doing things and like any other change these too will create a new set of winners and losers. It will create opportunities but will also threaten entrenched interests.

Ultimately, the point is about making it easier for Indians to do business without the government distorting economic variables. For the government, the most effective way to play with the price mechanism (in its quest to achieve a welfare intention) has been to create rules such that the process of freely transmitting the price information becomes difficult within the system. At the extreme, governments have resorted to banning or distorting markets directly—something which continues to plague the agriculture sector most frequently. This has, as we will see across various transitions, forced the onus and price of change on private individuals.

We have used the example of 'public goods' here to identify the challenges citizens and businesses face in dealing with the welfare intentions of the government but this conflict of objectives remains valid across a wide swathe of the economic landscape (closed land markets for farmers or difficult hiring and firing laws for industries). The answer, as we shall see, will lie in devising solutions such that the welfare intention is not mixed up with price distortion. The role of the government should not be to be an economic player but to be a facilitator of governance between different economic players. For the government to play that role, it needs to be clear on its objectives and the choices it is willing to make.

Making governance work—defining the choices India needs to make

There are phases in the history of a country which shape its character and destiny. Such a phase offers moments to a country that it needs to seize so as to convert possibilities into opportunities. For a country of the size of India, decisions and choices made during such times will shape not just its own history but that of humanity as a whole.

India's articulation of a vision of its future is important. It is a *sine qua non* so that we know the direction that we are headed to and whether we are indeed traversing that or not. In a noisy and boisterous democracy that India is, creating a common dream is in itself a tremendous act of bringing together various thoughts, ideas and aspirations. This requires its leaders to synthesize the message that the voters and citizens are saying or indeed, keeping unsaid. It also requires leaders to shape what it is that the citizens should want. The leaders must plant the dream in the minds and hearts of the citizens of India.

India's leaders started the country's journey as an independent nation by labelling dreams of the citizens as a tryst with destiny; a tryst is a private romantic rendezvous between lovers. India believed, rightly so, in the superiority of means over the end. The journey was its own reward. There was no end point in the rendezvous with destiny: it was the journey, the rendezvous itself that was to be cherished. India laid down major pieces of social agendas: mending the reality of illiteracy, casteism and religious dissention, strengthening the country against the fissiparous tendency of internal and external forces to break it and fighting against its abject poverty.

India has been spectacularly successful in its objective of keeping the country together. This has surprised many of its obituary writers. It has fought bravely in its fight against illiteracy and ill-health; its affirmative actions have tried to mainstream many communities. Projects of building a society and preserving its unity never reach a conclusion, they require constant nurturing. However, India's successes in these projects have sharpened the focus on its third agenda: its fight against poverty. In spite of a bout of very healthy economic growth over the last quarter of a century, India still remains a relatively poor country. Poverty, we must note here, is not just a material concept or about the lack of money, it is about the unavailability of opportunities and the inability to have aspirations for a better life.

It is increasingly clear, indeed clichéd, to say that Indians are now more aspirational. Their aspirations and desires have been unlocked, we are told, by economic changes (or as they are popularly called, reforms) over the last quarter of a century. It is considered reasonable to draw the causation that since the growth spurt of the last quarter century unleashed the aspirations, the aspirations themselves need further and faster growth to satiate them. Economic growth, the narrative goes, is an end in itself as it will help meet current aspirations and stoke further desires. This cycle will evolve into a vortex of virtuous cycles and take India into the land of material comfort and well-being.

What is not clear in such an apple-pie and motherhood statement is the inherent contradictions of aspiration. Are these aspirations about individual wealth or for society as a whole? Are the aspirations only about material wealth or to borrow a phrase from China, about a more harmonious society? How are the gains of the economy to be shared?

Are the gains being shared at all or are they getting concentrated in the hands of a few? Indians have aspirations for a good life but are we willing (or indeed, in many cases, able) to pay for our aspirations? The pay here refers, as we can well imagine, not just to money but to the willingness and ability to invest our energies and time in meeting our collective aspirations.

There are, as these preliminary questions show, many ways to think about our path of growth and then also to think about how to distribute the fruits of that growth. The choices that a nation faces and then goes on to make are made in the context of history and the expectations of a future. The history of a nation and its people shape its thoughts and ideas, its fears and aspirations. The vision of the destination it wants to reach and also the path it wants to take to reach there will determine the choices a country makes today. Choices made today will lead to more choices in the future. All this makes it important that we have a good grasp and articulation of both the direction that we want to take and the path that takes us there.

There is no fixed or final destination that India needs to reach: like its social and unity projects, the economic project too will remain a continuous work-in-progress. The process of solving many of the conundrums listed earlier is a gigantic task. Many questions will need to be asked, ways of doing things will need to change, old hierarchies will need to give way to new structures, many trade-offs will need to be made, many compromises sought and finally, a path will need to be cleared and trod upon.

On a more practical and every-day level, the way Indians deal with their government is changing and this relationship will need to continuously evolve for the better via increased transparency and responsiveness. India's government is helping create a digital identity for all Indians and is moving many of its interactions with the citizenry online. The way India banks (or currently a large number of them don't) will change as money moves online and on to the mobile. As Indian citizens' identity, their interactions with their government and their money digitizes, they will get an opportunity to easily and effectively communicate their aspirations. There will be glitches on the way but the path of change has already been taken.

Framing the discussion for more fact-based decisions

India is sitting on a momentous opportunity. Its rate of growth may have slowed somewhat over the last few years but the promise of the great Indian growth story has not gone out. In chapter after chapter, we explore the size of the opportunity, and more important, the potential that such an opportunity has to change India's economic and social face.

The change will not be painless. It will create its losers and winners and hence agitations and celebrations. Sections of societies will benefit and some will lose out and the intermediation between the winners and losers will be the key to political and social stability. Those who lose out will need to be co-opted back into the game of India's growth. For example, as industrialization and urbanization proceed apace in India, farmers should be able to benefit from the rapid rise in value of their land. Forced land acquisitions will only threaten and derail the process. The ability to spread the benefits of growth will be key to its stability.

It is important to emphasize that the losses need not necessarily come because someone else won, though this is not to deny that such transfers-of-value have indeed taken place and hence, vitiated the cause of change and growth. Economic growth is, by definition, not a zero-sum game as there is more to go around. Losses can happen if the signals are read wrongly or if a way of doing business disappears. For example, millions rushed into getting engineering degrees creating a supply shock which led to a stagnant salary base and lack of jobs for newly qualified engineers. However, the price mechanism continues to point out that there is still a severe shortage of doctors in the country. Similarly, manual agricultural labour will increasingly get priced out. The solution has to make them battle ready to be employable in other sectors and to connect them to jobs there.

The agenda for Indians and their leaders will be to keep a sharp eye out on the evolution and develop a deep understanding of the changes that come along with rapid economic progress. Such changes typically bubble under the surface before suddenly manifesting themselves. The changes that come about may themselves not be what society decides it wants and there will be mid-way course corrections and reversals. In all of these, the leaders and the citizenry will need to keep an eye on the bigger picture. It is critical hence that the bigger picture is clearly understood and communicated and this presents a crucial challenge of its own: India is a land of opinions.

Everybody has the democratic right to have and express an opinion and in a vast majority of the cases there is a tendency to jump to offering opinions with gusto. Indians possibly do justice to the saying that if you ask five for opinions, you will get six different ones and with the caveat to change it every time. As television and internet spreads in India with their ubiquitous surveys, questions and debates, opinion making in India is fast turning into an instant coffee. It is wanted here and now and strong! In the rush to have and air instant opinions, we sometime lose sight of the facts on which to base an opinion. We end up opining on the current crisis, the current issue-at-hand, the current fad without sometimes delving deeply into the inter-connectedness of the issue with other aspects.

Let us, for example, look at the issue of urbanization. Urbanization and industrialization will, even under optimistic projections, double the land required from current levels of 3 per cent to 6 per cent of India's land area. For some context, almost half of India's area (48 per cent) is under cultivation. Even a doubling of the area under urbanization from 3 per cent to 6 per cent will mean that the proportion of arable land will fall to 45 per cent from the current 48 per cent (that is also assuming that urbanization does not proceed on fallow land which accounts for 13 per cent of India's land area). For the people who benefit or lose, the changes will be life-altering but the overall context needs to be kept in mind and highlighted at frequent and relevant forums.

In many cases, the state is non-existent or under-prepared and overwhelmed by these changes. The onus will be on private individuals to create a discussion based on facts and reasoned opinion and bring in transparency and accountability.

Pursuing dreams and happiness

This book is not an exhortation to mindless pursuit of economic growth at any cost. We have, simplistically, come to associate our project of drawing ourselves out of poverty and into economic well-being with one single statistic: the rate of growth of India's GDP. Looking at this statistic is like looking at the rate of sales growth of a company. It conveys valuable information in and of itself but does not address many other critical nuances. To carry forward our analogy, just knowing the rate of sales growth in a company does not tell us, for example, whether it is paying its employees better or rewarding its shareholders more. Indeed, it does not even tell us if the company is growing profitably such that there is enough to share with all the stakeholders. And yes, what we have just measured is a 'flow-statistic', it does not tell us how strained or well-kept the balance sheet of the company is. This is not to trivialize the importance of the metric. Indeed, if there is no growth in the sales of a company, most probably all stakeholders will suffer (or at the very least, fight amongst themselves for a share of an ever-smaller pie). It is easy to see how simplifying the narrative of our discussion takes away the complexities of the discussion and how the nuances can get lost.

The end goal of growth in any country should be to create better lives for its citizens. What is a good life is a complex question? It includes, among other things, income and wealth (everyone should have enough of material goods and the ability to pay for them), social order (a reasonable and equitable distribution of wealth, incomes and most important, equal opportunities), health outcomes (longer life expectancies, lesser pollution, better gender ratios) and basic freedoms. As these indicators point out they will continue to remain a work-in-progress without an end destination.

India's dreams of where it wants to go and how will shape the lives of not just one-sixth of humanity that lives here but will influence the world. The choices we make and deliver upon will create large ripples across the economic, social and political fabric of the world. If India does indeed employ its upcoming millions well it can create a consumption, savings and investment boom. More important, it can lead a massive surge of humanity out of the current gut-wrenching poverty and appalling social indicators. A strong economy with well-to-do citizens will command the respect globally that India believes it should get.

This book is an attempt to lay down the facts and create a discussion. We hope that the churning of the facts and analyses in this book will give you the basis of making your own vision of the path and destiny for India. So, let the dialogue begin.

CONNECTING INDIA'S YOUTH TO JOBS

Period of transition

TWO DECADES OF strong economic growth has changed the structure of the economy even as many facets of it have struggled to keep pace. As an economy doubles in size (which in India's case has happened twice over—once every decade), it meaningfully alters the fabric of society and the type of employment opportunities that are available. Social rules and laws which held the society together tend to burst at the seams as a new reality takes hold.

Along with India's youth joining the workforce in increasing numbers, various transitions are simultaneously required in India's labour market:

(1) A move away from agriculture.
(2) A need for moving to organized employment from unorganized employment.
(3) A more knowledge-and training-based workforce than just application of traditional skills.
(4) A gravitation to urban India for work from the rural birth place.

These transitions are typical of economic growth anywhere. Ensuring that India capitalizes on these transitions will be the key to harnessing the demographic dividend.

(1) **Transition from agriculture.** As the nature of India's economy changes, we expect to see the profile of Indian labour shift to

manufacturing and services from agriculture. Indian agriculture, while employing approximately half of its 484 million strong workforce (as of end of financial year 2012), produces only a sixth or less—and falling—proportion of its GDP. There is a significant opportunity to transition India from its agricultural base to a more diversified industrial and services-oriented space. Given this disproportionately low contribution of agriculture to final output, it should come as no surprise that a large portion of India which is dependent on agriculture is poor.

An enabling support structure of this transfer (or rather, an important precondition) is the ability of farmers and their next generations to sell off their existing (in a vast majority of cases, suboptimal) land parcels. This will require significant investments in (a) strengthening property rights via, among other things, digitizing property records and (b) making a more transparent and liquid market in agricultural land transactions (for example, by doing away the artificial restrictions of a farmer selling to another farmer).

A massive shift of the labour force from agriculture needs to take place to improve productivity per person in this sector, which is among the lowest in the world. Every other developing economy has taken the route of moving its population from agriculture to manufacturing and then on to the services sector. India has followed a unique path in that it has a services-dominated economy in value terms even as a large majority of the labour force still stagnates in agriculture.

(2) **Transition from an unorganized to an organized workforce**. Only 18 per cent of India's labour force is regular wage or salaried according to the sixty-eighth round of the NSSO survey for 2012. An even smaller proportion of this is the organized workforce (a large proportion of the salaried/regular wage people are also part of the informal workforce).

To understand the poor conditions of work in India, we turn again to NSSO. NSSO's sixty-seventh round data for the year-ending June 2011 estimated that India had around 58 million non-agricultural unincorporated enterprises (this basically means that these were enterprises that were not in the field of agriculture and they were not incorporated as a company or as a partnership, or very simply, they were basically small entities). They were almost equally split between the sectors of manufacturing, trading and other services; 49 million of these 58 million enterprises were own account enterprises (OAEs, or simply, proprietorships) which represented the famous (forced) entrepreneurial spirit of India. This is more a matter of survival than risk-taking as these enterprises suffer from lack of scale and capital and work at poor productivity levels. These enterprises employed 108 million workers or more than a fifth of India's 484 million workforce. Each non-OAE had no more than five employees on an average. More than two out of five operated out of homes of households/proprietors and one-seventh of them had no fixed location of business. Less than two in five of these enterprises had any permanent structure to run their businesses. On an average these enterprises had a top-line of less than Rs 0.5 million and produced a gross value added (GVA) of around Rs 0.1 million only and employees got paid around Rs 0.06 million, much lower than the per capita income in India.

Unfortunately, in the last decade for which data is available (as we note in Table 2.1) the transition has not yet started to take place. This has led to multiple instances of labour fights across various factories in India where 'contract' labour was paid much lesser than the 'on-roll' workers for pretty much the same task. India has made it terribly difficult for companies to hire and fire employees based on demand conditions. The industry responded by developing a 'flexible' unorganized market. We later look at the implication of a small 'organized' workforce which corners most of the value-add. If more than a fifth of the workforce is stuck in these low-end activities, this can be a low-hanging fruit to propel economic growth. Allowing firms to build scale by (a) up-skilling OAEs, (b) providing easier access to capital and (c) making property and business rights more secure, India can kick-start its growth engine as well as provide better quality of life for a large number of its workforce. The upcoming demographic dividend should not be lost to the trap of forced low-scale entrepreneurship.

Table 2.1: A majority of India's workforce continues to remain self-employed; only a small proportion has a regular job

Employment status, various NSSO rounds, June year-ends, 2005, 2012 (%)

	Rural	Urban	Total
NSS—68th round; July 2011-June 2012			
Self employed	56.0	42.0	52.0
Casual labour	35.0	15.0	30.0
Regular wage/salaried	9.0	43.0	18.0
NSS—61st round; July 2004-June 2005			
Self employed	56.5	43.4	51.0
Casual labour	34.6	11.8	33.5
Regular wage/salaried	8.8	44.8	15.6
Difference between 68th and 61st rounds			
Self employed	(0.5)	(1.4)	1.0
Casual labour	0.4	3.2	(3.5)
Regular wage/salaried	0.2	(1.8)	2.4

Source: Various NSSO rounds; Kotak Institutional Equities research

(3) **Transition from traditional skills to knowledge and training based occupations**. India's current labour market is not knowledge-intensive. It is dominated by traditional skills like farming and manual labour. A transition linked to India becoming a larger player in the services and/or manufacturing space, will require the movement of the Indian labour pool from these traditional skill-based activities to more knowledge-based activities.

At a more fundamental level, as the growth over the last quarter century has changed the nature of India's economy; it opened up various avenues of work that were previously non-existent. Typically the signal of price helped identify the sectors where there was a supply-demand mismatch of skills whether it was in the case of engineers or pilots. Wage levels of unskilled or semi-skilled workers have grown significantly over the last few years signalling their requirement in the economy. Market dynamics in this field have been closely influenced by government policies of welfare: we will delve into this in more detail later in the chapter.

(4) **Transition from rural to urban India**. Around two-third of those becoming eligible to work currently live in rural areas as 69 per cent of India's population still lived in rural areas as of 2011. However, as many other countries have seen, India too will see a migration of working age people from rural India to urban India. As we will see later in the chapter on urbanization, urban India too will grow and expand and encompass what are currently rural areas. If the services-led model of growth continues for India, the ability to quickly skill people who are moving out of agriculture, will be critical. We explore another geographical aspect (north versus south India) in a subsequent section.

Addressing these transitions partially or individually is suboptimal. For example, India is seeing a move out of agricultural labour but the labour force is accumulating as informal workers in urban India. This does not increase productivity; it merely transfers the issue from one area to another. Government schemes sometimes militate against the creation of jobs: the large increase in minimum wages due to NREGA has led to pricing out of millions of women from the rural workforce in India. The populace needs to be equipped with the right skills to capitalize on the transitions. When an agricultural labourer with uncertain employment prospects moves to an urban/semi-urban area with a more secure job (secured via a skill that is valued in the manufacturing or services sector), he/she contributes actively to gain in productivity and thereby, is an active contributory to the economic growth and the making of the country.

Deep-diving into the numbers

Over the next ten years till 2025, 250 million people will be eligible to join the workforce. We count people over fifteen years of age, the minimum legal age for employment in India, or the completion of their studies, whichever is later (see Figure 2.1). This means that more than 2 million people will become eligible to work every month. India will be one of the very few large economies which will see such a significant rise in its labour force. Many of the larger economies will see a stagnation or even decline in their workforces, especially China. Surprisingly, even as India is expecting to see such a large inflow of people looking for jobs, it is not uncommon to hear of labour/employee shortages in India. This paradox is what makes it fascinating to explore whether India will be able to reap the benefits of its youthful population by matching these young people with employment opportunities.

Figure 2.1: Education investments paying off—the population is expected to get more educated with time

Chart showing potential quality of work force joining each year (mn)

	Illiterate	Till V	Till VIII	Till IX	Till XII	Diploma	Graduation	PG
2015	5.1	4.7	3.6	2.8	4.6	0.2	2.5	0.5
2016	5.0	4.4	3.7	2.9	4.7	0.2	2.6	0.5
2017	4.9	4.1	3.8	3.0	4.9	0.3	2.6	0.5
2018	3.5	4.0	4.0	3.1	4.9	0.3	2.7	0.5
2019	3.2	3.8	3.9	3.2	4.8	0.3	2.8	0.5
2020	3.1	3.7	3.8	3.2	5.1	0.3	2.8	0.5
2021	2.6	3.7	4.0	3.2	5.1	0.3	2.9	0.5
2022	1.8	3.5	4.0	3.3	5.4	0.3	3.0	0.6
2023	1.6	3.3	4.2	3.3	5.8	0.3	3.0	0.6
2024	1.5	3.0	4.5	3.6	6.0	0.3	3.1	0.6
2025	1.5	2.8	4.6	3.8	6.1	0.3	3.2	0.6

Source: Census of India; NCERT; Kotak Institutional Equities research

If India is able to get all or most of these young people decent income-generating opportunities, it will see a massive boom in both its GDP and the income earned can be used for consumption and savings thereby triggering a boost to both these sectors. If, on the other hand, India continues with its no or low job growth scenario, there can be strong social order consequences. Even without sounding alarmist, it is clear that not generating enough employment opportunities will at the very least mean a significant delay in pulling millions above the poverty line and condemning many more to a poorer life. Co-opting the large number of youth who will now be looking for employment opportunities in the India growth story can pull a large number of households who are still precariously perched close to the poverty line.

Around 12–15 million people will actively look for employment opportunities every year. To understand how the number of more than 2 million a month suddenly compressed to around a million or so a month, two factors need to be taken into consideration: (1) around 5–6 million people will 'retire' every year (though the concept of retirement in a highly self-employed and unorganized labour market country like India needs to be understood slightly differently) and (2) the abysmally low labour force participation by women in India means that around two-thirds of them will not look out for jobs. Our numbers currently assume that there will not be a meaningful increase in the proportion of females looking for jobs. If, however, more women do decide to actively look for jobs (and that will happen primarily because they are now bearing lower numbers of children), India will need to create substantially more job opportunities.

The crux of the solution hence is whether India can create a robust and flexible enough economy to generate these many employment opportunities. Keep in mind that in any economy jobs keep getting created and destroyed so that the gross number of jobs that need to be created every year is significantly higher than the numbers that we just mentioned. At the very outset, this will help us to be clear on one point: the solution will not lie in asking whether a centrally planned government can create so many opportunities. A government—or any bunch of people—cannot simulate or replicate the diverse changes that take place in a high growth economy and hence cannot a priori plan out the emerging jobs. What can at best be done is to facilitate growth in the economy and make it easier to do and scale up business which can then absorb all in the growth story.

What is a demographic dividend?

A youth bulge, that is, when the population of the economically active youth is high in proportion of the old and the children, is called a demographic dividend. For any country to enjoy demographic dividend, its death rate has to fall (that is, life expectancy has to increase) and its high birth rate has to fall sharply. The death rate typically falls with improved access to medical facilities and timely interventions (for societies and economies that are at the frontier of medical research, death rates also fall as technologies improve; for India this is, at best, a marginal contributor). High birth rates typically fall when infant mortalities improve. As people realize that their kids will grow into adults, they start having lesser of them. As (a) India's investment in its rural and urban health missions has started showing some impact on its infant mortality and (b) general technological advances and access to medical care in India has improved, India is set to see a healthier, younger demographic which is denoted by the term demographic dividend.

The implication is that a large set of the population that is born in a given time period lives and works longer than the previous generation. Given falling birth rates, the next cohort of people turns out to be smaller. India enjoyed its baby boom between 1981 and 2001 and this cohort now forms India's demographic dividend. India's population is growing but growing much more slowly. India's population rate of growth is expected to come down dramatically over the next 15 years from an annual growth rate of 2.2 per cent per annum in 1981 to 0.8 per cent per annum in 2026. This is significant but not enough to arrest population growth which is expected will reach 1.4 billion people by 2026 from the 1.2 billion that the census counted in 2011. The number of children born in India in the decade ending 2011 is almost exactly the same as those born in the decade ending 2001. Now every time the decadal census counts the people in the 0–10 years age range, it will find a smaller cohort than was born in the last decade. The reason for increase in population will slowly shift towards increased life expectancy, rather than new births.

Before we move ahead, we look at one more technical term. Dependency ratio refers to the ratio of those typically not in the labour force (dependents) and those typically in the labour force (participants). We refer to the age group 0–14 years as 'young dependents' and those above sixty as 'old dependents'. The 15–59 years age bracket is the working age population on which the young and the old populations are traditionally assumed to depend. As India's young got added to the population and they moved into the productive age group of 15–59 years, the dependency ratio plummeted and will continue to fall across the country (see Table 2.2). Not surprisingly, over time the 'old' dependency ratio will be on the rise. As the demographic dividend comes into the workforce and smaller cohorts are born, the young dependency ratio is also coming down.

Table 2.2: The overall dependency ratio has come down meaningfully

Age structure of India's population, Census year-ends, 1991-2011 (mn)

Age ranges	1991	2001	2011
0-15 (A)	312	364	372
15-59 (B)	465	586	730
60+ (C)	61	79	108
Total population	839	1,028	1,211
Young dependency ratio [(A)/(B)]	0.67	0.62	0.51
Old dependency ratio [(C)/(B)]	0.13	0.14	0.15
Total [(A+C)/(B)]	0.80	0.76	0.66

Source: Census of India; Kotak Institutional Equities research

A related question to ask in today's age of increasing life expectancy and longer period of studies, is whether the cohort of 15–59 years of age correctly represents the 'working age'. We will however work with this definition as this is currently the norm. But as is happening across the world, the definition of this cohort will also change in India.

The overall dependency ratio in India will continue to fall. However, the composition of the ratio is very different across states. The 'old' dependency ratio is growing in the South which suggests that South India has already 'expensed' a significant part of its demographic dividend even as the North continues its youthful expansion. India is and will remain a young country with half its population below the age of twenty-four years in 2011. To understand the North-South divide better, one needs to look no further than the median age of the various large states. Median age refers to the age of a person who would stand right in the middle if all the people were sorted on the basis of their age. The 2011 census pointed out that while the median age in the northern and eastern states of Uttar Pradesh (population of ~200 million people) and Bihar (~100 million) was 20 and 19 respectively, it was 29 and 26 in the southern states of Tamil Nadu (~72 million) and un-divided Andhra Pradesh (~85 million) respectively. No surprise then that the larger increment in the workforce will come much more from the younger northern and eastern states than from the older southern states.

Better educated youth—more aspirational

Conversion of raw demographic dividend into human capital that can enhance India's productivity growth requires massive investments in education and skill development. India runs a largely successful primary-level enrolment programme, the Sarva Shiksha Abhiyaan (India spent Rs 2.3 trillion on SSA over the financial years 2009–13). India in general and some large states in particular need to ensure that (1) the children continue in school and (2) they are imparted the relevant education/skill development programmes.

We mesh data from two different sources to derive our estimates of how Indian children are being educated. Taking census' age-wise data and the data of the All India School Education Survey, a survey of schools across India conducted by the Ministry of Human Resource Development, we estimate the proportion of children in various age groups who are in school. Since we draw data from two completely unrelated sources, we believe it gives us more confidence in the numbers and proportions though sometimes this may throw up some absurdities.

Our analysis makes a simplifying assumption: children of age six should be in class I, those of age seven in class II and so on. We then cumulate this data over various ages (primary school: class I to V, secondary school: class VI to X and higher secondary school: class XI and XII). Practically all children are now enrolled for primary education: the ratio ranges from 90 per cent to 100 per cent across all states with the national average being 97 per cent. However, this proportion falls to 66 per cent by the time the children go to secondary school and it further falls to 31 per cent when we look at higher secondary schools. These proportions are, not surprisingly, better for urban areas than for rural areas. States like Assam, Bihar, Jharkhand, Odisha and Uttar Pradesh have their work cut out in controlling drop-outs (see Table 2.3).

Governments have been cognizant of the requirement to push for access to higher education. The government has, since 2010, started a new scheme, *Rashtriya Madhyamik Shiksha Abhiyaan* (RMSA; National Middle Education Mission) which focuses on middle education by helping improve infrastructure and impart training to teachers. The government in 2013 launched the *Rashtriya Ucchatar Shiksha Abhiyaan* (RUSA; National Higher

Education Mission) where it along with the private sector is expected to invest around Rs 900 billion in colleges and universities over the Twelfth plan period of 2012-17.

Table 2.3: Drop-outs are still very large across the country; large eastern states are significantly below the national average

Proportion of children in school, March fiscal year-ends, 2011 (%)

	Class I-V			Class VI-X			Class XI-XII		
	Boys	Girls	Total	Boys	Girls	Total	Boys	Girls	Total
Assam	82	84	83	59	65	62	13	13	13
Bihar	94	94	94	46	43	45	11	11	11
Jharkhand	104	107	105	54	52	53	12	8	10
Odisha	102	101	101	69	66	67	9	8	8
Uttar Pradesh	93	97	94	53	52	53	27	26	26
All-India averages	97	98	97	67	65	66	31	30	31

Source: All India School Education Survey, Ministry of Human Resource Development (2008); Census of India; Kotak Institutional Equities research

The focus needs to move to integrating education with vocational training which focuses on skill development. The government is already funding the National Skills Development Corporation (NSDC) which aims to help private institutes impart vocational training/skill development courses which lead to employment.

Employment generation has remained stagnant

Even as the youth of the country knock at its doors seeking jobs, employment creation has remained stagnant at the 6.5–7 million per annum range since 1983 (see Table 2.4). Over the last seven years to 2012, the situation worsened with almost no meaningful employment growth (see Table 2.5). The government was so surprised with the findings of the sixty-sixth round survey of the National Sample Survey Organization (NSSO) in 2010 which showed that there was practically no job creation between 2005 and 2010 that it ordered another large-round survey in 2012 (which would otherwise have been scheduled in 2015)—the sixty-eighth round survey showed that around 15 million jobs were created in the two years 2010–12.

Table 2.4: India has historically created only ~7 mn employment every year

Table showing the simple average annual growth in employment per annum across sectors over time (mn)

Sector	1983 to 1993-94	1993-94 to 2004-05
Agriculture	3.3	0.8
Mining and Quarrying	0.1	0.0
Manufacturing	0.7	1.3
Electricity, water, etc.	0.0	0.0
Construction	0.5	0.9
Trade, hotel, and restaurant	0.9	2.1
Transport, storage, and communication	0.3	0.7
Finance, insurance, real estate, and business services	0.1	0.4
Community, social, and personal services	1.1	0.2
Total	**7.1**	**6.5**

Source: Planning Commission XIth plan document

Table 2.5: Do Indians not want jobs? Over 7 years, only 10 mn new jobs created!

Labour force population in the NSSO 61st and 68th round surveys, June year-ends, 2005, 2012 (mn)

	Rural		Urban		Total		
	Male	Female	Male	Female	Male	Female	Total
NSS—68th round: June 2012	239	104	113	29	351	132	484
NSS—61st round: June 2005	227	129	92	26	319	156	474
Difference between 68th and 61st rounds	**12**	**(25)**	**21**	**3**	**33**	**(24)**	**10**

Source: Various NSSO rounds; Kotak Institutional Equities research

India's overall elasticity of employment growth consistently fell from 0.16 to practically zero over the period from 1994–2000 to 2005–10. The elasticity of employment refers to the ratio of growth in employment to the ratio of the growth of the economy. If, for example, the employment in the economy rises by 2 per cent when the economy is growing at 8 per cent, the elasticity is 0.25 (that is, 2 per cent/8 per cent). Once there is a good understanding of the economic forces that underpin labour force elasticity, this number can then be used to forecast the proportion of jobs that will materialize if the economy grows at a particular rate.

A low elasticity means that one needs a much higher growth rate to absorb the growing numbers in the labour market; a higher elasticity means that the economy is significantly labour dependent and hence well positioned to absorb labour when its growth rate increases. Many social, legal, economic and demographic factors help in shaping the elasticity of growth in an economy. In the specific case of India the elasticity has been kept low by the fact that the overall number of jobs has not grown meaningfully even as there is a significant churn in sectors that create jobs.

This churn in the sectoral composition of jobs shows up in the very different rates of elasticity of various sectors. Sectors like trade, hotels and restaurants and construction have consistently shown high elasticity while the elasticity in agriculture has been very low or even negative. India which wants to free up a large number of people from agriculture needs a significantly negative elasticity for agriculture and very high ones for the other sectors.

However, if the overall elasticity were to remain low (even if there are large inter-sectoral variations), the burden of creating more jobs, by definition falls on the growth rate of the economy. The growth in the labour force in the country is almost preordained given the number of people who were born many years earlier. To provide jobs to all those who are looking out means that the economy has to continue to grow fast enough for it to generate employment opportunities.

High employment growth, coming from the right sectors, is critical

The sixty-eighth round of NSSO estimated the unemployment rate in 2012 at 5.1 per cent of the labour force on the current daily status (cds) basis; government numbers highlight 2.2 per cent unemployment rate on the primary plus secondary basis, but we don't need to digress here. Keeping the unemployment rate from growing makes GDP growth of 7.5 per cent per annum imperative (at ~3 per cent labour force growth/0.4 average elasticity). There are two implicit calculations and assumptions in this: (1) the calculation of 3 per cent labour growth is simple to calculate. Around 15 million people will enter the workforce every year over the next many years. On a current base of a 484 million labour force, this amounts to a 3 per cent annual rise in labour force and (2) the elasticity of employment has been closer to zero while we assume it to be around 0.4, which will require a very large elasticity from non-agricultural sectors.

A corollary of high employment elasticity is low growth in productivity. If a sector requires 1 per cent more people to produce 1 per cent more output (which means an elasticity of 1), this means that the average productivity of the sector has not increased at all. As the economy searches for more productivity, it is naive to assume that elasticities can be increased at will or even by specific policy inducements (more fiscal benefits for employing labour, for example). What is required is reimagining and introducing new work streams that can open up (both in manufacturing and services).

Any setback to this minimum GDP growth requirement has the potential to derail India's tenuous employment situation. As the demographic dividend joins the workforce year after year over the next decade or so, the economic growth story has to play out to absorb them all. The other alternative is to continue with the 'disguised unemployment' that has played out in agriculture over the last many decades. This refers to the large number of people who are not really required for a job but hang around nonetheless since they have nothing better to do. This excess supply of labour in any sector brings down the average and marginal wages for all in that sector.

Why do women not want to work?

India's labour force participation rate (LFPR or the ratio between the labour force and the overall population of that cohort), suggests a massive gap between the population and those who are actually a part of the labour force. In India, 39.5 per cent of the population is currently in the labour force (484 mn of the 1.2 bn people). Since this data is typically collected by NSSO and reported as a percentage of the total population in the country, it is conventional to talk of this ratio as the LFPR of India.

It is also conventional to calculate this ratio on the base of the cohort of people in the 15–59 years age range. This is especially true for a country that is going through a demographic dividend phase because it has a large pool of people in the 0–14 age range. Even when we recalculate the ratio, India's LFPR stands at 66.3 per cent (that is, of the 730 million people in the age range of 15–59 years, 484 million people are actively looking for employment). We can further segregate this ratio into men and women and find that the LFPR stood at 94 per cent and 37 per cent respectively in 2011.

India's working population hence is primarily represented by males. Indian women, if they do take up employment, tend to get into labour-intensive employment in rural India. Quite counter intuitively, the urban Indian woman is relatively less likely to participate in the labour market. These proportions have not materially changed for the past two decades; if anything they have continued to fall. However, as fertility rates come down, more women typically enter the workforce. South Korea's experience of this trend is illustrated in Figure 2.2. If this indeed changes and a larger percentage of women in India aspire to work, it could increase our estimate of the number of people looking for work every year to around 20–22 million.

Figure 2.2: As fertility rates fell, female labour force participation rose in South Korea—Indian women too may start demanding a place in the workforce

Experience of South Korea and India, calender year-ends, 1960-2000

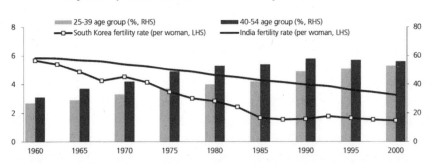

Source: Bloom et al. (2007); Census of India; Kotak Institutional Equities research

Where will the jobs be created?

It is clear that irrespective of whether India's labour force participation ratio increases or not or more women join the workforce or not, India needs to be prepared to create a very large number of employment opportunities. The question, hence, to ask is the segments where the incremental job opportunities will be created.

The future is, of course, unknowable but various industries do try to plan the requirements for their manpower. The National Skill Development Corporation (NSDC) commissioned a study across twenty-two large industries to get a sense of the number of people that these industries expect to employ by 2022. Aggregating the numbers from these various industries gives a good bottom-up picture in terms of what the work profile in India will look like in 2022 (see Appendix 1 for details).

Two points stand out: (1) The industries that will generate the largest number of jobs are building, construction and real estate (48.7 million), transportation, logistics, warehousing and packaging (41.1 million) and auto and auto components (35 million) leading the pack, apart from a large requirement in the unorganized sector (102 million). Of the 330 million employment opportunities that are expected to be created, two-thirds will be in these sectors and (2) Most of the employment opportunities will be in what are, at least relatively speaking, lower-level skills (levels 1 and 2). The definitions of the various skills are mentioned in Table 2.6.

As with every forecast, it is good to keep in mind that forecasts are typically good in indicating the direction and broad magnitudes and not necessarily the actual final result. Given the number of people that we expect will join the workforce (12–15 million every year), India seems poised to create as many job opportunities as will be required to absorb the large demographic dividend. If it indeed does work out as expected, India will have reaped a significant demographic dividend. The more important point is whether India has moved towards preparing its youth to harness the opportunities that are opening up.

Letting the price mechanism work

A pertinent question to ask is whether policymakers should even bother with setting up any such training goalposts or should they let the market forces (increasing and falling wages or creation and destruction of jobs) tell the economic participants (employers, employees, etc.) where to identify a skill shortage and retrain themselves accordingly. We look at a few examples of how the labour market has altered dramatically over the last decade or so: one because of government intervention, one because the government got out of it and another because regulations are so strict as to keep the labour market closed. In all cases, one can argue the outcomes have been potentially suboptimal.

At the bottom end, NREGA may have hurt who it intended to help

Over the past seven years, India has vigorously implemented a minimum-wage regime via NREGA. We hypothesize that this may have driven rural women out of the workforce leading to 'jobless growth'. Both the NSSO and the Labour Bureau surveys have pointed out the low or declining labour force participation of women, especially in rural India. There is limited clarity on why women were dropping out of the workforce. Some experts thought women may have started spending more time in education and skill development, or the data collection itself may have been faulty.

Table 2.5 showed that the declining labour force participation ratio, when juxtaposed with the population, meant that almost no employment opportunities were generated in India in the five years to 2010. Breaking up this data shows that while men found new employment opportunities, women lost out, especially in rural India. The dropping out of women in such significant numbers from the workforce has meant that at an all-India level almost no new jobs have emerged.

Data series from the Labour Bureau points out that across many agricultural activities, the premium that men used to command over women in terms of per-day wage has shrunk significantly. This is seen most prominently in ploughing but is also true for sowing, weeding, transplanting and winnowing. The harsh reality of the effort required in agriculture is that men could physically do more work than women and hence were paid higher. As the minimum wage under NREGA was fixed the same for men and women (and wage equality has long been fought for), women bore the brunt of job losses the most. Across many agricultural activities, the average wages were sometimes lower than the minimum wages legally specified then. The situation has dramatically changed where average wages now are above the minimum wages specified. An economic enforcement has been more powerful than the legal statute, which was patchily implemented.

Even as mechanization of agriculture has taken place over the last decade, there is still significant physical labour involved. The labour productivity has not meaningfully increased in many of the occupations noted earlier. In such a case, women, whose wages have both in absolute and relative terms gone up much more than men's, become less profitable to employ for a farm owner. We hypothesize that the implementation of a minimum wage has meant workers with low productivity have been priced out of the market, reflecting in fewer employment opportunities for women.

Women form a disproportionately large group in NREGA person-days (around 49 per cent of the person-days are women) as compared to their proportion in the rural labour force (around a third). This possibly points to the fact that women who are increasingly being priced out of the agricultural labour market are taking shelter in NREGA work schemes. Ideally the focus should be on improving the productivity of the female workforce via skill development. This will enable them to move beyond the minimum-wage band and command an employment opportunity on merit.

At the top end, we have excess engineers and MBAs

The government's focus on primary and secondary school education is paying off as India produces a larger number of students who are now eligible to enter colleges. Governments across the board also encourage students to study in colleges. The recent example of the Uttar Pradesh government wanting to gift laptops to students who pursue college degrees after clearing their Class XII exam symbolize the inducements that are offered.

An analysis of the demand-supply scenario in the higher education industry shows significant capacity addition over the last few years: 2.4

million higher education seats in 2012 from 1.1 million in 2008. A very large graduating class of engineers and MBAs worries us about their job prospects; India in 2016 will graduate more engineers annually (1.5 million) than China (1.1 million) and the US (0.1 million) combined. The MBA cohort will increase to 0.4 million from 0.1 million in the same time period. This has (1) reduced the importance of 'capitation fees' and (2) led to under-utilization of investments in college infrastructure.

India faces a unique situation where some institutes (IITs, IIMs, etc.) are intensely contested while a large number of the recently-opened institutes struggle to fill seats. This becomes clear when we look at the ratio of actual student intake to the approved student intake, especially in the case of engineering colleges. Across India less than four-fifths of the capacity is used and this spare capacity is unevenly distributed. It is not surprising that over the last few years, anecdotes and instances of 'capitation fees' at engineering colleges are not heard of as much as they were earlier.

Indian parents, as tiger-moms everywhere, one would assume, have believed and inculcated in their progeny the belief that more education is their way out of the morass of poverty. With most of the 3 million people wanting to pursue higher education now having an opportunity to do so, the big question that should have be asked of the truism of education is: are all these trained personnel required? Our analysis seems to suggest that India may be over-educating its people relative to the current and at least the medium-term forecast requirement of the economy.

The excess supply has corroded the pricing ability of the students of some of the finest institutes of higher management education in India. Over the placement cycle of 2012 over 2011, mean salaries at the Indian Institute of Management, Ahmedabad dramatically corrected in the 'banking, financial services and insurance' space and the mean salaries for fresh talent are (1) settling down in a small range across industries and (2) not growing significantly more than inflation. Graduates of the school who may have taken an education loan may find a quarter of their initial take-home pay being spent in repaying the loan even as their return on investment from education is lower than previous batches.

This reality is even starker for engineers. A four year engineering degree from a private college could cost anywhere upwards of Rs 1 million. With average starting salaries at Rs 0.2 million per annum, the payback period can be as high as five years.

The structure of the Indian economy currently is such that it requires around 1 million graduates a year, compared to the around 2.5 million being trained every year. The severe glut does not show up because there is significant concern on the quality/employability of the educated people. Across industries, the employability of graduates is typically reckoned to be between 15–60 per cent of all the graduates. In spite of their having spent large sums on their engineering and/or their management degrees, many of the students will not get an adequate return on investment or a significantly enhanced pay. Incidentally, neither will the employers feel that they have enough choice!

There are discussions that the government wants to increase the gross enrolment ratio of college going students to 30 per cent. This will imply that India will graduate ~6 million people every year. We have already noted the lack of employment opportunities for such a large cohort of graduates both currently and in the future, assuming the NSDC study is pointing us in the right direction. India would do well to invest this money not so much at the higher end of its education pyramid but at the middle end. Skill development opportunities still abound in India: it is just that they are at a level below.

Disparity between the organized and unorganized sectors

The organized sector employs only 10 per cent of the workforce in India's manufacturing sector and generates 65 per cent of the gross value added. The unorganized labour economy employs 90 per cent of the workforce to produce only 35 per cent of the output. The average organized worker is hence 17 times more productive than an unorganized worker. Unfortunately, these proportions have remained broadly the same over the last few years and they can have meaningful consequences on equality.

A recent ICRIER working paper (#286 'Creating Jobs in India's Organised Manufacturing Sector' by Radhicka Kapoor, September 2014) estimates that in the manufacturing sector, organized labour produced 65 per cent of the output even as only 10 per cent of the overall workforce was organized. The own-account-manufacturing (OAM), non-directory manufacturing establishments (NDME) and directory manufacturing establishments (DME) (all of these refer to units employing less than ten workers) account for 90 per cent of the workforce but produce only 35 per cent of the output. The average organized worker hence produces 17 times the value-add compared to an unorganized worker. Incidentally, the average organized workplace is also small by global standards: it employs only seventy-six workers.

If 10 per cent of the population produces 65 per cent of the value-add on a consistent basis, income generation and hence wealth accumulation also becomes similarly skewed: the die is cast against unorganized labour. We take the example of two people who join the labour force this year—one in the organized sector and the other in the unorganized sector. Given that the organized labourer works typically in the services sector, his takeaway from the share of value-add is also higher than in the case of an unorganized labourer working in the agriculture and manufacturing sectors. We assume that higher the income, the higher is the ability to save (and this is indeed, empirically true).

Our calculations (which we showcase in Appendix 2) show that by the end of their careers, those working in the organized sector can generate more from the financial return on their savings than the wealth of 'active' workers in the unorganized sector. Those in the unorganized sector are hence almost *ab initio* condemned to a situation of life-long working even as those in the organized sector can contemplate issues like a financially independent life and retirement. Continuation of this skew in the labour market is a recipe for social distress.

The reason why India has had difficulties in expanding the organized labour pool are the harsh hire-and-fire rules in India. A business model has been created to subvert these harsh rules. Businesses now hire temporary employees so as not to keep employees on their rolls and hence there is no need to offer them 'permanent positions'. The variability associated with business changes (fall in demand, seasonal surge, etc.) is absorbed at the level of an agency that employs these low-skilled employees on its rolls and offers them to companies as required. Such agencies typically charge the corporate client a fee for their services, typically, a percentage of the employee's pay. For many low-skill or high-attrition jobs such agencies of temps, along with training services for these temps, may present a more successful business model than just training them and expecting them to find a job.

It is pertinent to note though that while it helps the companies involved in having a flexible labour force, the employees are worse off. There is (1) no certainty of employment, (2) limited investment in their training and (3) deduction of statutory dues (which typically tend to be a dead-weight loss) leading to much lower cash in hand. However, all of this is assuming that agencies themselves are compliant with rules. There are many a 'contractors' who do not pay any of the statutory levies.

The mechanization and productivity imperative

According to the Annual Report of the Ministry of Labour and Employment in India for the financial year 2015, the average productivity of Indian labour is low when compared with its foreign counterparts. The productivity of India's labour force has been rising in the range of 4–5 per cent per annum which compares unfavourably with China where the labour productivity has grown in the range of 8–10 per cent per annum over the last decade. India has hence not been able to inch towards China's labour productivity. An Indian worker is around half as productive as China's. India's labour productivity (gross domestic product at purchasing power parity per person employed per hour) was US$ 4.46, as compared to China's at US$ 8.04 and US' at US$ 55.18 in 2013.

There is a wide variation in labour productivity among different countries in the world owing to a host of factors, most of which are directly and positively related to the level of economic development of the countries concerned. It is important to underscore the fact that differences in labour productivity levels have essentially nothing to do with differences in how hard workers work—on the contrary they indicate differences in working conditions. A poor worker in a developing country can work long hours, strenuously, under bad physical conditions, but yet have low labour productivity and therefore receive a low income because he or she lacks access of technology, education or the factors needed to raise productivity. Similarly a worker in a highly developed economy may have high labour productivity despite working relatively fewer hours.

On the other hand, wages are increasing fast across India. The rise in productivity is not as much as wages. The rise in wages is anecdotally blamed on the lack of availability of both general and skilled labour. Implementing increased wages at the lower end has prompted agriculture and the manufacturing industry to get more capital intensive (see Table 2.6). The labour intensity in production has been falling led by increasing use of capital in the production process which means that the quality of labour required to operate the equipment needs to be superior than what it was when the process was more manual or labour-intensive. Increasing cost of labour will hasten the process of deploying more capital to make the work of labour more productive to justify the higher wages.

Table 2.6: Labour prices have risen dramatically compared to tractor prices—which has aided the trend of mechanization

Cost of labour (men, annual average, Rs/day) and tractor prices (Rs)

	2007	2013	% increase
Well-digging	82	244	
Ploughing	73	194	
Sowing	65	171	
Harvesting	69	169	
Transplanting	68	158	
Winnowing	66	155	
Weeding	65	153	
Average wage	70	178	155
Average tractor price (Rs)	313,369	452,550	44
Tractor HP (average)	37	39	5
Tractor price (HP adjusted)	8,458	11,594	37

Source: Labour Bureau reports, various issues; Industry estimates; Kotak Institutional Equities research

Employability is the new education

The key learning from these observations is that creation of more jobs in the organized sector is required in industries that can employ the upcoming youth. Creating large-scale unorganized or labour-dependent rural jobs cannot upscale the large number of rural youth. A massive binge of improving higher-education supply has also not improved employment outcomes for students who went through the portals of these institutions. Similarly, a tightly controlled labour market which has not facilitated the entry of more organized workers has kept both productivity and incomes low.

A critical element hence is the creation of matching centres which will prepare the youth for the jobs that are or will be required in the market. The employment centres of yore need to convert into skill development centres which allow people to quickly pick up skills that are in demand. As we note in Appendix 1, a very large part of India's requirement of labour will be in areas that can quickly be learnt and picked up.

The profile of new Indian labour is significantly more educated than its previous generation. With the success of government schemes like Sarva Shiksha Abhiyaan (SSA) and the mid-day meal scheme, drop-out rates in India's primary and secondary schools have fallen dramatically. This will lead to the profile of the workforce upgrading over the course of this decade and beyond as we saw in Table 2.2. Education will make the new labour desire urban/semi-urban jobs with employment contracts in manufacturing or services.

However, the employability of Indian graduates is very low across a variety of sectors. This has to do with the lack of soft skills (communication, English language, etc.) in the services industry and lack of technical skills in the manufacturing space. This can be traced to a variety of reasons, including (1) absenteeism by teachers in primary schools, (2) outdated teaching methodologies and curriculum, (3) lack of interface between industry demand and education supply and (4) a general aversion or reluctance to join vocational training programmes (driven by a perception issue between 'degrees' and 'diplomas' where the former is considered more prestigious).

Poor employability creates a difficult problem for the various stakeholders in the employment market. A candidate is not well-trained but has still spent some money on formal education and in many cases is unwilling to invest further without clear job prospects. Employers are unwilling to pick up untrained students and are loathe to investing in their training as there is lack of certainty on whether the trained youth will stay back. Hence, the focus has now shifted from education to employability. Vocational training and employability enhancement will become big opportunities for players who can bring in scale. Many of the 'consumers' of education are natural consumers of vocational training institutes.

Deep-diving into the vocational training market

We estimate in Table 2.7 that the vocational training market is around Rs 900 billion annually. We look at the number of people who will require to be trained over the period till 2022 and also look at the requirements of re-training some of the current workforce as they upgrade their skills (50 per cent of the current labour force) or re-skill themselves (30 per cent of the current labour force). Our estimate of the pricing of vocational training is driven by industry estimates as they exist for the four levels of skills. The skill levels are defined by NSDC and given in Appendix 1.

Our analysis suggests that the vocational training business could be represented by a set of two inverted pyramids: most of the 'numbers' lie at skill levels 1 and 2 (our estimate is 84 per cent) while they contribute only 24 per cent to the top-line potential of the business. This pareto (80 per cent of the value residing in 20 per cent of the higher skill-levels: levels 3 and 4) is what has attracted a wide variety of private players into the skill development market. With the industry willing to pay high salaries for skilled or qualified workers, the increase in prices of education or vocational training at the higher end has been significant, and has seen active participation from the private sector.

The government as a large player at the lower end (ITI course prices can be very low) has also vitiated the economics of the vocational training market at this end. With the government now opening up its purse-strings for private companies to receive grants (low-cost debt, equity funding via NSDC) and zero-cost debt (Rs 25 million interest free loan for each ITI) for starting training institutes at the lower end, there is now an active interest by the private sector in the training space in low-end skill development.

Table 2.7: Inverted pyramids of quantity and value have led to capacity-creation challenges

Dichotomy between numbers and value in skill development over the period between FY2008-22

	Level 1	Level 2	Level 3	Level 4	Total
New potential employment opportunities created (mn)	208	59	47	16	330
Upgrading a part of the current work-force (mn)	67	15	8	2	92
Re-skilling a part of the current work-force (mn)	40	8	3	1	51
Total number of people requiring skill development (mn)	315	82	57	19	474
"Annual numbers" (mn)	21	5	4	1	32
Revenue projections					
Revenue from skilling (Rs per person)	5,000	20,000	50,000	400,000	
Value (Rs bn)	1,575	1,645	2,867	7,540	13,628
"Annual revenue" (Rs bn)	105	110	191	503	909
Inverted pyramids					
Proportion of people (%)	67	17	12	4	100
Proportion of value (%)	12	12	21	55	100

Source: National Skills Development Corporation reports; Kotak Institutional Equities research

Vocational training versus general education

In India, there is a significant demand for 'general' education as opposed to 'vocational training', with the latter not considered at par with the former. The current school curriculum is outdated and does not bring in elements of vocational training. Globally, vocational training tracks are moulded into the general education track, or alternatively, link back to the university system. 'Degrees' as awarded by universities as opposed to 'diplomas' awarded by vocational training institutes are preferred in India. This is leading to more graduates than needed by the economy.

India requires that more of its students get into vocational training. The target segment is of students who (1) are going ahead to do their higher schooling or graduation (Class XII or graduation and above) without a clear employability plan in place and (2) those who can be trained in vocational training at the primary or secondary level (Class V or IX) while still in school. This is consistent with the requirement of lower skill level employees as are required by the industry.

Supply of training

The current capacity to train or provide vocational skill is fragmented and small compared to the overall need of 22 million per year. As the National Skills Development Corporation notes in its 2014 annual report, they helped train a million people in the financial year ending March 2014. The issue that affiliated institutes face is the lack of trainers which is driven both by the broken economic model as also the general unavailability of trainers: training institutes do not attract the talent that gets absorbed in industry. Skill development, especially at the lower end, has traditionally been the preserve of the government and it is only now that the private sector is getting interested in this space.

Even in programmes run by government ministries, there is focus on training those who have completed primary or secondary education. Courses at ITIs, which range from short term (running for 1–4 weeks) to as long as two years, require a basic education certificate in many cases. Given the massive need to train people in level 1 and level 2 skills, this non-alignment of expectations between the candidates and the training institutes is surprising.

Vocational training systems: An international perspective

Countries around the world have devised various ways to give their youth vocational training. Typically, this requires that the employers contribute their inputs on the type of talent required, which are then incorporated either as part of the schooling curricula or as part of training institutes, which can loop back into the university system for formal completion of education. The government acts as a facilitator in the interactions and also serves as the accreditation body.

The important elements of successful vocational education programmes include an active engagement by employers and a system designed to effectively deliver the training to students. The focus has to be on outputs (whether the students are fit for a job after their training) rather than on the inputs provided by the training institutes.

We look at the various models of providing vocational education across the globe. Switzerland has strong industry linkages and a very significant majority of its students enrol in vocational training programmes. New Zealand has focused on developing 18,000 competency-based standards to assess the skills of graduates. China, on the other hand, has seen dramatic improvement in enrolments in its vocational and training programmes driven by rising demand from students even as the government has taken over the responsibility of training from the state-owned enterprises that used to run them earlier.

Switzerland—ensuring students get many options

After the initial years of compulsory education, the Swiss education system offers vocational education and training (VET) at the upper-secondary level. Professional education and training (PET) is provided at the tertiary level. Education and training begins at the upper-secondary level with learners having the option of continuing through the tertiary level. VET and PET are based on clearly defined curricula and national qualification procedures, providing learners with specific qualifications and prepares them for technical and managerial positions. They are also characterized by a high degree of permeability: a credit system to keep track of prior education and training makes it much easier for learners to pursue additional education and training opportunities and change the course of their working lives. Continuing education and training (CET) courses are also made available at all levels.

VET provides two-thirds of young people in Switzerland with a solid foundation in a given occupation. Most programmes are of the dual-track variety (that is, part-time classroom instruction at a VET school combined with a part-time apprenticeship at a host company). As the 2014 report of the Federal Department of Economic Affairs points out, there are around 250 such programmes to choose from. The less common variety is an entirely school-based programme (full-time classroom instruction, no apprenticeship) which are generally offered by trade schools or commercial schools. The VET programmes closely match the needs of the labour market, both in terms of skills and the number of available jobs. Switzerland's State Secretariat for Education Research and Innovation (SERI) is working with India in its first expertise transfer project where aspects of the dual-track approach of VET are being implemented.

New Zealand—quality assurance of providers

Quality control in accreditation requires a control over the processes of the accrediting bodies. Countries like New Zealand have created the New Zealand Quality Control Association (NZQA) which uses a quality assurance framework that assesses both the providers' quality and the trainees' competencies. NZQA has developed 'Standard One' criteria as a comprehensive framework of provider quality, which assesses the educational mission, inputs, processes, assessments and outputs. As part of this, NZQA (along with industry associations) has developed 18,000 competency-based standards to assess the skills of graduates (for example, student can 'draw and explain simple electric diagrams').

China—rising wages propelling need for skill education

In a report sponsored by the Planning Commission in India, 'Understanding Skill Development and Training in China: Lessons for India', the Institute of Applied Manpower and Research in April 2014 highlighted the details of the Chinese vocational training set-up.

Vocational education in the Chinese school system is introduced at the junior secondary level (or junior middle school) for students in the age group of 12-14 years. Junior level secondary schooling is the last 3-year stage of the nine years of compulsory schooling mandated by the Nine Year Compulsory Education Law of 1986. Unlike India, after the junior secondary level, each student is required to undertake the Senior High School Entrance Examination called the 'Zhongkao', the score in which determines the entry into general academic and vocational education schools. Typically, middle school graduates with lower marks end up in the senior secondary vocational stream.

After completing nine years of compulsory schooling, only about

11.6 per cent junior secondary graduates entered the workforce (2012). Out of the 88.4 per cent continuing senior secondary education, the proportion of those entering the vocational stream was about 47 per cent: almost half the junior secondary graduates entered the vocational secondary schools—this is in significant contrast to the situation in India.

India—starting to take small steps in skilling its youth

Sector skills councils: India is setting up sector skills councils which will be industry bodies that will help codify the types of skills required in upcoming entrants. The objective will be to ensure that the industry gets to mould the type of talent it needs. Setting up these councils will require significant inter-firm coordination. Industry associations are participating in making this happen.

Participation of employers: Many ITIs now work in collaboration with corporate clients who provide machinery and equipment to the ITIs with the understanding that the students trained will be available to work with the corporate. Similarly, many are now providing access to their shop-floors so that students can see the application of their learning first-hand. In many cases, many engineering colleges are doubling up as places where ITIs are run. These ITIs make use of some of the college teaching resources as well as equipment and other infrastructure. As noted earlier, the government is also providing grants and low-cost loans for upgradation of ITIs. Many Confederation of Indian Industry (CII) members have taken upon themselves to 'adopt' ITIs across the country.

Finding the right faculty: The biggest challenge is to find competent faculty. More than the costs, the availability of faculty is a big challenge. Significant time and effort needs to be spent by a company engaged in the vocational training business in 'training the trainer'. Attracting the right talent to become trainers is difficult. The pay scales of a trained student and a trainer tend to converge quickly, especially at low-end skill levels.

Accreditation: Accreditation requires that the government or sector skill councils create the right mix of output indicators on which to measure the effectiveness of the schools. India focuses too much on inputs. For example, the guidelines of the Directorate General of Employment and

Training (DGET), Ministry of Labour for opening up of new ITIs gives the detailed process of verification of inputs (facility, trainers, financiability of project, etc.). Students, however, look at the employability post their training at an ITI and hence focusing on standardizing and strengthening the quality of the output, rather than focusing on the input, is the key to creating more market-friendly institutes.

Lack of accreditation and standardization across training institutes, increases the cost of reaching out to students. In case of an accredited institution, instead of spending on reaching out to students, students end up paying the institute for enrolling in its course. Over time, for organizations that achieve scale or create a large well-placed alumni pool, the cost here can dramatically reduce: word-of-mouth advertising works best in this sector as students look up to peers or seniors who have been placed.

GameChangers

Find the right value equation for all four stakeholders

Getting the value equation right for all the stakeholders will determine the success of the vocational training model. Employers want trained employees but are afraid of losing them to attrition, students need assurance of employment and corporates in the business of training need to make decent returns or their investments, which can be facilitated via scale, technology or fiscal incentives. The common objective is to convert manual labour into trained technicians which increases incomes and productivity.

A successful business model of skill development requires that the aspirations of the four stakeholders: (1) students, (2) employers, (3) training companies and (4) government are met. The central objective of all four is increased productivity and income. However, defining a business model requires defining who pays when, and how the costs of delivery can be controlled.

Students: A student comes into the vocational training programme with the objective of an assured job (or as close to it as possible), or in cases where people come for re-skilling or upgrading skills, an increase in salary. Typically the value of a course gets determined not only by accreditation but by the ability of the course to tangibly add value to the income stream of the student. Skill development needs to take place at the lower end of the skill spectrum and possibly will involve students from poor or impoverished backgrounds. In many cases a student may not be in a position to afford the fees of a training institute. Our discussions with industry players indicate that if students find that a short-term course (1–6 months) that yields tangible benefits (increased pay or getting a job) it is not difficult for the student to generate internal or external financing.

Employers: Employers face a situation where, while wanting trained students, they are typically unwilling to pay for the development of what would be a personal skill-set for the employee. This stems from (1) the limited ability to control attrition and (2) the employment of temporary labour (in order to circumvent arduous hire-and-fire rules) in many low-end jobs.

Many employers, especially in industries that have a large scale like IT and BPO, have set up internal units for training and skill development. Skill development is hence done on the job and with support from seniors in the field, with some help taken from outside agencies.

The employer base in some of the large, absorptive industries like transport and real estate is very fragmented. For companies engaged in training, the skill required needs to be customized according to the needs of every employer. However, if a common skill-set is agreed upon by various members of the industry, the issue of fragmentation can be solved and the skill (and the employee) will become more portable.

Training companies: For companies engaged in this sector, the challenge is creating a process that is more efficient and cost-effective than the internal training programmes that the employers have created. Training companies need to constantly be in touch with employers with respect to new training needs. Finding, retaining and adequately compensating trainers are major challenges for companies. Developing 'train the trainer' programmes are critical at this juncture.

Private companies also struggle to compete with the regulated and subsidized ITIs. Students are required to choose between the 'low cost' government training institutes and the 'higher cost' private institutes. Given that many of the students choosing to go for vocational training programmes come from poorer background, they end up choosing the lower-cost option. This is a good example of the government using its rather visible hand to vitiate the prices in the market.

Government: The government is interested in ensuring that the population is well-trained and adequately employed in high productivity jobs. The government also wants to ensure that the spread of vocational training institutes is far and wide so that they reach out to the more remote and far-off places. The government has its own inclusive growth agenda of encompassing minorities, scheduled castes and tribes, backward and extremist-infested regions, etc.

Getting the revenue equation right

One rule of thumb that many in the industry follow is that the cost of the programme that a student can bear is around 3–5 months of his/her pay (if it is his/her first job) or equivalent enhanced pay, the rest needs to be borne by the employer or the government.

For example, industry discussions suggest that if a person trained say in accounting can be placed with an employer for a monthly salary of say Rs 15,000, the student will be willing to be pay around Rs 50,000–Rs 60,000 for such a course. In case the cost of delivery is more than that, the extra amount needs to be recovered either via placement fees (recovered from employers) or some support from the government (tax breaks or grants, etc.). However, given (1) the economic backgrounds of the students who enrol and (2) the low (in absolute terms) income potential of the jobs at skill level 1 and 2, this model tends to break down and requires intelligent extraction of value.

Creating an enabling environment

The cost of vocational training needs to be borne by one or more of the stakeholders. Across different skill levels, income levels of students, etc. different proportions of money need to be contributed by each of the stakeholders. In the low skill market, which is where, as we noted earlier, 80 per cent of the students lie, there is a significant need to co-opt the government and/or employers. For acquiring higher skill levels, employers can be in a position to fund a programme by paying placement fees to institutes in return for providing trained resources. In many cases, given the higher value attached to the skill level, funding for the cost of the programme is easily available.

At the low-skill level, where a student has a limited ability to pay, the typical way in which a student pays is through a poorly-paying apprenticeship. For example, a person would spend say 2–5 years as a labourer with a head carpenter/mason or a truck driver and then turn into an experienced technician himself. This informal learning is not only very time consuming for the student but may also not prepare him for all aspects of the trade. If the 2–5 year long leanings can be compressed into a 3–6 month long course, a student as well as the employer can benefit. Ensuring that a student is able to attend the course (the loss of pay at such levels can be debilitating) is a challenge.

Creating a model where the vocational training market takes off making it viable for the employee, employer and corporates will help create the right skill-sets required in the country. Having too much government control or intervention will only reduce the ability and the incentive of companies to bring quality to low-priced courses.

Conclusion

As India grapples with providing its large demographic dividend employment opportunities, it will need to rethink and rework many of its laws and make its organized labour force more accessible to the upcoming surge of young workers. A report by The United Nations Economic and Social Commission for Asia and the Pacific (UNESCAP) highlighted that India's Gini-coefficient worsened to 0.339 from 0.308 over the period of early 1990s and the late 2000s (a higher Gini-coefficient reflects a more unequal society). The best antidote to increasing inequality is access to better and productive wages for a large majority and that can only happen when the skills of the workers are matched to the demand of the market. Let us now attempt to link the demographic dividend's job hunt to job creation opportunities that exports can throw open for India.

BRINGING HOME THE DOLLARS

A run on the currency

INDIA WENT THROUGH trying times in 2012–13 when there was a sudden realization that the country's current account deficit may be unsustainable and possibly significantly under-funded by capital flows. This led to both a 'run' on the currency causing the rupee's value to swiftly collapse from around 45–48 to a US$ to closer to 68–69 and also a reduction in the value of the foreign exchange holdings of the country. In this chapter, we link this phenomenon with the cause of developing manufacturing that we alluded to in the previous chapter.

Current account is basically the difference between the value of exports and imports of goods and services. In a world where services were not a very large component of imports or exports, trade account was the preferred mode of analysing a country's balance of payments vis-à-vis its trading partners—it took into account only trade in goods. However, as the world economy is moving towards being dominated by services and countries like India are becoming significant exporter of services (primarily IT), the current account presents a better picture. If a country exports more than it imports, the current account will be in surplus or else, it will be in deficit.

Another way for a country to enhance its foreign exchange reserves is if investors bring money into the country. This money can come in either as remittances by the Indian diaspora or portfolio investments in equity and debt markets or by companies which bring in foreign direct investment. Movements in these accounts refer to the capital account. If more money comes into the country than what leaves it, the capital account will be in surplus or else, it will be in deficit. Putting both the capital and current account balances together, we get the net foreign exchange gained or lost by a country in a particular period of time.

India's balance of payments presents a study in contrasts—large deficits in the current account are financed by large inflows on the capital account. India spends the foreign exchange it receives from capital inflows on financing its current account deficit (CAD). As we note in Figure 3.1, India has practically always been a current account deficit country. When capital inflows become volatile on the back of turmoil in global financial markets, 'financing' the current account deficit, at times, become a challenge.

Figure 3.1: India's current account and trade account deficits had worsened to their worst levels in 2013

Trade deficit and CAD as a percentage of GDP, March fiscal year-ends, 1991-2014 (%)

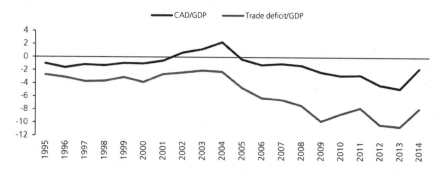

Source: CEIC; Kotak Institutional Equities research

Bringing in the dollars via exports and remittances

We make a case for a dramatic increase in exports notwithstanding the relaxed view of many policymakers and strategists who take comfort in the country's robust capital inflows that are used to finance our CAD. The increasing consumption demand in the country (especially of items like electronics, coal and steel, apart from the usual suspects of gold and oil) is being met by imports rather than by domestic capacity development and expansion. India's export industry has remained constrained by historical policy and infrastructural problems. It is critical for India to develop its productive capacity for both local and global consumption. This will shore up its CAD as well as provide employment for its growing demographic dividend. This model will build a more resilient economy that will sustain through the vagaries of capital inflows or of domestic or global downturns.

The development and growth of India's IT services industry rescued its trade deficit from tipping over the edge over the last two decades. The industry has been bringing in foreign exchange through the export of its services and its employees across the world have contributed meaningfully to India's strong inward remittance pool. Over the financial years 2001–2014, India's net software exports rose to US$ 67 billion from US$ 6 billion.

Non-resident Indians (NRIs) sent in US$ 65 billion in fiscal year 2014, making India the largest recipient of inward remittances in the world. This is up from US$ 13 billion in 2001. Importantly, remittances in India equal almost a fourth of the trade exports, making them an important component of the current account. We highlight that during the great financial crisis of 2009, remittances remained stable while capital account flows (on account of FDI and FPI) saw wild swings.

Non-resident Indians have responded to the country's overtures and helped it tide over foreign exchange crises: of course, at the right price. After India's nuclear explosions in May 1998, when it faced the brunt of global sanctions, the Reserve Bank of India and State Bank of India were able to raise ~US$3 billion via the Resurgent India Bonds in August 1998. India had to offer 7.75 per cent (in USD) and 8 per cent (in GBP) while the corresponding sovereign yields in these countries were ~5.5 per cent (in USD) and ~6.2 per cent (in GBP). Similarly, the India Millennium Deposits floated in December 2000 were priced at 8.5 per cent (in USD). Both these bonds were also exempt from income and wealth taxes in India. In the recent crisis, India was able to raise almost US$ 35 billion in 2013 by offering rates which were at a similar premium to the then market rates in these currencies.

Understanding the CAD

The current account deficit can be understood as a difference between national savings and investments. We look at two equations:

GDP = C+I+G+(X-M)	GDP = C+S+T
where,	where,
C = private consumption,	C = consumption
I = private investment	S = savings
G = government goods and services	T = Taxes
X = exports	
M = imports	

Putting them together, we get:

X-M = (S-I)+(T-G)

(X-M) is the current account (in absence of transfers, etc.), (S-I) represents private savings and (T-G) represents, in a sense, government savings: the equality of the equation denotes that CAD is nothing but the difference between national savings and investments. If a nation's savings are less than its investments, this will end up reflecting in a current account deficit. A key element of moderating the CAD is hence to increase savings in the country.

A school of economic thought argues that CAD will automatically get financed by capital account inflows. The objective from a macroeconomic point of view of running a high CAD is to attract more investments into a country by increasing its 'absorptive capacity'. This school argues that if there is a large inflow of capital, the currency will appreciate (if there are no interventions by the central bank), thereby increasing imports and reducing exports and hence increase CAD, thereby maintaining equilibrium in the balance of payments. Similar logic applies to the large outflow of capital. The equilibrium unfortunately works over long periods of time and does not present itself in response to sudden changes in capital flows.

Other economists view CAD as the potential output loss in the economy (that is, what could have been produced within the economy is now being imported). They worry not about financing the deficit but about the loss of jobs and output in the country. From their perspective, the capital account and current account are two different entities, which while they merge into the balance of payments, require different strategies. They expect the surplus and deficits to be kept in a narrow band, rather than letting them be volatile. Excess appreciation of the currency due to capital inflows discourages exports and increases imports, leading to deindustrialization and loss of employment.

Understanding India's current growth model

India's growth model is based on consumption rather than on manufacturing-driven export growth. The composition (C+I+G+X–M) of India's GDP vis-à-vis China is very instructive (see Figure 3.2). The South East Asian miracle was engineered by keeping exchange rates low, even as these countries saw significant inflows of foreign exchange on the capital account. China sees significantly higher capital inflows than India but has been able to maintain a cheaper currency, thereby providing a boost to exports and dampening consumption. This is also what has helped China amass its multi-trillion dollar foreign exchange reserve. China, after reaching a middle-income level for its population, is now trying to change track from being an export powerhouse to a more local consumption-driven one.

Figure 3.2: India's GDP composition is tilted in favor of consumption, markedly different from China

Break-up of GDP of India and China, March fiscal year-ends, 2013

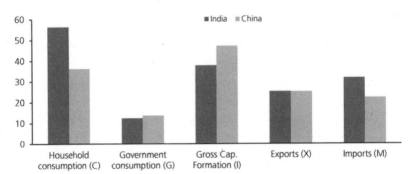

Source: CEIC; Kotak Institutional Equities research

The upside of a consumption-driven model is that growth can continue even during a global downturn, while an export-driven model requires the world economy to be healthy and growing. The difficulty in a consumption-led model is its sustainability especially if it is held hostage to foreign capital flows determining policy variables like the exchange rate.

India faced a unique situation over a large part of the last decade: till the Great Financial Crisis (GFC) struck, it received significant capital inflows which held the rupee steady against the USD. The Indian rupee remained in the 45–48 range to the USD for a better part of the decade. This was surprising given the inflation differential between the US and India was reasonably high (around 2–5 per cent per annum). However, inflows in the form of large foreign portfolio investments and foreign direct investments kept the value of the rupee stable. A stable rupee attracted foreign capital inflows and also significantly facilitated consumption (as seen in the higher imports in India). India hence could not capitalize on the export opportunity on the trade side as its currency remained strong. On the services side, India has had non-currency advantages like an English speaking population, a large number of engineers and the telecom revolution which it used favourably in its IT revolution.

India's foreign exchange reserves rose significantly over the early part of the last decade (see Figure 3.3). This rise in reserves was driven by a strong inflow of capital into the country, driven by increasing growth and investment opportunities that it provided. Over the last five years, however, the rate of growth of reserve accumulations has virtually stagnated as the current account deficit has broadly equalled capital account inflows. In a year like 2009, the reversal in capital account inflows also meant that there was a reasonable drawdown in reserves.

Figure 3.3: India's foreign exchange reserves stagnated in the US$ 250 bn to US$ 300 bn range over the last half a decade

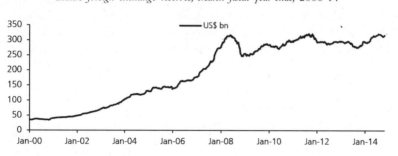

India's foreign exchange reserves, March fiscal year-ends, 2000-14

Source: Bloomberg; RBI; Kotak Institutional Equities research

Understanding the inflow and outflow of dollars

India has been an energy-starved country and hence has been significantly importing energy resources, especially oil. However, recent environmental and allocation related concerns have led India to becoming a large importer of coal. Similarly, environmental and illegal mining concerns have led not only to the stoppage of exports of iron ore but India has also started importing both iron ore and steel in meaningful quantities and value. As a developing country, it is only to be expected that India will be a large importer of capital goods. However, surprisingly, the import of capital goods is only broadly equal to the combined import of consumption items like electronic goods and bullion. We look at the trends of these numbers in Figure 3.4. A coming together of all these factors created a flutter in the foreign exchange market over the earlier part of this decade.

Figure 3.4: Commodities form a much larger proportion of India's imports than capital goods

Major components of imports, March fiscal year-ends (US$ bn)

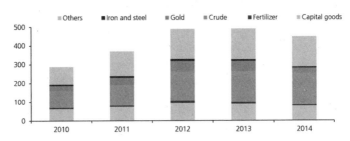

Source: CEIC; Kotak Institutional Equities research

India's CAD/GDP ratio in financial year 1990 had reached 3.3 per cent at a time when the country was not a hot destination for capital flows effectively triggering a run on the currency. This forced the RBI to devalue the rupee to Rs 24.5 /US$ from Rs 17.9 /US$, a depreciation of 37 per cent in financial year 1992. A CAD of 4.2 per cent of GDP in financial year 2012 followed by a CAD of 4.7 per cent of GDP in financial year 2013 triggered a run on the currency from ~Rs 48 /US$ to an eventual stabilization of ~Rs 61 /US$, a depreciation of a fifth of its value over a two-year period. This sharp depreciation made imported products expensive, made exports somewhat competitive and coupled with a series of restrictions on import of gold led to an improvement in the CAD to 1.7 per cent of GDP in financial year 2014 (see Table 3.1 for many of these and subsequent details).

Table 3.1: India has had a very volatile CAD

India's balance of payments, March fiscal year-ends, 2018-14 (US$ bn)

	2008	2009	2010	2011	2012	2013	2014
Current account	(16)	(28)	(38)	(46)	(78)	(88)	(32)
GDP	1,239	1,229	1,366	1,706	1,879	1,859	1,878
CAD/GDP (%)	(1.3)	(2.3)	(2.8)	(2.7)	(4.2)	(4.7)	(1.7)
Trade balance	(91)	(119)	(118)	(131)	(190)	(196)	(148)
Trade balance/GDP (%)	(7.4)	(9.7)	(8.7)	(7.7)	(10.1)	(10.5)	(7.9)
- Exports	166	189	182	250	310	307	319
- Imports	258	309	301	381	500	502	466
- Oil imports	80	94	87	105	155	170	168
Invisibles (net)	76	92	80	85	112	107	115
- Services	39	54	36	49	64	65	73
- Software	37	44	48	53	61	64	67
- Transfers	42	45	52	53	63	64	65
- Income (net)	(5)	(7)	(8)	(17)	(16)	(21)	(23)
Capital account	107	7	52	62	68	89	49
Percentage of GDP	8.7	0.5	3.8	3.6	3.6	4.8	2.6
Foreign investment	43	6	50	40	39	47	26
- FDI	16	20	18	9	22	20	22
- FPI	21	(15)	29	30	17	27	5
- NRI deposits	0	4	3	3	12	15	39
Short-term credit	16	(2)	8	11	7	22	(5)
ECBs	23	8	2	13	10	8	12
External assistance	2	2	3	5	2	1	1
Other capital account items	11	(4)	(13)	(11)	(7)	(5)	(11)
E&O	1	1	(0)	(3)	(2)	3	(1)
Overall balance	92	(20)	13	13	(13)	4	16
Average USD/INR	40.3	45.8	47.4	45.6	48.0	54.4	60.5
Average crude (US$/bbl)	78	84	70	85	112	108	108

Source: RBI; Kotak Institutional Equities research

Over the two financial years of 2012–13, the trade deficit was upwards of 10 per cent of GDP at 10.1 per cent and 10.5 per cent respectively.

In simple terms, 10 per cent of the GDP was generated from the excess of imported goods over exported goods—a very large proportion by historical or any peer-set comparison. Imports of goods were up 6.3 times to US$ 491 billion in financial year 2013 from US$ 78 billion in financial year 2004; in the same period exports grew only 4.7 times to US$ 300 billion from US$ 64 billion. In effect, this is India's 500–300 problem: India imports ~US$ 500 billion worth of goods but is able to export back only ~US$ 300 billion. A sharp crackdown on imports, as noted earlier, led to imports coming down to US$ 449 billion in financial year 2014. Of the US$ 42 billion contraction in imports, US$ 15 billion came from lower imports of gold.

Any strategy to tackle the current account deficit holistically needs to be a sum of parts. For that, we break India's CAD according to the geography of its deficit. India's largest deficit is driven by the Middle East (oil), China (a range of products), Russia (defence and machinery), Australia (coal), Nigeria (oil), Indonesia (coal) and South Korea (electronic goods). India should aim to attract fund flows from these countries: either on the portfolio side via sovereign wealth funds or through FDI. On the other hand, India runs a large positive trade balance against countries like the USA. It is hence no wonder that countries like the USA want more openness in India's trade or capital account so that they can have a more balanced trade with India.

Imports

The trade account has been constantly in the deficit driven by a larger import bill as compared to India's exports. The composition of India's imports has shifted in favour of importing even those goods that are available in abundance here (see Table 3.2). India spent US$ 16 billion and US$ 7 billion in financial year 2014 on coal and steel import respectively, even when it has large reserves of both the ores. Delay in coal linkages has made India one of the largest importers of Indonesian and Australian coal. Similarly, large projects in the steel sector are stuck at various levels due to environmental clearances (though now there are challenges of financial closure due to the turning steel cycle).

India has been spending in the range of US$ 30 billion annually on importing electronics and telecommunication equipment over the last three years. If current trends continue, India's electronic imports could well rival India's oil imports by the end of this decade (especially if the price of oil remains low after the recent collapse in late 2014). India is a large captive market for both these sectors: it would have added significantly to India's technical capability and absorption of its large labour pool if these items had either been indigenized or if the process of clearing FDI for the companies operating in these sectors had been made easier.

India's current account deficit is significantly impacted by the fluctuations in the commodity market. India is the fourth largest importer of oil and the largest consumer and importer of bullion—the last decadal trend of significant upswing in the prices of these commodities has had an adverse impact on India's CAD. The cool-off in the prices of these commodities will provide India with some buffer on its foreign exchange position.

Exports

India's traditional export items have come from industries like: (1) textiles and readymade garments (financial year 2014 exports at US$ 31 billion, CAGR over the last decade: 10 per cent), (2) leather and leather manufactured exports (US$ 6 billion; 10 per cent) and (3) gems and jewellery (US$40 billion; 14 per cent). Countries like China (in leather) and Bangladesh (in textiles) have taken a significant lead over India. India, however, has been successful in becoming a large exporter of petrochemicals, automobiles and engineering goods (see Table 3.3). One large industry that has opened up for India for the export market is the refining and processing of crude. India now boasts of the world's fifth largest refining capacity. Across the world, construction of new refineries has been stuck because of environmental reasons. The last new refinery to become operational in the US was in 1976. With significant export incentives available in this field, India has been able to create the most complex of refineries. We however note that the large export industries in India are not necessarily very labour intensive.

Table 3.2: More than 6X rise in overall imports over the last decade

Imports into India, March fiscal year-ends, 2004-14 (US$ bn)

	2004	2005	2006	2007	2008	2009	2010	2011	2012	2013	2014
Petroleum crude and products	21	30	44	57	80	94	87	106	155	164	165
Capital goods	17	22	31	40	55	69	64	75	95	90	80
of which, machinery	5	7	10	14	20	22	20	24	30	28	24
of which, electrical machinery	1	1	1	2	3	4	3	4	5	4	4
of which, electronic goods	8	10	13	16	20	24	21	27	33	31	31
of which, transport equipment	2	3	4	5	8	13	12	11	14	16	14
Other items	6	9	14	23	28	41	29	36	48	46	40
of which, fertilizer	1	1	2	3	5	14	7	7	11	9	6
of which, non-ferrous metals	1	1	2	3	3	6	3	4	5	5	5
of which, metalliferous ores and metal scrap	1	2	4	8	8	8	8	10	13	15	14
of which, iron and steel	1	2	4	6	8	9	8	10	11	10	7
Others	17	25	31	35	46	58	64	85	120	122	97
of which, gold	7	10	11	14	16	21	29	41	56	54	29
of which, coal, coke and briquettes	1	3	4	5	6	10	9	10	18	17	16
Mainly export related items	14	18	20	19	22	34	33	55	55	49	51
of which, pearls precious and semiprecious stones	7	9	9	7	8	17	16	35	29	23	24
of which, chemicals: organic	3	4	5	5	7	8	9	12	13	14	16
Consumption goods	3	3	3	3	5	5	9	9	12	14	12
Manufactures of metals	1	1	1	2	3	3	2	3	4	4	4
Total imports	**78**	**112**	**148**	**186**	**251**	**304**	**288**	**370**	**489**	**491**	**449**

Source: CEIC; Kotak Institutional Equities research

Table 3.3: Exports have risen less than 5X over the last decade

Exports of manufactured goods from India, March fiscal year-ends, 2004-14 (US$ bn)

	2004	2005	2006	2007	2008	2009	2010	2011	2012	2013	2014
Manufactured goods	48	60	73	86	103	125	117	161	190	186	194
of which, engineering goods	10	15	19	26	33	40	33	53	59	57	62
of which, chemical products	9	12	15	17	21	23	23	29	37	39	41
of which, gems and jewellery	11	14	16	16	20	28	29	38	45	43	40
of which, textiles	12	13	16	16	18	19	19	23	27	26	31
of which, electronic goods	2	2	2	3	3	7	6	9	9	8	8
of which, leather goods	2	2	3	3	3	4	3	4	5	5	6
of which, cotton	0	0	1	1	2	1	2	3	4	4	4
of which, paper, wood products	1	1	1	1	1	1	1	2	2	2	2
Petroleum and crude products	4	7	12	19	26	28	28	42	56	61	62
Primary products	10	13	16	18	25	25	24	31	41	43	44
of which, agriculture and allied	7	8	10	11	16	17	16	22	33	37	39
of which, ores and minerals	2	5	6	7	9	8	9	9	8	6	6
Other Commodities	2	2	3	3	4	8	9	13	18	10	9
Total exports	**64**	**84**	**103**	**126**	**163**	**185**	**179**	**251**	**306**	**300**	**313**

Source: CEIC; Kotak Institutional Equities research

Attracting short- and long-term foreign money for investments

Capital inflows into India are divided into two parts: foreign direct investment (FDI) and foreign portfolio investment (FPI). FPI inflows refer to portfolio flows while FDI covers the longer term investments in companies. The process of investing via a FPI route differs significantly from the FDI route, as it is driven by different regulators with differing priorities. Over the past many years, the regulator in the capital market, SEBI, has progressively made it easier for foreign funds to register and trade in India. The current process of registering and starting trade can be accomplished in as little as two months (including time to acquire a PAN and signing up with the custodians).

The process for FDI is still significantly rule-driven with detailed rules for various sectors. In many cases, the investments need to be approved by the Foreign Investment Promotion Board (FIPB), and in certain cases, the regulator or the ministry overseeing an industry also has a say. The rules are periodically modified (a consolidated FDI policy document is released every six months) and can be driven by various considerations that have kept many sectors outside the purview or influence of foreign investment. A FDI investee needs to deal with local land acquisition, labour and environment laws, all of which are in a state of flux given their socioeconomic and political sensitivities.

In this scenario, inevitably, the money coming in via FDI is broadly similar in quantum to the more volatile FPI component (for a series of FDI and FPI inflows, see Table 3.2). Over the financial years 2008–14, the total FDI amounted to US$ 126.5 billion compared to the FPI net inflows of US$ 114 billion. Even as we appreciate that the colour of money is green, FDI brings with it benefits of technology transfer, more employment, reinvestment and more stability. Large swings in the FPI inflows between the financial years 2008–10 give policy makers a cause of concern over this type of money being 'hot' which would rush out in times of any crisis.

India also became, for a small period of time, a large exporter of capital. Indian companies became very active in the field of foreign acquisitions over the latter half of the last decade. Indian outbound FDI flows cumulated to US$ 79 billion over financial years 2005–10 thanks to several iconic purchases of global entities by Indian entities in sectors like automobiles and auto components, steel, sugar and telecom. This trend has now reduced as the availability of cheap money has stopped, the acquisitions themselves have brought significant learnings (and in some cases, significant debt) and the expectation that the business environment in India is expected to improve.

Given the high growth of India's (consumption-driven) economy, we find it surprising that a developing country would want to export capital, or that its entrepreneurs would want to find challenges in different economies rather than consolidate or grow in their home base. The strategy reflected a need for entrepreneurs to spread their risks geographically by extending themselves into different global economies. The government and industry were finding themselves increasingly at odds over issues like environmental regulations and allocation of public resources.

By 2011 India progressively liberalized the remittance of monies that Indians could send abroad to US$ 200,000 every financial year without any approvals: this started from as little as US$ 25,000 in 2004. However, the recent foreign exchange run on the Indian rupee meant that this limit was clamped down to US$ 75,000 in September 2013. It was relaxed later to US$ 125,000 in June 2014.

What is India's X factor?

India almost never created any advantage in the export of manufactured goods. The reason for losing export competitiveness can be traced to a whole set of issues like small scale reservations, harsh labour laws (which are duly circumvented) and abysmal infrastructure development (delays in road transport, port congestions).

As India moves into the phase of absorbing its demographic dividend, it needs to review its growth strategies. It is important for India to build its manufacturing base as a means of employing its upcoming demographic dividend. India's GDP composition has moved to being dominated by services from agriculture, without a growth in manufacturing/industry. This has created a peculiar situation—while there is significant surplus manpower in agriculture it is not able to move directly into the services sector. Globally, the movement of workers has been from agriculture into manufacturing. In India between 11 million and 13 million people will be looking for employment opportunities every year for the next 15 years and services can at best absorb only 5 million new entrants every year.

India is now globally recognized for its software exports, a stature it has not earned for its goods exports. On the trade side, a few examples of auto, engineering and pharma stand out. India's export strengths have emerged from technologically advanced engineering (or reverse engineering) capabilities. China's model, on the other hand, is based on high volumes of goods manufactured by deploying a massive scale in its operations. China is also steadily building export leadership in telecom equipment, white goods and increasingly, automobiles.

The X factor for India will be higher exports of manufactured goods (in the field of economics the shorthand for exports is 'X'). Not only will this reduce India's CAD but it will also help create employment opportunities. Many global auto firms and capital goods companies have made public announcements of making India one of their global hubs for manufacture. India's large well-educated talent pool (which will need to be trained vocationally for specific roles in various industries) means that it enjoys an advantage in industries that are significantly more complex. Over the next few years as these industries' plans fructify in India, it could create significant incomes and wealth in the country.

Bringing the traditional industries back on the radar

From being a virtual nobody in the international leather market in the 1980s, by the end of the last decade, China had gone on to control a third of the world trade. Leather is a very labour-intensive industry, something that serves India's demographic development interests well. India was the largest exporter of leather and leather goods in the 1980s. It accounted for 8.8 per cent of the world's leather trade in 1981 (when China barely accounted for 0.4 per cent). By 2006, India's share had fallen to 2.6 per cent while China accounted for 31 per cent of the world's leather market.

There are structural reasons why India has not been able to stand up to China's aggression in manufacturing. In labour-intensive manufacturing, the variability in demand (demand for leather products goes through seasonal variations and significant demand fluctuations as fashions change) gets passed on to the number of people employed by a company. Having flexible hiring and firing laws (so that the entrepreneur is not burdened with a fixed cost in times of slack demand) can help. Similarly, since a successful line in leather requires millions of a similar product to be made, scale can bring down per unit costs and increase efficiency. The productivity of labour also increases as the scale increases: India, as noted in Chapter 2 (page 39), suffers from low labour productivity.

China has, over the last few years, allowed its currency to gradually appreciate from the peg it set against the USD. As the Indian rupee depreciated against the USD the yuan appreciated; the rupee has lost almost a fourth of its value against the Chinese yuan over the last five years. This will, of course, make Indian exports more competitive in the global market. However, the world trade market has been growing slowly over the last few years driven by the slow growth rates in the US, Europe and Japan. As growth revives, this change in currency dynamics should help spur India's exports position.

We should address here an issue that typically crops up: rates of interest in India are very high. Currency, interest rates and inflation are macro-economically linked. The cost of funds in China are indeed optically low (typically in the range of 3–4 per cent) compared to India (upwards of 10 per cent). However, this argument does not hold in light of the significant inflation in India as opposed to China. Indian entrepreneurs still enjoy low to negative real interest rates. Hence, this lament should be healthily questioned whenever heard.

Replicate Brazil's success in agriculture

India has the largest arable land in the world and is one of the largest producers of a variety of grains and agricultural commodities. However, India's agricultural net exports have remained in the range of US$ 35–40 billion over the financial years 2012–14 and the variety of exports has not materially changed over the last few years. In fact, imports are rising to meet the increased demand for edible oil.

India's role-model in the field of agriculture should be Brazil, which harnessed the oil crisis of the 1970s to emerge as one of the largest producers of agricultural commodities. Given the surge in prices of inputs for fertilizers, Brazil focused on intensive and modern farming thereby creating its agricultural miracle. Given Brazil's climate, its emergence as the world's largest producer and exporter of soy is truly remarkable, a strategy that dovetails nicely with the world's growing hunger for protein-rich food.

India created its own Green Revolution in the 1970s motivated by a mandate for self-sufficiency—which was driven by the conditions attached to food grain imports. India is slowly beginning to see a revival in the fortunes of its farmers. However, the revival has come from increased prices rather than via meaningful yield gains. India's own increasing prosperity is reflecting in fast-growing demand for protein content in its food which is most obvious in the rising demand and prices for dairy and poultry. A similar trend is also visible in edible oil, for which India has come to depend on imports.

Given India's low yield in agriculture (across commodities), it will need to aggressively invest in the sector. This creates the potential of not only feeding India's rising population (which is expected to stabilize at 1.5–1.6 billion by the middle of this century), but also in creating an export powerhouse. Processed foods command significantly higher valuations and margins, so we expect this to be a focus area for the industry and the government as Indian agricultural exports move beyond mango and rice. We will return to this point in our discussions in a later chapter on agriculture.

Making the most of the flat world through exports and remittances

The steady growth in Indian software exports continues. A significant proportion of India's investment and consumption boost has come from the spin-off effects of the software boom. From being an insignificant contributor to the Indian economy less than a quarter of a century ago to being a key component of India's growth story, the software industry, both on its own and via its employees' remittances, has created a mega inflow of dollars. The IT services industry clocked revenues of US$ 67 billion in financial year 2014. Many of the off-shoots of India's growth story, whether increased automobile sales, housing demand or demand for electronic items, can be attributed to the multiplier effect of the fortunes of the IT industry.

As other countries, most notably, South East Asian countries like the Philippines and Malaysia and Latin American countries like Mexico begin to position themselves in this space India is beginning to face competition from them. Growth for India will need to be driven by moving its software exports to higher value-added services; countries like the Philippines have done well in capturing the lower-end market.

India's current account is also supported by large inward remittances from its widespread diaspora. India's diaspora has seen a dramatic change over the past few decades with software professionals in the US significantly matching Indian labourers in the Gulf in their quantum of remittances. India's inward remittances in financial year 2014 were US$ 65 billion. The remittances exhibited low volatility even during the financial crisis.

Despite India being a large recipient of such remittances, its economy is not dominated by them as is the case with some other economies like the Philippines, where the proportion of remittances to GDP can be as high as 8–10 per cent (though the proportion has increased from 1.7 per cent in 1995 to 3.5 per cent in 2014). India has, as we noted earlier, successfully tapped its diaspora in times of crises.

Dealing with the various commodity conundrums

India's import bill is dominated by the commodities that it needs for its consumption. A third of India's import bill is driven by oil imports and about a tenth by bullion imports. Half of India's imports are hence priced by the demand-supply dynamics in the real and financial world, something which it has to take as an exogenous variable, that is, one over which it has no influence or control. As India grows richer, its energy needs are increasing and so is the ability of its citizens to buy gold, one of its most favoured assets.

India's energy consumption was 622 million tons of oil equivalents (mtoe) in financial year 2014—up from 491 mtoe in financial year 2010. India's indigenous supply of energy to meet its 622 mtoe demand will be only 365 mtoe, leaving an import requirement of 258 mtoe. We include coal, natural gas, petroleum products and electricity in our demand-supply calculations. The consumption demand is expected to go up to 941 mote by 2020 and the internal supply to 466 mtoe. This will increase the import dependency to 475 mtoe from 258 mtoe currently. Significantly increasing the production of coal and getting gas out of sea-beds will form a key part of any future strategy. Getting environment clearances, putting in place a proper system of allocation and pricing of these resources right is critical for India.

India's needs to move towards the unlocking of value from large accumulated reserves of gold with its citizens. According to the World Gold Council estimates, as at end of 2013 Indians had accumulated gold of around 20,000 tons which is worth ~US$1 trillion. Various organized gold loan companies have emerged which facilitate converting gold into cash (loans). Also, with the rise of exchange traded funds (ETFs) in India, a new way of holding gold is emerging. However, neither of these trends has dimmed demand for physical gold in any material sense. India needs to make it easier to monetize gold via gold loan companies. Putting in place a cascading tax system on gold can help reduce its position as a store of black money.

With such high dependency on oil and bullion in India's import bill, it is held hostage to commodity price upswings; though one must concede that it also benefits from the downswings.

Leveraging India's own market to attract industries

One of the largest non-commodity imports for India is capital goods. Going back to the basic macroeconomics concept discussed earlier, we believe this is an important component of India's transition to a developed economy, wherein India imports technology and know-how. The growth in capital equipment is dominated by non-electrical machinery and transport equipment—imports of these rose to US$ 80 billion in financial year 2014 which is more than four times the import of US$ 17 billion in financial year 2004. The more interesting element of India's import growth story comes from the increased demand for electronics: items worth US$ 31 billion were imported in financial year 2014 which is also up four times over the same period.

India's telecom industry is expected to spend US$ 20 billion over the next three years on new equipment and upgradation. Given the large Indian telecom market (at more than 900 million SIMs at the end of October 2014 India had the second largest number of mobile subscribers in the world), this presents an ideal opportunity for the industry to base itself in India. However, India has been importing large chunks of its requirement from vendors in China (Huawei, ZTE) and Europe (Nokia Siemens Networks, Ericsson). For many of these technologies, not only does India have the skill-sets, it also has a booming market. Free trade agreements (FTAs) have made it easier for India to import but this should not become a substitute for creating a manufacturing base in India.

Many auto manufacturers have been lured to India with the expectation of learning and implementing 'frugal engineering'. India has demonstrated excellence in 'high value engineering' and it is time for many other industries to set up and take notice.

What is holding this back?

Economics 101 points out that there are four factors of production: capital, land, labour and organization. Unfortunately for India, stakeholders in all these four factors have faced difficulties in carrying on production efficiently and effectively.

Hard decisions are hard to take

Given the increasing need for energy (power generation), India has started importing coal. This is despite there being 110 billion tons of proven coal reserves (out of a total resource base of 277 billion tons) in India. India extracts only about half a billion tons of coal annually so it will not be running out of this resource in a hurry. The reason for imports is the slow development of coal mines in India which is driven by (1) pending environmental clearances and (2) non-development by many private players that have been allocated coal-blocks (which were de-allocated by the Supreme Court in September 2014). Similarly, India is importing steel while many projects for converting India's iron ore to steel are still stuck at various stages of environmental or other clearances.

India's slow development on this front does not necessarily stem from its need to protect its natural reserves as a strategic asset but from its unwillingness or inability to take hard decisions and see through the implementation. Unless India begins to develop its abundant resources, it will end up spending a large proportion of its foreign exchange reserves on importing goods which could have been produced in India. This requires that owners of capital who invest in these projects get some certainty that the projects that they are backing will get off the ground. Faster decisions on approval of projects, a clear title to the (mineral) resources and certainty of regulations are all aspects where India has not delivered convincingly over the last few years.

Land as a holy cow

One of the hardest decisions that India needs to take is on framing its land acquisition policy; 48 per cent of land in India is devoted to agriculture, a proportion which is significantly large for a country its size. In comparison only 15 per cent of land in China is devoted to agriculture. As India builds its industry, it will require a harmonious process of transfer of farm land to industry. India has seen a lot of heated debate on land acquisition. Given the large scope to improve yields, a few percentage points of area transferring from agriculture to industry/urbanization will hardly dent India's food security.

The process of land acquisition needs to be fair and its remuneration transparent. India is debating and discussing various alternatives: imposing a 26 per cent tax on mining profits for the development of the local community, annuity payments to farmers on acquisition of their land (rather than just an upfront payment), project equity for landowners in the projects set up on the land sold by them.

Many of these well-intentioned proposals are stymied by ambiguous titles to ownership which makes the process of compensation and rehabilitation arduous and error-prone. This also makes the process of digitizing land records an uphill task in India; only a few states have made beginnings in this area. The biggest reform in land acquisition will be to ensure that owners can enjoy unencumbered titles to their land.

Given the low productivity of Indian farms, the financial return on agricultural land is very low (~3–4 per cent if we take into account the market value of the agricultural land). Any change in the use of land from agricultural to industrial purposes can lead to a multi-fold jump in the value of the land. According to research by my colleagues at Kotak Institutional Equities, the ROE earned by BSE–30 companies in financial year 2014 was 15.8 per cent. Such a multi-fold jump in returns will lead to an obvious increase in the value of land for the acquirer. However, permission for land use change is one of the biggest sources of 'rent' in the system.

Sentenced to being small

India's economic policy makers have traditionally believed that employment is generated through SMEs. In order to facilitate the existence and growth of SMEs, India explicitly created a policy of reserving many items that could be manufactured only by small scale industries (SSIs) as defined under the law. The policy came into effect from 1967 with a list of 47 items so reserved, which had risen to 807 items by 1978. It is only over the last decade that the controls have been effectively abolished, allowing large-scale manufacture of these items.

According to the annual report of the Ministry of Micro, Small and Medium Enterprises for the financial year 2014, the following items are still reserved for exclusive manufacture by the micro and small enterprises sector: (1) food and allied industries: pickles and *chutneys*, bread, mustard oil (except solvent extracted), ground nut oil (except solvent extracted), (2) wood and wood products: wooden furniture and fixtures, (3) paper products: exercise books and registers, (4) other chemicals and chemical products like wax candles, laundry soap, safety matches, fireworks, *agarbatties*, (5) glass and ceramics: glass bangles and (6) mechanical engineering (excluding transport equipment) items like steel almirahs, rolling shutters, steel chairs (all types), steel tables (all other types), steel furniture (all other types), padlocks, stainless steel utensils, domestic utensils (aluminium).

This list serves to highlight the level of detail to which the government goes to help shape the scope of manufacturing in India. A perusal of the list of more than 800 items that were once reserved shows the extent to which Indian industry was controlled by the government. An SSI unit is envisaged as a very small entity. The size of a firm was determined by the capital deployed by it and even at its peak, the definition of a SSI implied an upper limit capital deployment of Rs 10 million. Many entrepreneurs got around this restriction by having multiple units in the same premises but operating under different names (and with different 'gates' all opening into the same main work area).

Over time it was realized that small scale, while having an ambivalent impact on employment generation, created very little scope for lowering costs or enhancing profits, which could be reinvested back into the unit. Reinvestment was anyways un-remunerative for the entrepreneur: if the capitalization of the unit crossed the thresholds set for it, it would lose fiscal benefits.

The policy lasted through the decades of 1970s to the late 1990s shackling the growth of Indian industry. Over the 1980s and 1990s, other countries, most notably China, pursued a policy of scale, thereby lowering unit costs of the goods produced. This allowed them massive advantage in the international market and China went on to become the 'manufacturing hub' of the world. Not surprisingly, Indian companies not constrained by SSI regulations in the services sector, prospered and made a mark.

Hire, but don't fire

Labour protection is another emotive issue in India. Successive governments have been loathe to radically changing policies aimed at protecting labour. This has manifested itself in the creation of various rules and acts which protect the workforce. These laws have been circumvented, in many cases, with the use of temporary labour to whom these protections do not apply. What started out as a measure to protect the workforce has actually helped keep it more unorganized and insecure. In turn, the tenuous nature of temporary employees makes companies reluctant to invest in skill development and training, which in turn impacts productivity.

The plethora of well-intentioned legislations has created a bureaucratic nightmare for entrepreneurs and stunted the growth of the organized workforce in India. These rules come in the way of creating scale. Factories in China routinely boast of tens of thousands of workers, however, the largest companies in India, across all their plants, employ less than a few thousand workers. The services industry, which is outside the purview of many conventional labour laws, has a much larger employee base.

Given the unintended requirement of having smaller workforces, Indian entrepreneurs have increased their dependence on capital. Labour intensity in manufacturing is falling and is being replaced by capital. With bank finance and capital markets easily accessible, entrepreneurs are making the right micro choice of choosing capital over labour. At the macro level, this leads to unemployment.

Understanding India's attempt at driving up exports

Indian policymakers have tried to address the issue by creating oases of manufacturing excellence with special facilities and policies through special economic zones (SEZs). SEZs have slowly picked up in strength for India but even after a decade of their launch, they account for only less than 25 per cent of the country's overall exports (see Figure 3.5). This proportion is small when compared to exports by China from its SEZs (which is closer to the 40–45 per cent range). Large proportions of exports are still IT and petrochemical exports and not as much manufacturing exports as India had hoped for when it started out on its SEZ policies.

Figure 3.5: SEZ exports have stagnated at between 20% and 25% of overall exports

Exports from SEZ or otherwise, March fiscal year-ends, 2008-14

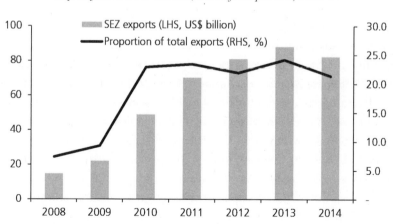

Source: CEIC; SEZ India; Kotak Institutional Equities research

As of December 2014, India had 352 notified SEZs of which 196 were operational. The notified SEZs occupied 51,056 hectares of land area. To put the 510 sq km of land area in perspective, this is similar to a city of the size of Pune (430 sq km) or Jaipur (485 sq km). Chinese SEZs, though fewer in number, are much larger—each SEZ is basically a province dedicated to being one SEZ.

The last decade (the financial years 2004–14) can be divided into two parts to appreciate the exports story. Between 2004 and 2009, exports grew ~3 times to US$ 185 billion from US$ 64 billion, or at a CAGR of 24 per cent. In the last half of the decade (from 2009–14), exports went up only 1.7 times to US$ 313 billion, or a CAGR of only 11 per cent. In the second half of the decade, however, exports from SEZs went up ~4 times to US$ 82 billion in 2014 from US$ 22 billion in 2009. SEZ exports, hence went up by US$ 60 billion in the last five years even as overall exports went up by only US$ 128 billion. Almost half the incremental exports over the last five years came from SEZs.

Exports from Indian SEZs have seen phenomenal growth, significantly greater than the overall export growth of the country. This possibly demonstrates one of two things: (1) SEZs have made exporting easier and more remunerative and hence more of the action is moving to those locations or (2) the activity which would have continued in the normal course of business at non tax-exempt locations has moved in to take advantage of the more liberal laws of the SEZs.

To put the latter point in perspective, there are some advantages of situating an export unit in a SEZ: (1) duty free import/domestic procurement of goods for development, operation and maintenance of SEZ units, (2) 100 per cent income tax exemption on export income for SEZ units for the first five years, 50 per cent for the next five years thereafter and 50 per cent of the ploughed back export profit for the next five years, (3) exemption from minimum alternate tax, (4) external commercial borrowings by SEZ units up to US$ 500 million in a year without any maturity restriction, (5) exemption from central sales tax and service tax, (6) single window clearance for central and state level approvals and (7) exemption from state sales tax and other levies as extended by the respective state governments.

India's export policy push with SEZs resulted in the notification of

352 SEZs. However, two-thirds of these SEZs (228 of the 352 notified SEZs) cater to the IT and ITES segment, thereby reinforcing India's position in the services export space. There has been limited development in the export of goods via SEZs, except for petrochemicals.

The SEZ policy has been criticized for several attributes that were obvious at the time of inception. The small dispersed areas of SEZs, allowing them to come up away from ports, lack of provision for building connecting infrastructure, creating hundreds of SEZs rather than concentrated zones, all stand out as glaring oversights. SEZs, in effect, ended up serving as tax shelters and a tool for creating land banks.

An export policy push not only requires a rethink of or a tinkering with the current SEZ policy but also a concentrated push in creating true SEZs. A typical SEZ needs to (1) be large (the largest Chinese SEZ, Shenzhen is 493 sq km, which is broadly equal in area to all Indian SEZs put together), (2) be near a port, (3) have internal connecting infrastructure and (4) concentrate on items of manufacture that India has or can develop expertise in. SEZs should also be allowed to 'export' to the domestic tariff area (DTA) after paying the appropriate customs duty, if any. Therefore, if a telecom equipment plant or a consumer electronic goods plant is created as a SEZ to take advantage of the infrastructure and favourable laws, the benefit of that can accrue to India—the gains coming in from both technology transfer and gainful employment.

India has been signing free trade agreements (FTAs) with countries across the globe. These FTAs need to be followed up with active diplomacy to ensure that Indian exports become a prominent feature. Visits of the premiers of all the five nations in the Security Council over the last few years can serve as a template for Indian diplomats. All the foreign prime ministers and presidents focused on the Indian market helping pave the path for their national corporates to gain entry.

GameChangers

Incentivizing local production

Across various infrastructure industries, government or public sector enterprises have started pushing for indigenization. The National Thermal Power Corporation (NTPC) and the Power Grid Corporation of India

(PGCIL) have taken the lead in helping indigenize technology used in power generation and transmission respectively. NTPC now requires indigenization in the >500 MW plants, a segment that Indian operators could not develop capably in due to cheaper Chinese imports. Similarly, PGCIL has mandated that in the >765 kV segment, a foreign company needs to have some Indian operations, or a joint-venture with local firms.

The Telecom Regulatory Authority of India (TRAI) released a consultation paper on 'encouraging telecom equipment manufacturing in India' in December 2010. The paper points out that 'given the right initiatives by all stakeholders, the manufacturing sector can make rapid strides. The telecom system/hardware equipment market is much bigger than the telecom software market and domestic production can not only reduce our imports, but also create a large export opportunity with the consequent benefits to the telecom industry and the country.'

India annually has around US$ 30 billion of defence expenditure and a significant amount on the import of defence equipment, which provides it an ideal opportunity to offer off-sets to its vendors, or better still, offering them to set up local production here.

Given the consumption nature of India's economy and the increasing middle class, Indians will continue to increasingly consume electronic goods. India needs to provide incentives for this industry to set up manufacturing bases, possibly in SEZs in India. This will not only allow technology to be transferred to India (and in due course, be developed in India) but will also provide meaningful employment to its labour force. The auto industry is expecting to make India its export base, especially for Africa and Europe. A similar model needs to be developed for the electronics goods industry.

Focus on natural exports

India needs to revitalize its agricultural production with a dual objective: to feed its growing population (which itself is getting richer and demanding foods with better nutritional value) and to become an export hub. India lost the advantage in the field of agriculture to Brazil but it can recapture the advantage in select commodities (like dairy products, fruits and vegetables). India has become an importer of foreign pulses and edible oil; especially in pulses which practically India alone consumes in the world, it is a trend that it needs to reverse.

India stands a good chance of making it big again in its traditional export sectors of gems and jewellery, textiles and leather. These sectors are labour-intensive and are areas where India has skilled labour and traditional advantages.

India needs to focus on value-addition in its own economy rather than exporting basic raw materials and importing finished products as in the case of iron-ore and steel. Similarly, it needs to reduce its import of coal when it has its own large reserves. Development of the mining industry will require a thought-through process of environmental clearances (also involving rehabilitation) and right-price auctions: this will motivate parties to start and complete projects on time.

Open up to FDI

India's FDI has been concentrated in the services and in the real estate sectors. It needs to consider opening up FDI in capital starved sectors like banking, insurance and retail. These sectors require large commitment of capital over long periods of time, making India less susceptible to wild swings in foreign inflows/outflows. India also requires huge investments in its infrastructure—a suitably structured infrastructure asset can be a big opportunity to attract patient (and low-cost) foreign capital.

How India's economy shapes with respect to its contribution from manufacturing will also determine the shape and size of India's urbanization, a topic that we explore in the next chapter.

THE RISE OF THE CITIES

The size of the urbanization opportunity in India

INDIA'S STEADY URBANIZATION has the potential to absorb investments of Rs 120–150 trillion over the course of the next eleven years till 2025 (see Table 4.1). City expansions will call for a dramatic increase in (1) housing stock, (2) transport infrastructure and (3) last mile connection of utilities (like power and water). We estimate investment in these segments at US$ 2–2.5 trillion over the next eleven years to 2025. For context, we note that India's GDP in financial year 2014 was US$ 1.9 trillion. India will therefore need to invest between 8 and 10 per cent of its GDP every year on developing its urban infrastructure.

Our projections for India's urbanization call for 2.5 billion tons of cement, 650 million tons of steel and 4.6 million tons of paint over the next eleven years. To put this in perspective, installed capacities in these sectors as at the end of financial year 2014 were 369 million tons of cement, 94.3 million tons of steel and 2.5 million tons of paint (see Table 4.2). We would encourage you to look at these numbers to get a sense of the orders of magnitude involved, rather than to get a very precise estimate of industry sizes. The magnitude of investments required for this scale-up in urban infrastructure in terms of capital goods as well as services is large enough to kick-start India's moribund capital cycle and trigger the next leg of economic growth.

Table 4.1: India's urbanization can throw up large investment opportunities

Estimates of investments required due to India's urbanization,
March fiscal year-ends, 2025

	Demand	Pricing (Rs /sq ft)	Potential market size	Private or public
Real estate				
Residential	35 bn sq ft of new property required	1,000-1,500	Rs 35-52 tn	Mainly private investment; significant government intervention in bottom-of-pyramid segment possible
Commercial and retail	As for residential	1,000-1,500	Rs 35-52 tn	Private-sector spending
Potential investment in real estate			Rs 70-100 tn	
Transport				
Urban roads	1.4 mn kms and associated infrastructure (traffic signals, pavements, lighting)	Rs 25-30 mn/ km.	Rs 35-42 tn	Investments by local urban bodies, financed by property tax, land auctions and perhaps user charges
Mass transit systems	63 cities with 1 mn+ population, about 40 kms of metros/city. Investment in buses, BRTS and mono rails will complement investment in metros	Rs 2-3 bn/km.	Rs 5-8 tn	Mainly public investment or PPP if the model stabilizes. We have not estimated investment in private two and four wheelers and other intermediate transport, in which the private sector will invest
Potential investment in transport			Rs 40-50 tn	
Infrastructure				
Power utilities	Transmission and distribution		Rs 1-3 tn	Mainly public investment; user charges will need to fund infrastructure
Water	Supply of clean water and clean-up of sewage		Rs 1-3 tn	Mainly public investment; user charges will need to fund infrastructure
Potential investment in infrastructure			Rs 2-4 tn	
Total urbanization spend potential until FY2025E			Rs 120-150 tn (US$ 2-2.5 tn)	

Notes:
(a) The pricing refers to current estimates; they do not take into account inflation.
(b) In real estate calculations, we do not take into account the price of land.

Source: Kotak Institutional Equities research

Table 4.2: India's urbanization can throw up very large investment opportunities

Estimates of investments required due to India's urbanization,
March fiscal year-ends, 2025E

	Steel		Cement		Paint	
	Comments	mn tons	Comments	mn tons	Comments	mn tons
Real estate						
Residential	4.5 tons of steel required per 1,000 sq ft	157.5	20 tons of cement required per 1,000 sq ft	700.0	1.3 ton of paint required per 20,000 sq ft	2.3
Commercial and retail	5.5 tons of steel required per 1,000 sq ft	192.5	20 tons of cement required per 1,000 sq ft	700.0	1.3 ton of paint required per 20,000 sq ft	2.3
Potential investment in real estate		350.0		1,400.0		4.6
Transport						
Urban roads	200 tons of steel required per km	280.0	800 tons of cement required per km	1,120.0	NA	NA
Mass transit systems	10,000 tons of steel required per km	25.2	2,000 tons of cement required per km	5.0	NA	NA
Potential investment in transport		305.2		1,125.0		
Total cumulative urbanization spend potential until FY2025E		655.2		2,525.0		4.6
Capacity of the relevant sectors (end-FY2014)		94.3		369.0		2.5

Source: Kotak Institutional Equities research

How do you fund such massive investments?

These investments will need to come from private and public sources. As Indians invest in improving their own housing stock, they will demand better transport infrastructure and associated utilities. Over the past two decades, India has experimented with public-private partnerships in developing infrastructure like roads, metro trains, power and water. The success of these partnerships has been patchy at best given that the state has been keen on shielding its citizens from paying the actual cost of delivery of an infrastructure project.

Cities and their governments will need to be inventive in raising resources to meet the aspirations of its citizens. User charges, property taxes and land auctions will all need to play a critical and complementary role in funding cities for their growth. Many commentators have pointed to the idea of developing the municipal bond market to augment the resources at the disposal of urban local bodies. We are more circumspect about the development of this market given the currently still-born corporate bond market. As Indian cities acquire more financial powers and local governance institutions, maybe a municipal bond market will become meaningful but till such time, it will at best be a marginal resource base.

New cities or organic expansion?

As India re-imagines its urban landscape, we argue that it needs to focus on making its large cities liveable rather than creating new ones. Indian cities rank very poorly when compared to their international counterparts. The idea of 'creating' new cities belongs to the era of manufacturing-led growth, something that has not been the case in India. Even if this evolves with the development of infrastructure like the Delhi-Mumbai Industrial Corridor (DMIC), which is expected to give a big push to manufacturing, this will lead to the seeding of, at best, a handful of cities (seven planned currently).

India's services-dominated economy will see its current pint-sized cities burgeoning into massive urban sprawls. Consider Mumbai's density, where 17.7 million people live within an area of 546 sq km, while Shanghai's

22.7 million citizens sprawl across 3,626 sq km, an area 6.5 times larger than Mumbai. Tokyo, with twice the population of Mumbai, is 15 times larger; the world's most populated city has 37.6 million citizens sprawled over 8,574 sq km.

Even if India's area under urbanization doubles in the next decade, it is important to note that it will still account for 6 per cent of the country's land area. This should belie concerns that cities will over-run agricultural or forest land in India, fears that underpin many of the policy constraints in urban expansion.

Why does one come to a city?

As people move away from farming to seek work in manufacturing and services, the link with land as the key factor of production becomes tenuous making way for more densely populated regions.

A cost-benefit analysis of congregating in a city versus staying back in a rural area pits the private benefits of large groups living in proximity against the public costs imposed by such a congregation. Private benefits will include the facility to work, trade, collaborate and compete while the common costs will include congestion and pollution. A city continues to expand, according to this theory, till the benefits outweigh the costs.

We tag the benefits of city living as private (that is, benefits accruing to individual citizens of the city) and costs as public (that is, accruing to society as a whole). For an individual in a rural area, it makes personal sense to move to a city. However, for the city, the potential city-dweller must bring in more value than he will cost the city. There comes a time when cities become too large to accommodate growth; as their public services are capped, they become unattractive to live in.

Two factors can change this equation: (1) creation of adequate infrastructure helps reduce public costs (for example better roads lead to lower congestion and better refuse management leads to lower pollution) and (2) as communication and/or transport technology evolves, it changes the shape of the city. Infrastructure and technology can significantly reduce the costs of living in a city, thereby enhancing the utility of staying in one.

Pull 1: Mobility

Cities that latch on to the dominant employment trend benefit from it (think of IT for Bengaluru and Hyderabad, for example). A city that stops producing new jobs or remains stuck in obsolete employment structures stops attracting good talent. The exceptions to this are citizens who journey to a city to escape even worse prospects in their rural hometowns (think Kolkata). Over the last seven years, urban India has generated almost all of the incremental employment opportunities. A city must be an effective employment generator: the promise of a city has to be one of upward social mobility.

Employment creation is an outcome of a good business environment which allows for new economic opportunities to be readily converted into business ventures, leading to job creation. Employment creation depends on (1) an educated, skilled and employable workforce and (2) lower implicit and explicit costs of doing business.

Pull 2: Affordability

The largest costs of staying in a city are shelter and associated infrastructure services, for example, transport, power, water and sewage, power, education and health. To make a city liveable, it is imperative to keep these costs low. Keeping costs low for citizens does not mean offering any of these infrastructure services for free, which would only compromise the quality of the utility. Low revenue-generating utilities typically malfunction, compelling the poor to pay an even higher price for basic necessities. The rich survive by subscribing to private infrastructure. India has been trying to make its citizens pay for many of its utilities, a goal stymied by a history of free services and the contemporary reality of populist politics. However, there are encouraging signs of greater political will and support for the idea.

- **Housing:** Indian cities typically follow a master plan approach. These take a 15–25 year view of a city and planners envision growth and expansion to demarcate areas for various purposes. Unfortunately for India, the planning process itself is long drawn and plans typically get finalized deep into the vision period. For example, the 20-year Delhi master plan of 2001 (which was to update the 1980 master plan) was finally approved and promulgated on 1 August 1990. Similarly, final touches are still being given to the 2021 master plan for Delhi.

A key ingredient of housing cost is land. A rigid master plan makes it difficult to increase the availability of land quickly during a plan period. Similarly, as cities expand in area, they typically need to co-opt agricultural land. The process of converting agricultural land to non-agricultural land (popularly called NA land) is rife with hurdles tied into corruption. Even as a city's authorities need to be concerned about the provision of basic facilities as the city expands (roads, hospitals, schools, etc.), landowners in the surrounding areas should have some flexibility in deciding on how to use their land. Opening up the land market and reviewing building strictures (height restrictions for one) can help bring down the costs of city living considerably.

- **Transport**: Intra-city commute and freight movement are important for services-led urban development. The intra-city movement of passengers and freight needs to be fast and cheap. There has been significant emphasis on public transport globally and India needs to improve the quality and quantity of its public transport so that the newly emerging consuming class does not necessarily see the need for personal vehicles. India has invested a great deal in its many high quality inter-city roads but ironically, intra-city transport systems (roads, public transport, rapid transit systems, etc.) are woefully inadequate.

- **Water and sewage**: Water services (both delivery of clean water and sewage disposal) are all but free in India, leading to a collapse of urban utilities. It is not an uncommon sight across many cities (for example, in Mumbai) to see water tankers plying the streets to affluent housing societies as well as poor localities which do not have access to public water supplies. The populist approach to pricing water fails the poor who pay a high price for this basic utility. Sewage clearance is also not adequately priced and the breakdown in this service also hits the poor the most. Poor sanitation takes a toll on health as well as employment, burdening the individual, industry and the state.

- **Power**: Of late, many states have started increasing the price of power with the implicit promise of providing higher quality power (both in terms of voltage and also in terms of the number of hours that power will be available). Indian cities have large unmet needs for power even where electrification is largely complete (estimates suggest that 94 per cent of urban households have access to electricity). Many labour-saving and modern devices (mixer-grinders, vacuum cleaners, washing machines, dishwashers, refrigerators, air-conditioners, etc.) are making their presence felt in Indian homes only now. Cities that offer their citizens low priced access to uninterrupted electricity can ensure greater productivity from their citizenry.

- **Health and education**: It is difficult to classify health and education as private or public goods. Clearly, the benefits of good health and good education accrue to a person concerned. However, better education and health of its citizens creates a positive virtuous cycle for society as a whole. Indians across the board—and especially so in urban India—have started meeting their health and education needs through private means. This is a classic case of the private cost of public failure. Public services in the field of education and health should be credible competitors to private players.

We do not include issues like security (the police system) and justice (the legal system) in the cost of living in an urban area because they are necessarily public goods which the state is duty-bound to provide both effectively and efficiently. We will look at some of these issues in detail in subsequent sections; for now we turn our attention to sizing up Indian cities.

COMPARING INDIA'S URBANIZATION TO THE GLOBAL EXPERIENCE

India is no longer a land of villages

Census 2011 put to rest the faux-romantic idea that India lives in its villages as according to this census, for the first time in recorded Indian history, the absolute population of urban India grew faster than that of rural India. Importantly, this data does not factor in those census towns, which for all practical purposes are urban but are not recognized as such by the state. As we look ahead in time, we expect that the rural population will, in absolute terms, stagnate at the 833 million mark and all the incremental growth in Indian population will be urban. A large portion of rural working age persons will move to urban India, meaningfully changing the composition of rural India and shaping the new urban India. This is not surprising since most of the net employment creation in India over the last decade has been urban (this has also to do with the vast number of women who dropped out of the workforce in rural India which showed practically net nil job creation).

The big driver of urbanization across the world has been people giving up their agricultural vocations for more attractive prospects in manufacturing. This took place over multiple generations (indeed centuries) in the west and happened more quickly with the East Asian miracle economies. India has surprisingly seen little of both these phenomena. Even after a quarter of a century of liberalization of the economy, around half the labour force in India is still associated with agriculture, but producing less than a sixth of its GDP.

India has been a reluctant urbanizer

India's rate of urbanization has been very slow compared to most of the larger countries in the world. There are two important reasons for this: (1) a large part of India's labour force has still not been able to free itself from agriculture and (2) Indian rules do not recognize the extent of India's urbanization.

India still employs a large number of people in agriculture because of a dearth of opportunities in manufacturing. Over the past few years, the Indian government has demonstrated its keenness to make manufacturing the backbone of growth. The National Manufacturing Policy aims to raise the share of manufacturing to 25 per cent of GDP by 2025 from 14 per cent in 2014. Assuming that GDP growth averages 7 per cent over this period, this will imply a manufacturing growth rate of 12 per cent

CAGR. If indeed this target were realized, India could possibly spawn a few more new cities.

India's urban population is considerably larger than what official numbers indicate. This is because too many Indian towns are officially classified as rural areas as their status has not been updated in official records. To qualify as urban, a town must (1) be recognized as such by the government and have an urban governance mechanism (municipality, corporation, etc.) and (2) satisfy three criteria: (a) a minimum population of 5,000; (b) a density of >400 people per sq km and (c) >75 per cent of the main male working population should be engaged in non-agricultural pursuits.

Villages with >5,000 residents ('large villages') accounted for only 9.6 per cent of the rural population in 1961; by 2001, they accounted for 21.8 per cent of the rural population. By 2011 this proportion had risen to 23.5 per cent, that is, almost a quarter of the rural population now lived in 'large villages' or 'towns'. If such villages are labelled 'urban' (since they satisfy one of the three criteria required), as much as 49 per cent of India can be said to be 'urbanized', compared to 31 per cent as officially reported in Census 2011.

Services-led growth: Implications on space needs

India's services-sector led growth means that India may not create as many new cities as other countries which relied on manufacturing. Manufacturing has two interesting and critical features that help in the growth of new cities: (1) knowledge of manufacturing has matured and standardized across the world leading to spill-over benefits from agglomeration (or bunching up together in one place) and (2) land is a critical input in manufacturing and as more units and people start coming together, land begins to get expensive and industries are compelled to look beyond city borders for seeding their new clusters.

The services sector thrives where there is a large congregation of people in one place. Services, by definition, are offered by people to each other. Given its nascent nature in human history, significant new changes (inventions, developments, etc.) are taking place in the services sector and hence it helps if the people associated with this sector congregate.

Services typically do not require as much land as manufacturing. A typical manufacturing unit in India would be a discrete one-floor structure, while a high rise building could house a clutch of service businesses.

We see the impact of this clearly as we note the larger number of smaller cities that China has as compared to India. The prognosis by United Nations remains the same. It projects that by 2025 China will have 139 cities with a population between 1 and 5 million and 218 cities with a population between half a million and a million; India will have only 64 and 75 such cities respectively. UN estimates also note that by 2025, 21 per cent of India's urban population will live in cities which have populations of greater than 10 million; for China this proportion will be only 13 per cent. If the current growth trajectory of services-led growth continues, India will do well to focus on improving the lot of its current cities and their outgrowth and managing that well.

India's urbanization will more probably lead to mega-urban regions. In this context, the National Capital Region (NCR) and the extended city of Mumbai both of which have expanded in every direction that they could find or create land. We should expect to see cities start to coalesce towards each other (Indore-Dewas, for example). If infrastructure like the Delhi-Mumbai Industrial Corridor spurs manufacturing activities along its length, we may well see the phenomenon of an urban corridor develop. According to projections made by the United Nations, by 2025 five Indian cities will feature in the top 25 cities in the world (in terms of population).

Growth of cities: Rest of the world

The idea of a city brings to mind the cliché of a 'concrete jungle' with its implication of dense congregations, high rises and congestion. This is in contrast to the notion of rural living with its visions of vast fields, single-floor houses and single-storey buildings. As people leave rural lands for cities, it is critical to understand how Indian cities will evolve. Many countries have been urbanizing steadily over the past 200 years and there are lessons to be learned. We ask: (1) as more people come into cities, do cities typically become denser or do they start expanding outwards? Or (2) could they actually expand outwards so much that they decongest their old hubs? An understanding of these issues, their drivers and their projections can help guide India in its urban planning.

Cities in the developing world are far denser than those in the developed world. The order of magnitude of over-crowding in the developing world is 3–5 times the density of the developed world. The high-density urban phenomenon is a feature that defines the developing world. This is because it costs relatively too much in time and money for urban populations in the developing world to commute to work from distant suburbs.

Cities in the developed world have been losing density consistently over the last century. There has been a steady decline (at a gradual rate of between 1.5 per cent and 2 per cent annually) in the average annual density of twenty cities in the US over the twentieth century. The density of cities in the US in the early 1900s is similar to that of cities in India today. The de-densification of these cities took place even as the absolute number of citizens in these cities increased substantially. Cities have grown meaningfully in area to accommodate a larger number of citizens even as they have provided more space to each individual.

As cities expand, the other interesting feature is the distribution of density in a city. The centre of the city, not surprisingly, is typically the densest. The number of people who live away from the centre form a much larger proportion of the population than those who live near the centre. This requires good transport systems that allow people to move across large distances quickly and cheaply.

Cities de-densify as people can move around quickly and cheaply

The story of development of urban centres over the last century has been the development of cheap and quick public transport epitomized by metro/subway systems or railway lines across different cities. Many of the largest cities in the world (London, New York, Tokyo and Paris among the major ones) have famous metro/subway maps which are not just an essential ingredient of daily life but also works of art. High quality buses and taxis also incentivize people to use public transport.

If commuting is fast and cheap, a city naturally expands outwards as we can see from the example of several Indian cities, a case in point being Mumbai. Since independence, average distance travelled by a suburban local train passenger has increased dramatically. The average distance travelled in 2013 was 33 kms (or broadly the distance between Churchgate and Borivili) which is up from 16 kms (which corresponds to the distance between Churchgate and Bandra) in 1951. This allows people to live further away from work, allowing for geographic proliferation of the city. Indian cities are now investing in metros and bus rapid transit corridors. We explore this in greater detail in the section on transportation where we demonstrate how and why a good transport helps a city de-densify.

India's urban development is likely to mimic global precedents in many ways, while differing on account of twenty-first century influences. We foresee an increase in the organic emergence of satellite hubs spawned by specialized interests connected to primary 'flagship' hubs. Modern city development and expansion is defined by (1) the wide variety of jobs on offer and (2) the development of communication technologies. A variety of jobs calls for an equal number of skill specializations. No longer are cities known for only the single industries they are built around. New communication technologies will increasingly reduce preoccupations with commuting while nurturing the formation of multi-hub (or multi-modal) cities. This highlights the need for flexibility in the development plans for cities.

Table 4.3 shows the population of Indian cities and their sizes (unfortunately, there is no good data on the area of the cities in 2011). There is significant ambiguity on how and where city boundaries are drawn for the purpose of these calculations (the parameters may differ for the cities listed). However, it is easy to see that Indian cities are significantly denser than cities in the developed world.

Indian cities are small in size as compared to the larger cities in the world with which Indian cities compare in population. The geographic expansion of Indian cities will be driven by (1) easier intra-city travel, aided by increasing purchasing power and better infrastructure and (2) the growth of satellite hubs that focus on particular specializations.

Table 4.3: Indian cities are very dense

Area, population and densities of various Indian cities, March fiscal year-ends, 2001-2011

	2011	2001		
	Population	Area	Population	Density
	(person)	(sq km)	(person)	(person/sq km)
Mumbai	18,414,288	603	11,978,595	19,865
Delhi	16,314,838	431	9,879,290	22,917
Kolkata	14,112,536	186	4,580,513	24,596
Chennai	8,696,010	174	4,343,562	24,963
Bangalore	8,499,399	226	4,313,266	19,065
Hyderabad	7,749,334	173	3,658,477	21,184
Ahmedabad	6,352,254	281	4,514,988	16,063
Pune	5,049,968	430	2,538,290	5,903
Surat	4,585,367	213	2,702,404	12,716
Jaipur	3,073,750	485	2,322,395	4,792

Source: Census of India; Demographia World; Kotak Institutional Equities research

How will urban India look like in 2025?

Table 4.4 shows the various scenarios that may play out depending on how Indian cities develop. If Indian cities grow by becoming denser, contrary to our thesis, India will likely convert around 10,000 sq km of virgin territory into urban land over the next decade to 2025 (or more than the current area of the city of Mumbai being converted urban every year). However, if India follows the global model of more people in more space, India will need to double in size from its current urban land area. Even if cities don't de-densify, they will nevertheless expand their coverage area as populations increase. In all scenarios, India has little choice but to plan for large new urban tracts. Regardless of the specific lay of urban land in India, by 2025 the density of population in Indian cities will still be meaningfully higher than that in developed countries.

Table 4.4: Minor changes in urban densities can have mega outcomes

Calculating the urban land area of India, March fiscal year-ends, 2011-25E

	2011	2015	2020	2025
Projected urban population (mn)	377	424	485	548
Further densification scenario—Urban population density increases by 2% every year				
Urban density (people/sq km)	3,689	3,993	4,409	4,868
Urban area (sq km)	102,220	106,099	109,892	112,647
De-densification model—Urban population density decreases by 2% every year				
Urban density (people/sq km)	3,689	3,403	3,076	2,780
Urban area (sq km)	102,220	124,511	157,519	197,222
Mid-way scenario—Urban population density remains the same				
Urban density (people/sq km)	3,689	3,689	3,689	3,689
Urban area (sq km)	102,220	114,845	131,331	148,635

Source: Census of India; Shlomo Angel; McKinsey report on urbanization in India; Kotak Institutional Equities research

In absolute terms, the Indian urban cover will likely be between 110,000 sq km and 200,000 sq km, up from the current ~100,000 sq km. We would allay the fears of civil society and policymakers who foresee this determined urbanization eating into the country's agricultural interests. Even the most aggressive urbanization growth numbers imply total urban land in India at 200,000 sq km, which represents around 5–6 per cent of the overall area of the country (on a base of 3.3 million sq km). India's cropped area is ~160 million ha or ~1.6 million sq km. A doubling of urban land, from 0.1 million sq km to 0.2 million sq km, will shave but a whisker off India's land under cultivation. This perspective reinforces the case for governmental and political will to meet India's growing urbanization needs head on.

Growing cities: Scaling-up more robust than seeding

India's urbanization is more a fact than a mission which puts the spotlight on space. In the absence of defined spaces, this juggernaut will roll where it will. The government has started talking of creating 100 new cities triggering important discussions on the merits of creating new cities versus scaling-up the old ones.

India's urban development history has many examples of manufacturing spawning cities in the past century. Like elsewhere in the world, manufacturing plants create their own ecosystems around themselves, becoming the kernels of cities and small towns. This took place in several sectors: iron and steel (for example, Bokaro, Jamshedpur, Rourkela), automobiles (Chennai, Pune), oil and gas (Digboi, Jamnagar) and mining (Asansol, Bellary, Dhanbad) among others. If India's manufacturing sector grows exponentially in the next decade, India may spawn a few new cities. Apart from government expectations, there is little to indicate this kind of growth. On the contrary, manufacturing's contribution to India's GDP has remained rather stagnant. There has been a rising share of services-dominated growth in the past decade and also in most projections: this phenomenon favours the strengthening and scaling-up of existing cities.

India has had little success in seeding new cities. Mihan near Nagpur, for example, was created from scratch and invested with roads, power and associated infrastructure is beginning to see a glimmer of economic activity after around a decade of lying fallow. Lavasa, a city near Pune, saw a slow pick up despite having in place all the infrastructure people look for in a city. It remains to be seen whether Gujarat International Finance Tec-City (GIFT) near Ahmedabad will see large private companies set up shop there. In most cases the cities require an economic engine for people to congregate which may or may not be available or may or may not take root in a new city.

India is hoping to seed seven new cities along the Delhi–Mumbai Industrial Corridor. Any manufacturing activity that picks up in this corridor will attract investments in local infrastructure as well as workers with skills that are in demand. Thus, indeed, are cities born. However, corridors like this one cannot absorb all of India's urbanization needs and potential. On the other hand, smaller cities in India are growing briskly with residents aspiring for better services and employment. Its census towns are demanding a greater share of attention from authorities and India would do well to focus on these centres and provide urban amenities and governance to these areas. In our view, new drivers of employment favour expansion as a more sustainable urban development model than planting of new cities.

Growing cities: Global experience of planting cities

Government cities: Many countries have tried to seed new cities by moving their seats of government away from existing cities to new virgin territories. This is typically done to decongest an old city and to give the administrative machinery more room. Given that most of the activity is related to the business of government, these cities tend to have very limited populations compared to the main cities. Table 4.5 shows that most of these capital cities, even though they are almost a fourth or a fifth of the size of the main city, host only a tenth of the population of the economically important cities. The densities of these towns are hence significantly lower than the densities of larger towns.

Table 4.5: The administrative cities are meaningfully small in size and population compared to the large cities

Area and population of administrative city and largest city of various countries, May 2014

		Area (sq kms)	Population (number)	Density (people/sq km)
Australia				
Administrative capital city	Canberra	472	382,000	809
Largest city	Sydney	2,037	3,980,000	1,954
Brazil				
Administrative capital city	Brasilia	673	2,426,000	3,605
Largest city	Sao Paulo	2,849	20,273,000	7,116
Canada				
Administrative capital city	Ottawa	502	956,000	1,904
Largest city	Toronto	2,287	6,345,000	2,774
Malaysia				
Administrative capital city	Putrajaya	49	67,964	1,387
Largest city	Kuala Lumpur	1,943	6,635,000	3,415
Gujarat, India				
Administrative capital city	Gandhinagar		560,497	
Largest city	Ahmedabad		5,585,528	

Note:
The data for Gujarat, India is based on Census 2011.

Source: Demographia World Urban Areas; Kotak Institutional Equities research

These administrative capitals require meaningful investments to develop infrastructure for buildings and transport which gets funded by the state. It is no surprise hence that most countries have shied away from this model because it is too expensive to maintain a city for such limited use.

University towns: The world has many examples of thriving university towns, among which are Boston in the US, Oxford-Cambridge in the UK, Konstanz in Germany and Manipal in India. However, a country can have only a handful of such towns at best and here too the reputation and size of the city takes decades to form. Also, unless the town cultivates another attractive specialization it is likely to remain limited in size without sufficient opportunities to attract new residents.

In twenty-first century India, nurturing organic expansion appears to be the appropriate model for expanding the country's urban footprint. This approach can be very successful if the government accords it the kind of strategic planning and investment that it appears eager to pour into creating new cities.

Creating homes

Urban India needs to almost double its built-up area to around 75 billion sq ft in 2025 from the current ~40 billion sq ft most of it in bad shape. As India builds out an average of 3 billion sq ft of residential supply every year over the next decade, it needs to improve its quality of housing dramatically as with increasing prosperity, buyer profiles and requirements will change rapidly.

These calculations are based on modest assumptions of housing space needs. Even at 1,500 sq ft of space for an average 'Real-rich' household, it amounts to a per capita housing space of around 300 sq ft. In the 'Survivor' category, the per capita housing is barely 60 sq ft, not much more than a prison cell in many countries. However, even these modest assumptions imply a significant upgrade of the current housing facilities for Indians. The NSSO sixty-ninth round survey had pointed out the average floor area of a dwelling was 40.03 sq m (or around 400 sq ft) in rural India and 39.20 sq m (similarly, around 400 sq ft) in urban India, reflecting the poor housing conditions that Indians live in.

Residential demand accounts for about half the demand in any urban development. There is concomitant demand for commercial, retail and to some extent, industrial buildings in a city. Applying this rule-of-thumb, it is easy to envisage the magnitude of construction required in urban India. If India is to build out 6 billion sq ft of buildings every year, at a current costing of Rs 1,000 per sq ft to Rs 1,500 per sq ft, it represents an annual construction industry valued at Rs 6–9 trillion. We have, in the introduction section, highlighted the amount of cement, steel and paints that will be required for this.

Housing paradox 1

India's housing represents a paradox between low floor space index (FSI) and high density. Indian cities have one of the lowest FSIs in the world (typically ranging between one to two in most cases, compared with four or more in many large urban locations). The paradox is that these small spaces accommodate among the densest populations in the world. Low FSI causes the price/value of land to surge, making it unaffordable for many and this leads to a large number of people squatting on the land. What people cannot afford economically, they try to grab politically through the sheer force of their numbers. In this context, it is instructive to look at the slum regularization policies that many governments have followed, especially near election time, particularly in cities like Delhi and Mumbai. The Census of 2011 notes that 65.5 million—more than the entire population of the UK—people live in slums across urban India.

Few in urban India can afford to purchase the newer, well-constructed but expensive homes. According to the sixty-ninth round survey conducted by NSSO, the average age of houses in urban India as of 2012 is around 25 years though there has been significant construction in the last decade with 30 per cent of all houses in urban India less than 10 years old. There has been significant improvement over the last decade in the quality of housing in India though a lot remains to be done.

Housing paradox 2

Thanks to its love for real estate investments, India is in the curious position of having more houses than it has households. As reported by

India's 2011 Census, India's households increased by 60 million to 247 million from 187 million between 2001–2011. Reflecting India's higher 'physical' savings, the number of houses went up by 81 million to 331 million from 250 million. The urban increase is telling: 38 million new houses for 24 million new households. This does not mean that the housing shortage problem has been solved. As of end 2012, urban India had a deficit of 18.7 million new houses and rural India was short of 43.1 million houses.

More than three-fourths of urban residents live cheek by jowl in cramped spaces. The irony of this amidst plenty arises from two critical impediments: (1) low FSI ratio which makes land very expensive and (2) the inability to commute cheaply and quickly, which means that people have to congregate in and around areas where they can find economic activity and public infrastructure.

Affordable housing: Not an oxymoron

As much as 70 per cent of the urban housing shortage arises from the bottom four deciles of households whose ability to pay is severely constrained. If one looks at the monthly per capita expenditure (MPCE) at the fortieth percentile and calculates the ability to pay for a house, we find that the buying capacity of such households is capped at ~Rs 300,000 (see Table 4.6).

Table 4.6: Low-cost housing needs to be very affordable given the low MPCE

Calculating the ability of the 40th percentile household to pay for housing, March fiscal year-ends, 2012

MPCE at 40th percentile (A)	1,028
Annual expenditure per capita (B*12)	12,335
Number of people in an urban household (average)	4.7
Total annual household expenditure (C)	58,469
Annual household income (125% of C, assuming some savings, etc.; D)	73,086
Housing to income ratio (E)	4.0
Possible value that the household can afford (D*E)	292,344

Source: Ministry of Housing and Urban Poverty Alleviation; Kotak Institutional Equities research

MPCE numbers, as we will see in the chapter on consumption, are typically significantly understated and even if we were to adjust for that, a large portion of the unmet housing needs are at an economic value of Rs 0.5–1 million. Assuming that households of five members can crowd into spaces of between 250–400 sq ft, housing stock in the range of Rs 1,250–Rs 4,000 per sq ft will be needed to address the needs of people up to the fortieth expenditure percentile.

Three significant changes can help keep costs in control: (1) availability of a larger land area on the periphery of a city, (2) cheap and fast transport to and from the city's commercial hubs and (3) higher FSI such that the available land can be made more productive. Raising the FSI ratio is in itself no panacea as a higher FSI will need to go hand in hand with improved access to infrastructure (of transport, schooling, health, leisure, water, etc.). Creation of infrastructure, especially transportation, creates its own positive externalities and this can be financially harnessed to develop infrastructure.

It is not very difficult to meet these pricing expectations, especially if these three aspects start getting addressed simultaneously. However, the ability to finance four times the gross income (as we have assumed in our example) typically does not exist as a household is not considered credit-worthy by conventional banking channels. Many unorganized or non-banking channels offer credit to such households but at significantly higher rates of interest and for lower tenures thereby reducing the multiple to gross income that households can get to buy their homes for. Developing a financing market for this segment can be a money-spinner.

Another alternative that India has rarely seriously considered (given the high 'ownership' rates) is the development of a rental market. Residential housing in India typically offers very low yield. This low yield expectation should be harnessed to develop a thriving rental market. The ability of many households to live in better conditions can be strengthened if they can move to secure long-term rental houses. Large rental colonies owned by investors populated by a population that is finding its economic feet in a city can be a meaningful game-changer.

The challenge of housing for the segment below the fortieth percentile of the expenditure bracket is daunting. We have noted earlier that more than 70 per cent of the housing deficit is in this segment. The solutions will lie in (1) making economic growth trickle down further via good education, employability and employment, (2) requiring development of low-cost housing nearby if a higher FSI is offered and (3) developing 'transit rental housing' strategies where the government can be the owner of well-constructed housing which is given out on rent for a set number of years, say for a decade or so, till a person/family can find its feet in a city.

It has never been a prudent or successful strategy to move people far from economic centres which defeats the main reasons why people move to cities—better opportunities and proximity to work. Delineating distant suburbs for the poor is therefore an unworkable or impractical solution as too many will chose to live in closely-packed quarters closer to their places of work. Cities have to have housing units at various price points in their various hubs, including the cheapest.

The South Korean model has some answers

When South Korea went through a phase of high growth in the 1980s, it faced similar housing problems. Good quality housing was restricted to few and the average quality left a lot to be desired. Having lost a fifth of its housing stock in the war of the 1950s, the Korean government had made multiple announcements in the intervening decades on the construction of new housing. By the mid-1980s, the number of houses to households was only around 70 per cent, leading to sky-high prices. Unaffordable housing became the platform on which President Noh won the presidential election of 1987. The presidency was clinched by his promise of creating 4 million new housing units on a base of around 6 million units. This plan was later scaled down to around 2 million units, of which 0.9 million were built in and around Seoul (see Table 4.7). A quarter of a million units were allocated for low-cost housing. Notably, the project relied heavily on private capital financing: 67.7 per cent was provided by prospective home buyers through pre-sales, 22.3 per cent by loans from the National Housing Fund and only a minor portion (around 10 per cent) came from the government.

Table 4.7: The Korean government massively intervened in the housing market—creating superior physical outcomes

Indicators of housing stock in South Korea, calender year-ends, 1980-2010

	unit	1980	1985	1990	1995	2000	2005	2010
Housing stock	'000	5,318	6,104	7,160	9,204	10,959	12,494	13,884
Housing space per capita	m2	10	11	14	17	20	23	25
Housing space per household	m2	46	46	51	59	63	66	67
Number of people per room	person	2.1	1.9	NA	1.1	0.9	0.8	0.7
Housing units with warm water	%	10	20	34	75	87	96	98
Housing units with water-borne toilets	%	18	33	51	75	87	94	97
Housing supply ratio*	%	74	70	72	86	96	106	113
Housing units/1,000 people	unit	142	151	170	215	249	280	302

Note:
(a) Housing supply ratio = (total housing units)/(total number of households); based on the 2010 census definition of a household.

Source: Cho (2013); World Bank Institute; Kotak Institutional Equities research

Land acquisition for the plan was a particular challenge. In the 1960s and 1970s, land supply for residential development was mostly done through negotiations between private parties—landowners and developers. Realizing the need for large-scale land acquisition for residential development, the government instituted a land expropriation system from the late 1970s. In particular, the Housing Construction Promotion Act was revised in 1977 to empower the Korea National Housing Corporation (KNHC) to conduct housing construction and supply projects. The Act gave KNHC the right to expropriate land for housing development.

The Land Development Promotion Act in 1980 further enabled the government to (1) re-zone large tracts of agricultural land or forested areas, allowing for their conversion into residential land and (2) mandated that landowner sells such land to the government at prices determined by a publicly certified appraisal organization. The compensation was determined before the designation and up-zoning, which led to heated differences between landowners and government agencies.

Co-opting landowners into the urban growth story

It is moot that governments need to make land more easily available and then generate a supply shock such that housing does not end up becoming a luxury. The history of land acquisition in India suggests that government expropriation will not work. Co-opting landowners in the periphery of a city as it plans its growth is hence critical.

Most often the land on the periphery of a city is agricultural. Land designated for urban use—commercial, industrial or residential—is valued at 30-50 times the value of agricultural land. As the unit of measurement gets calibrated more finely, switching from hectares to square feet, a lot of value gets created in the process.

Cities can expand more easily if the landowners are able to benefit from this value transition. This requires two critical things to fall in place: (1) clear and enforceable title to land and (2) easy tradability. India has started digitizing its land records, but it will take a while before we see the benefit of this through more efficient and transparent property trading. Easier tradability requires that the state does away with the artificial distinction of what is agricultural land and what is not. Given the wide arbitrage in value, the current distinction only creates scope for corruption. More important, a closed market where only a farmer can buy agricultural land from another farmer creates less liquidity and poorer price discovery; people anyways find ingenious ways to change their vocations in official records.

If the owners of land on the periphery of a city can be made champions of urbanization, the process of development of a city can be quick and rewarding for all (as the famous Magarpatta example of Pune illustrates).

Transporting people around

A city's roads are its arteries. The economic vitality of a city depends on the ability of its citizens and goods to move around the city to create economic value. A quick and cheap way to move both makes for a thriving city. An efficient transport system allows the city to expand further from its business district. More important, in an economy dominated by the services sector, different services congregate in different places in a city so the ability to quickly and cheaply move around to and from various hubs is important.

The importance of mobility can be gauged from the fact that urban planners now talk of 'transit-oriented-development' rather than 'development-oriented-transit'. The current thinking in urban planning suggests the primacy in developing transit modes such that they guide the development of a city. This is in stark contrast to the earlier thought process that transit should follow development. 'Build and they will come' is now the guiding philosophy.

The potential build-out

Modern cities go significantly beyond conventional conduits of transport like roads. Many have successfully introduced modes like the metro, trains and waterways. Even if we focus on the two big aspects of transport, that is, urban roads and metros/trains, we find that the build-out will be quite meaningful both in terms of physically expanding the current networks and also in terms of the money that will be required to be spent on this.

Indian urban planning guidelines (service level benchmarks of the Ministry of Urban Development) propound that roads should occupy 11 per cent of every sq km of urban area in a city (7 per cent for towns). The other service level benchmark of the same policy is that the road density should be 12.25 km per sq km of area. Using the 12.25 km per sq km criterion, we find that (1) Indian cities fall significantly short of planned road acreage (Indian urban roads total a length of only 0.4 mn kms) and (2) the build-out will need to be 5 times the current available stock of roads over the next ten years.

If India were to build roads to these specifications for its expected urban spread of 150,000 sq km by 2025 and we take a conservative costing of Rs 30 million per km for urban roads, it will need to budget Rs 40 trillion for roads. For our calculations to come true, India will need to build more than 350 km of roads every day—such is the order of magnitude of deficiency in India. Given that we have struggled with the creation of 20 km a day of highways, we need to seriously rethink how urban roads will get created. A more effective solution will be to build infrastructure in peripheral areas where the city is likely to expand and create suitable infrastructure there.

Given that by 2025, sixty-three cities in India are expected to have populations of more than a million people, all such cities will, according to the current thought process of the Ministry of Urban Development, be eligible for metro systems of their own. If we add this component —metros under consideration and construction—India's transport spend on roads and metros will be upwards of Rs 50 trillion.

India has successfully been able to communicate to its citizens the idea that for inter-city roads, a toll needs to be paid to make the projects economically viable. This is not necessarily the case with urban roads which are typically provided to citizens as a free common public good. Even if the idea of tolling urban roads is both a difficult sell and a difficult one to execute, India needs to move towards congestion pricing, high parking charges, property taxes, etc. to generate revenue for maintaining and developing its roads. Railway/metro pricing is increasing though the current spat in Mumbai between the operator and the state government shows that a wide chasm remains between what the state thinks its citizens have a capacity (or willingness) to pay and what makes a project economically viable.

Transport in urban India—in a sorry state

The rationale for making these large investments is to offer an urban consumer better quality travel facilities. Unfortunately, there are limited large-scale surveys on this and the best data that is available comes from a 2007 report commissioned by RITES (earlier known as Rail India Technical and Economic Service, an engineering consultancy company, specializing in the field of transport).

Table 4.8 shows the quality of commute in urban India in terms of (1) the mode of commute, (2) the average speed of travel and (3) the average distances travelled in various types of cities. Larger cities see much longer commutes in terms of distance. If we juxtapose them with the slower speeds in larger cities, the travel time expands exponentially. Pollution caused by transport ranks as one of the most important contributor to overall pollution across large Indian cities. Investment in infrastructure is hence critical if cities are not to choke on themselves. A detailed substantial debate is required on the relative merits and de-merits of the various modes of transport.

Table 4.8: Two-fifths of transport in India is still non-motorized

Mode share of trips in urban India, March fiscal year-ends, 2007 (%)

City category	Population	Mode of transport						Average speed (km./hr)	Average trip length (kms)
		Walk	Cycle	Two wheeler	Public transport	Car	IPT (a)		
Category-1a	>0.5 mn with plain terrain	34	3	26	5	27	5	26	2.4
Category-1b	<0.5 mn with hilly terrain	57	1	6	8	28	—		2.5
Category-2	0.5-1.0 mn	32	20	24	9	12	3	22	3.5
Category-3	1.0-2.0 mn	24	19	24	13	12	8	18	4.7
Category-4	2.0-4.0 mn	25	18	29	10	12	6	22	5.7
Category-5	4.0-8.0 mn	25	11	26	21	10	7	19	7.2
Category-6	> 8.0 mn	22	8	9	44	10	7	17	10.4
National		28	11	16	27	13	6		7.7

Note:

(a) IPT = Intermediate Public Transport

Source: Study on Traffic and Transportation Policies and Strategies in Urban Areas in India; Wilbur Smith and Associates, Ministry of Urban Development (2008)

Even as India improves its public transport, it needs to take into account the large influx of private vehicles. As in the rest of the world, as more Indians become financially stronger, they aspire for private transport. India's penetration rate of cars is so low currently that if it were to go the way of the developed world, its car population can grow more than 50 times the current size!

Two-wheelers have been the favourite mode of private transport in India even as cars pick up steadily. This is symptomatic of the low purchasing power in India but more important, it is because the road space is so limited that a two-wheeler is a more efficient mode of transport than a four-wheeler.

It is important to note that the carrying capacity of two-wheelers and four-wheelers in India is now much more than the carrying capacity of buses (see Table 4.9). This shortage in public transport manifests itself on Indian roads where buses almost always carry significantly beyond their certified capacity as do suburban railways.

Table 4.9: Carrying capacity of buses is significantly lower than that of private transport

Registered motor vehicles in India and their carrying capacity, March fiscal year-ends, 2012 ('000)

	Two wheelers	Cars, Jeeps and taxis	Buses
Number of vehicles	115,419	21,568	1,677
Typical carrying capacity (#)	2	4	40
Total carrying capacity	230,838	86,272	67,080

Source: Ministry of Road Transport and Highways (2011-12); Kotak Institutional Equities research

The cost of public transport is kept significantly low, in many cases much below the economic cost of operating it. This leads to deterioration in the public service and forces people to opt for personal transport clogging the streets. Converting citizens to public transport requires (1) changes in economic incentives in favour of public transport and away from private transport, coupled with (2) improving the quality of the commute. The suggestions here are obvious and have been reiterated in multiple committee reports.

Telecommuting for work, entertainment, shopping

The nature of regular travel is undergoing a sea-change and is likely to evolve rapidly in the immediate future. Planners would do well to take cognizance of these changes.

Communication technology: Most travel is on account of work, education or leisure all of which require the physical presence of a person. As communication technologies evolve, it allows people to enjoy many of these things from the comfort of their homes.

Multi-hub city models: Cities are seeing the development of satellite hubs that are increasingly self-sufficient. As cities move towards a mixed-development model, distances travelled will potentially reduce even as the frequency of trips may increase.

Urban freight: City design needs to take into account the movement of freight in a city. The pattern of intra-city freight movement is changing dramatically thanks to the development of e-commerce. Earlier where consumers went to shops and lugged their purchases home, we now have e-shopped goods being delivered to consumers' doorsteps. E-commerce valuations hitting the headlines these days are an indicator of the potential of this business. Freight forecasting will be required to take this sudden but dramatic change into account.

Typically freight movement in an Indian city is enabled by fleets of vehicles of all sizes as well as non-motorized transport (handcarts, rickshaws, etc.). Freight movement requires the planning of loading and unloading points. Warehouses located close to a city can interfere with the flow of passenger traffic while those located too far compound heavy vehicle traffic and increase costs. Given the importance of non-motorized freight in India means that the average speed on roads for both people and freight typically gets determined by the slowest moving vehicle.

Sudden and unexpected changes can shape cities

In an exceptional paper, 'From Horse Power to Horsepower', Morris (2007), then a Ph D student at the University of California, identified the challenges that urban centres were facing in the late nineteenth century: horse manure.

By the late 1800s, the problem of horse pollution had reached unprecedented heights. The growth in the horse population was outstripping even the rapid rise in the number of human city dwellers. American cities were drowning in horse manure as well as other unpleasant byproducts of the era's predominant mode of transportation: urine, flies, congestion, carcasses, and traffic accidents. Widespread cruelty to horses was a form of environmental degradation as well.

The situation seemed dire. In 1894, the Times of London estimated that by 1950 every street in the city would be buried nine feet deep in horse manure. One New York prognosticator of the 1890s concluded that by 1930 the horse droppings would rise to Manhattan's third-story windows. A public health and sanitation crisis of almost unimaginable dimensions loomed. And no possible solution could be devised.

In ten major US cities, the number of teamsters rose 328 percent between 1870 and 1900, while the population as a whole rose only 105 per cent…This situation was made even worse by the introduction of the horse into an area from which it had been conspicuously absent: personal intra-urban transportation. Prior to the nineteenth century, cities were traversed almost exclusively on foot. Mounted riders in US cities were uncommon, and due to their expense, slow speeds, and jarring rides, private carriages were rare; in 1761, only eighteen families in the colony of Pennsylvania (population 250,000) owned one. The hackney cab, ancestor of the modern taxi, was priced far beyond the means of the ordinary citizen.

Horses need to eat. According to one estimate each urban horse probably consumed on the order of 1.4 tons of oats and 2.4 tons of hay per year. One contemporary British farmer calculated that each horse consumed the product of five acres of land, a footprint which could have produced enough to feed six to eight people. Probably fifteen million acres were needed to feed the urban horse population at its zenith, an area about the size of West Virginia. Directly or indirectly, feeding the horse meant placing new land under cultivation, clearing it of its natural animal life and vegetation, and sometimes diverting water to irrigate it, with considerable negative effects on the natural ecosystem.

And what goes in must come out. Experts of the day estimated that each horse produced between fifteen and thirty pounds of manure per day. For New York and Brooklyn, which had a combined horse population of between 150,000 and 175,000 in 1880 (long before the horse population reached its peak), this meant that between three and four million pounds of manure were deposited on city streets and in city stables every day. Each horse also produced about a quart of urine daily, which added up to around 40,000 gallons per day for New York and Brooklyn.

There were many other issues: flies that bred in the filth, over-crowding of the horses in the stables, high death rate of the horses (average life expectancy of only 2 years), the inability of the coach-drivers to control their vehicles leading to deaths of pedestrians, etc.

But something completely unexpected took place which changed the situation: the internal combustion engine began humming in cars.

Contemporary observers calculated that cars were cheaper to own and operate than horse-drawn vehicles, both for the individual and for society. In 1900, 4,192 cars were sold in the US; by 1912 that number had risen to 356,000. In 1912, traffic counts in New York showed more cars than horses for the first time. The equine was not replaced all at once, but function by function. Freight haulage was the last bastion of horse-drawn transportation; the motorized truck finally supplanted the horse cart in the 1920s.

As difficult as it may be to believe for the modern observer, at the time the private automobile was widely hailed as an environmental savior. In the span of two decades, technology eradicated a major urban planning nightmare that had strained governments to the breaking point, vexed the media, tormented the citizenry, and brought society to the brink of despair.

Infrastructure for the city

The key to making city life affordable lies in providing access to all citizens to high-quality but affordable infrastructure services like power and water. Citizens don't necessarily look for the cheapest (or free) delivery of these services; what is valued more is the consistency, quality and quantity of delivery. Traditionally, these services have been significantly subsidized in

India and in many cases these low resources compromised the quality of the utility: what is provided free is not valued by the consumers.

Water: Drinking water demand

India's National Water Policy 2002 prioritizes drinking water over other uses of water. However, as with many policies Indian, there is a sub-clause which allows for a reprioritization, if so required. The drinking water segment has been stealthily privatized due to the failure of urban water utilities.

India prices its water low and compounds this sin by failing to collect these charges efficiently. The all-India average (twenty cities) price of water is less than Rs 5/cu metre. However, 31.8 per cent of this is unaccounted for water (UFW), that is, it is not billed. The water availability is limited to an all-India average of only 4.3 hours in a day. Unfortunately, such is the state of apathy towards data in this sector that the last benchmarking exercise in this sector was done by the Asian Development Bank in 2007 as part of its 'Benchmarking and Data Book of Water Utilities in India' from where this data has been cited. We saw similar apathy towards data in the previous section on the urban transport sector where we worked using 2007 data.

Larger cities like Chennai, Mumbai and Bengaluru are more 'profitable' than others, their operating ratio (the ratio of their costs to their revenues) being less than one. Jamshedpur, the only city whose water utility is in private hands, is also able to recover costs. Across India, however, water utilities are plagued by water theft and high operating ratios.

The failure of public utilities is evident from daily scenes of bulk water delivered to some residential societies by water tankers in towns and cities. Each carrier bears a load of up to ten cubic metres of water. The tankers source their water from groundwater or from municipal supplies and provide it to localities which are not connected to the urban water supply grid, or which get less than they need from allocated supplies. They charge anywhere upwards of Rs 1,000 in Mumbai for a payload of ten cubic metres, as against municipality charges of Rs 50 for a similar volume.

The failure of utilities has also fuelled the growth of the packaged water industry and water purifiers. In effect, the failure of a public utility has posed a private cost on its residents who now need to spend time and money cleaning up the water that comes to their homes.

India also does not treat its waste water. According to estimates by India's Central Pollution Control Board in its report 'Status of Water Supply, Wastewater Generation and Treatment in Class-I Cities & Class-II Towns of India', as much as 69 per cent of India's water went untreated in 2009. The same report also states that 39 per cent of the actual operating capacity does not meet the government's standards for the safe disposal of water.

Municipalities across the world price water significantly higher than the current price in India: the typical pricing of water is close to US$ 1 per cubic meter. The pricing of water by municipal bodies in developed economies typically includes charges for cleaning the waste water that is generated after consumption, not so in India. Some water utilities like Delhi have over the last few years, raised water charges by up to 50 per cent, imposed fixed monthly service charges and added sewerage maintenance charges. Mumbai has made only tepid attempts to price its water effectively. Tentative steps to create water utilities get discussed in cities like Delhi and Mumbai, but so far there has been no tangible movement. If the creation of water utilities takes off, just like the creation of distribution companies in the case of the electricity sector, it can open up investment opportunities.

Privatizing water services is a sensitive issue, and not just in India. Attempts to privatize water services in Latin American countries have seen mass protests followed by city governments backing down. The rallying case for opponents of privatization is Cochabamba in Bolivia, where violent protests by residents on increased water-usage charges spooked the government into backing out of its agreement with a private company.

In India, Delhi and Mumbai have experimented with limited privatization of water services, without much success. Smaller towns, however, have taken a lead in experimenting with the privatization of water management and service delivery. Nagpur's water services are managed by Veolia, a private party. Veolia is also working with the Government of Karnataka in smaller cities like Gulburga and Hubli-Dharwad. As cities begin to get more comfortable with the idea of the private sector handling their water needs, the trend could pick up in earnest across the country.

The power situation

According to the 'Report on Eighteenth Electric Power Survey of India' by the Central Electricity Authority in 2013, Indian cities' demand for power was expected to grow meaningfully at 7 per cent per annum. This is significantly faster than the rate of growth of urban population, which is expected to be 2.7 per cent over the next ten years reflecting the latent demand in the power sector and current low usage. This estimate of power demand growth may prove to be conservative.

This demand push is coming from not just the consumer sector but also from the commercial sector. As the report points out: 'the increasing trend in commercial category is primarily due to rapid pace of increase in consumption due to development of malls and other related activities. The drop in industrial utilization is primarily due to shifting to service industries from manufacturing units.' Even as one arm of the government prepares to make manufacturing 25 per cent of India's GDP, other arms seem to have a healthy scepticism about this. Interestingly, the expectation of a shift of power requirement to malls may turn out to be misplaced if e-commerce takes off meaningfully. More pertinent, the latent demand in urban India is high with hardly any meaningful electrical mechanization having taken place.

Power utilities suffer from the same fate as water utilities. They are required to meaningfully under-price their services. Unlike water, where the pricing decisions rest with every urban local body, power is a state subject and prices typically get set at a state level. State electricity boards run into severe losses because of the policy of under-pricing power. States have, over the last couple of years, started raising power prices but a lot remains to be done to avoid losses.

In many cases, it is not just about raising the cost of power. Power is delivered as inefficiently as water and there is significant scope for improvement. A World Bank policy research working paper by Ghani, Grover, Goswami and Kerr (2013) notes the success of a Bhiwandi distribution franchisee (Bhiwandi is a textile hub in Maharashtra near Mumbai). In a matter of four years, AT&C losses fell to 15 per cent from 58.5 per cent, collection efficiency shot up to 99 per cent from 58 per cent and load-shedding became a thing of the past.

Finding the funding mechanism

Urban growth demands a brutal review of policies regarding local governance and funding. Many rural areas are morphing into census towns (or what for every practical purpose are urban areas but not recognized as such) while many cities are outgrowing their administrative or master plan boundaries. However, they continue to be governed by structures like gram panchayats or powerless municipal corporations.

The seventy-fourth amendment to the Constitution of India assigned local governing bodies a larger responsibility in governance. This was intended to give greater responsibility to municipal corporations and their equivalent in rural areas (gram panchayats) to bridge the distance between citizens and state and central governments. However, these institutions still lack the financial and legal muscle required to put in place effective programmes for growth in their jurisdictions. City councils in particular (municipal corporations) find themselves at the mercy of a plethora of agencies differing in purview, scope (national, regional or city-level) and purpose. A consolidated city plan typically has no identifiable champion.

A few Indian cities do have mayors, whose roles are purely ceremonial. In many large cities including those in China and the US, city mayors have meaningful responsibilities and governance powers. In such cities, the mayoral position is often a stepping stone to national political office. A mayor who is directly elected by a city's populace can be held accountable for the well-being and growth of the city. More important, a mayor can provide a clear vision for a city's growth compelling all departments mandated to create and maintain public services to integrate their plans into an overarching vision.

Taxes collected from urban residents are an important revenue source for local state governments. These monies are then allocated across the state, particularly in the direction of important vote banks, which may typically be in the rural areas currently. As urbanization alters voter demographics, we expect a sharper focus on the governance of cities. Half of India could well have been urbanized already (depending on definitions) so it is a question of time when the semantic ambiguity is resolved and these areas are classified as urban. As the urban voter finds his/her voice being spoken in the political mainstream, Indian cities should expect to get the ability to determine their own destinies.

City governments, constrained to raise revenues on their own, are hence dependent on the state or on the centre or on schemes like the Jawaharlal Nehru Urban Renewal Mission (JNNURM) (see Table 4.10). A city dependent on external funding is typically beholden to the interests that fund it, the priorities of which (in terms of what projects need to be executed, where and when) can be very different from what a city needs. More important, different authorities typically end up working in silos which impede the development of a grand master plan for the city.

Table 4.10: Municipalities in India are significantly dependent on grants from state—and they run a deficit

Proportion of total revenues of municipalities in India, March fiscal year-ends 2008 (%)

'Own' revenues—primarily property tax	34
'Own' revenues—non-tax	19
Grants, assignments and devolution by sate government	33
Grants by central government	5
Grants from Finance Commission	2
Others	7
Total income	100
Revenue expenditure	64
Capital expenditure	42
Total expenditure	106

Source: Thirteenth Finance Commission quoted in Mohanty (2014); Kotak Institutional Equities research

Cities will have to turn to their residents for funds. Residents will have to be co-opted into development plans and funding for their cities. Good infrastructure raises the value of real estate in a city, which the city needs to harness to fund itself. We look at these funding options in some detail.

- **Usage charges:** A public good, by definition, needs to be available to all for use and its access should not be restricted by the inability to pay for it. We have noted earlier that utilities that under-price their services typically get run down rather quickly. This is true of power and water utilities. Roads are a public good that do not get priced appropriately even as larger numbers of private vehicles continue to ply on them. It is not viable for cities to give its citizens free infrastructure or price it so low that the revenues are insufficient either for maintenance or upgradation. Typically, a large chunk of city residents can afford to pay for the development and maintenance of infrastructure. The model followed by toll roads, telecom and to some extent the power sector set an example for how to price public goods.

- **Property taxes:** For most Indian urban households, the roof over their heads is the most valuable thing that they own, accounting for the largest chunk of their net worth. Cities could well tap into the net worth of their populations by instituting effective property taxes. As cities go about developing infrastructure, it leads to a surge in real estate prices. This is especially so of transport infrastructure to areas those were previously not connected or were poorly connected as illustrated by rising property rates near the metro in Mumbai and Delhi or around ring roads in cities like Hyderabad. This increase in capital value needs to be shared equitably between the city and its citizens. Of course, an increase in property taxes needs to lead to a concomitant increase in the quality of services which are not specifically billed, for example, road lighting, fire services, sewage, draining or garbage disposal.

- **Land auctions:** Cities can tap their new and old areas for funding. The new areas may develop either on their own or their growth can be calibrated through the development of infrastructure. If the areas develop spontaneously, cities miss out on an opportunity to shape their development and hence they can end up becoming haphazard. Cities would do well to imbibe a 'transport-oriented-development' model to nudge their populations to newer areas. Land in such areas can be auctioned for development. Similarly, as older parts of cities die, they need to redevelop those land parcels to continually revive the cities. Mumbai's conversion of its old mill area into a thriving business district demonstrates the potential for this. Future conversions need not be as protracted and challenging if approached more strategically and holistically taking into account contentious issues like rehabilitation, laws and litigation while creating a master plan for the area proposed for conversion. Auctions for high-value land like Mumbai's mill land can significantly enhance the resource base for cities.

The idea of city corporations accessing debt markets is a seductive one. However, we believe Indian city treasuries are quite far removed from accessing this pool of money as is evident from: (1) the corporate bond market, which is typically much larger across the globe, not having yet taken off in India for a variety of reasons and (2) their lack of stable or reliable cash flows to support the issue of debt. When cities show signs of financial independence through the measures outlined earlier, issuers will be more comfortable accessing bond markets while investors will have greater conviction as well. Even if a few municipalities manage to raise funds from the debt market, it is expected to remain a niche and marginal resource base for now.

New cities will find it even more difficult to generate funds. If built from scratch, such cities will see long gestation periods between investing and building smart infrastructure and attracting residents to live and pay for it. This can be costly, but more worryingly, it may turn out to be wasteful.

GameChangers

Pricing and collection are critical

Privatization of utility services conjures images of profiteering. However, it is important to highlight that it is the maintenance and operation of the utility that is up for privatization and not the commodity itself, whether water or power. Private participation needs to be combined with a strong state governance mechanism to prevent the private sector from using its natural monopoly position to make super-normal profits from essential utilities.

India needs to structure the pricing of its water and power utilities right. All developments on the demand side as well as conservation efforts will get a significant boost once the signalling mechanism of pricing is in place. Indian urban utilities also suffer from long delays in collecting their dues with average debtor days being more than half a year for both water and power utilities. Complete metering, economically viable pricing and ensuring that the sums due are collected require strict enforcement. This is critical for ensuring not just generation of revenue but also to foster a culture of compliance. If a few people get away without paying, it invariably creates a question in the minds of the compliant populace. Across the three segments of agriculture, industry and residential, the pricing and collection of these utilities can lead to the realization of their economic value prompting more efficient use.

Flexible and integrated master plans

Indian cities will grow significantly larger in area. Many city master plans take into account incremental growth in population around a single economic hub. India's urban growth will deviate meaningfully from its city blueprints on account of our forecasted trends in (1) de-densification and (2) multi-model (or multi-hub) development. The modern city must provide for flexible land use. It must create processes to facilitate the process of land conversion from agricultural to residential/commercial. This will also allow the city treasuries to benefit directly and officially from such conversions, currently a grey and shadowy area.

A consultative and flexible planning process could respond quickly to the changing needs of a city. This is easier said than done in light of the plethora of laws and agencies that currently govern the process of urbanization. The consultative approach must take into account the long-term growth of a city and offer its residents the opportunity to live and work outside the heart of the flagship city. This requires city limits to extend and build on land outside the city for developing new hubs. Stakeholders in a city's development therefore include not just its current residents but its future residents as well who live in adjacent areas. Inevitably and inexorably, a city will stretch to include these residents in due course.

City master plans must take into account projections for population growth and the character of the surrounding land, making provisions for new city centres.

Mayoral system—localized city representation

Robust cities need empowered and directly elected leaders for their governments. Whether the leader is called a mayor, city president or CEO is moot. A role like this comes with accountability and the responsibility to develop and execute integrated city development plans. As the gap between the number of urban and rural Indians begins to close, we will see a sharper focus on the governance of cities. The mayor's office can be the one that defines the overarching vision for a city's development and coordinates between all the providers of services and capital goods needed to realize the vision. We expect that as urban voters become stronger political constituencies they will demand locally responsive governments.

Financial prudence

Indian cities have typically very poor levels of governance because they do not have the ability to fund their own maintenance and development and hence remain vassals of the state or the centre. Property taxes and utility prices need to rise so that cities can create utilities that function.

Indian cities are small when compared with most of the other larger cities in the world. As India prepares to de-densify, it should use the building of infrastructure in the periphery of a city to complement its increase in property taxes or development charges. If Mumbai has to grow to the size of New York, it will need to grow five to twenty times its current land area (depending on what estimate we take of the land area of these cities). Covering such large areas will require pre-emptive setting up of infrastructure the value of which will need to be financed by eventual residents.

India remains a poor country and the pricing of utilities is an issue typically fraught with political sensitivities. However, there are examples of how utilities need to improve outcomes through effective and efficient management so that a larger populace is able to get the service from· the utility. Today, given the decrepit nature of various utilities, many neighbourhoods get excluded as there is no money to build infrastructure. In most cases, a well-regulated private entity is able to bring in efficiencies.

Development of housing capacity

The poor quality and quantity of housing in India means that there will be a massive push towards better housing. Our calculations suggest that

India will need to build an average of 6 billion sq ft of capacity every year over the next decade. The real estate industry in India remains tightly controlled while large parts of it remain unorganized. India needs to streamline rules for housing to allow more organized players and timely approval and completion of projects.

Low-cost housing involves two shifts in present thinking: (1) increasing the bankability of a large section of the population so that they are credit-worthy at low rates of interest and (2) opening up large areas of land so it is cheap and available for construction. The city must explore the idea of an easy, secure leased-housing market for new migrants. India can pick up helpful hints from South Korea which induced a massive supply shock in the mid-1980s to ensure that almost everyone owned a home.

Significant investment in moving people and goods within the city

A concomitant requirement of the increase in the land area of cities will be the need to develop very large-scale transport solutions. A large part of the transport need is currently being met privately (people buying their own two or four-wheelers). Cities must improve and then incentivize public transport to reduce congestion and pollution. Mixed-use housing (following a pattern of 'transport-oriented development') should mean that travel distances come down even as the frequency of trips may increase. The challenge in building transport infrastructure is to figure out how to make these utilities recover investments and pay for operational costs.

THE CHANGING FOOD PALATE
AND THE CHANGING FARM

Evolving food habits

INDIA'S AGRICULTURE IS changing. Large price changes in agriculture outputs over the last decade, some triggered by the government and some emerging from the changing demand pattern have changed the landscape meaningfully. Price increases of outputs at a time when the costs of many inputs (like fertilizers, water and to a large extent, fuels and power) were controlled and stable led to a massive profitability boost for the agriculture sector. This profit boost has been reinvested into the ecosystem thereby helping increase yields and capital formation in the sector.

This is not to say that all is rosy with Indian agriculture. It is still beset with a wide variety of problems: (1) a poor landholding structure, (2) layers of intermediation and (3) dilapidated or un-built logistics being some of the key challenges. A highly fragmented landholding structure means that change is difficult to come. Coupled with poor land title records (though this is changing), farmers are stuck to their land. Fragmentation of land also means that aggregation of produce becomes a challenge thereby requiring large number of aggregators which shows up in a large chain of intermediation. Poor warehousing and logistics cause massive losses in value.

We have pointed out elsewhere in the book that Indian agriculture needs to lose a large number of people. For half of the labour force to produce only around a sixth of the nation's economic output is a travesty as it keeps a large chunk of India's population poor. Two large changes will need to take place (though they are taking place at the margin, the pace needs to accelerate): (1) people need to stop entering and indeed, start leaving agriculture. This requires significant job creation in other sectors and (2) the output of agriculture itself needs to meaningfully expand. This will take place via increasing yields in staples but more importantly, through the changing output of agriculture (more horticulture, dairy and poultry). Over the next decade, Indian agriculture should see more large-scale farms coupled with a significant focus on food processing as Indian agriculture adapts to the rapidly changing diets.

Understanding the landscape

Given India's sizeable land mass (India is the world's seventh largest country in terms of land area), a large portion of which is arable, India ranks high in terms of total production of various commodities. In many cases, the yields are low which represent a significant opportunity for improvement. India is among the largest producer of various food items. While it ranks second to China in the total production of staples (like wheat and rice) and fruits and vegetables, India is the largest producer of milk. Even in the numbers of livestock, India ranks among the top two (see Table 5.1).

India's arable area as a proportion of its land area is at 48 per cent (159 million ha/329 million ha) which places India as the country with the highest arable area in the world. In comparison, US' arable land proportion stands at 18 per cent of its land area, while for China it is 15 per cent (both countries are roughly three times India's land area). This is important from two perspectives:

a. The debate in India on converting agricultural land into industrial and residential use has, at many times, turned violent. If India needs to move towards an economy not dependent on agriculture but having a healthy mix of manufacturing and services, a reasonable part of its land will need to move beyond agriculture. Even if the most optimistic scenarios of India's urbanization were to play out over the next decade or so, the total urban land area will be less than 6 per cent of its land mass, compared to the 48 per cent that is currently under agriculture.

Table 5.1: India's agriculture production compares well with the rest of the world

Measuring India's agriculture across various parameters, 2012

	India	World total	India's rank	Second to
Area (mn ha)				
Total area	329	13,442	7	
Land area	297	13,009	7	
Arable land	159	1,411	2	China
Irrigated land	86		1	
Crop production (mn tonnes)				
Wheat	86	701	2	China
Rice (Paddy)	157	722	2	China
Pulses	17	67	1	
Groundnut	7	38	2	China
Vegetables and melons	105	1,090	2	China
Fruits excluding melons	74	637	2	China
Sugarcane	342	1,800	2	Brazil
Milk	122	723	1	
Livestock (mn nos)				
Cattle	210	1,430	2	Brazil
Buffalos	111	194	1	
Agri equipments ('000)				
Tractors in use	3,149	29,320	2	USA

Source: Agriculture Statistics at a Glance (2013)

b. This large use of land highlights the low yield of Indian agriculture. In spite of such large land resources being devoted to agriculture, India still does not top the charts in overall production, which reflects poorly on its yield performance. India has a significant potential for increasing its yield. Indian farmers have started using the land more often (multiple-cropping is now increasing) but a lot more can be done. Indian farmers, on an average, cropped their land 1.4 times a year; Chinese farmers did so 1.6 times (as of 2009).

The changing production profile of India's agriculture

In 2013, India produced 500 million tons of food stuff for its population of 1.2 billion people, or around 400 kg per person (or, an availability of more than a kilogram a day per person). The half-a-billion tons production comprised almost equally of food grains and horticulture (fruits and vegetables) as we see in Table 5.2. Sharp increase in production over the last decade (4.7 per cent CAGR volume growth) handsomely beat population growth (~1.2 per cent CAGR). Milk production also went up meaningfully to 132 million tons a year (or ~300 gm per person per day) over the last decade thereby enhancing per capita food availability.

Table 5.2: India now produces a quarter billion tons of food and horticulture; an eighth of a billion tons of milk

Production of foodgrains, horticulture and milk, March fiscal year-ends, 2003-13 (mn tons)

	Foodgrains	Horticulture			Milk
		Fruits	Vegetables	Total	
2003	174.8	45.2	84.8	130.0	86.2
2005	198.4	50.9	101.2	152.1	92.5
2007	217.3	59.6	115.0	174.6	102.6
2009	234.5	68.5	129.1	197.5	112.2
2011	244.5	74.9	146.6	221.4	121.8
2013	257.1	81.3	162.2	243.5	132.4
CAGR (%)	3.9	6.0	6.7	6.5	4.4

Source: Ministry of Agriculture; National Horticultural Board; Kotak Institutional Equities research

India's agriculture season has traditionally been split up into the *kharif* (or monsoon-dependent crop; typically sown in June-July and harvested in October-November or around Diwali) and the *rabi* season (or the winter crop; typically sown in November-December and harvested in March-April, or just after Holi). *Kharif* used to be the dominant crop for India and hence its agriculture was very monsoon dependent. India's agriculture production profile is changing with the *rabi* food grains output now rivalling *kharif's*, and more important, horticulture catching up with food grains.

In the triennium (which means the average of a period of three years)

ending 1993, *kharif* was 56 per cent of the total food grains output while *rabi* was 44 per cent with an average total output of 175 million tons. Even as late as the triennium ending 2006, *kharif* was 53 per cent of the output of 207 million tons. However, for the triennium ending 2014, *kharif* output is expected to be 49.7 per cent of 260 million tons (see Table 5.3). The importance of *rabi* comes from the spectacular growth in the output of wheat. The winter *rabi* output is less linked to monsoon (as opposed to *kharif*, which is sown when monsoon strikes). This has also helped Indian agriculture to be less dependent on the vagaries of the monsoon. Horticulture output which used to be three-fourths of the food grains output in 2003 was almost equal to it in 2013. We expect horticultural output to meaningfully surpass food grain output as we go ahead.

Table 5.3: Kharif foodgrains output, which was 56% of total output a couple of decades ago, is now less than 50%

Output of grains in Kharif and Rabi season, March fiscal year-ends, 1993-2014

	Triennium averages (mn tons)			Proportion (%)	
	Kharif	Rabi	Total	Kharif	Rabi
1993	97.5	77.3	174.8	55.8	44.2
1995	101.0	84.1	185.1	54.6	45.4
2000	103.3	98.6	201.9	51.2	48.8
2005	102.5	92.9	195.4	52.5	47.5
2014	129.2	130.6	259.9	49.7	50.3

Source: CEIC; Kotak Institutional Equities research

The changes in agri–output pattern have been influenced by: (1) government interventions (which have had both positive and negative impacts), (2) free-market price signals and (3) changing demand patterns.

Government intervention

India is in the midst of a revolution in farmer incomes. This increase in incomes is characteristically different from the Green Revolution that India saw from 1967 to 1979 which was marked by sustained yield increases in staple crops like wheat and rice. The impetus for the first

Green Revolution came from high import dependency and the desire to achieve self-sufficiency. The current revolution (taken from the triennium ending in the financial years 2003 and 2014) has seen lesser traction in terms of yield increases but has seen massive price increases driven largely by increased global prices for agricultural goods and also the policy of the Indian government to increase minimum support prices (MSPs) across the board. As we see in Table 5.4, increase in realization due to price increases dominates the increase in yield.

Table 5.4: Significant boost to rural incomes, credit over the last decade

Computation showing the changing profile of rural incomes

	Prices			Production (mn tons)			Value (Rs bn)		Change	
	2004	2014	Chg (%)	2004	2014	Chg (%)	2004	2014	(Rs bn)	(%)
Agriculture—important commodities										
Wheat (Rs /qtl)	630	1,400	104	72	96	19	455	1,338	884	194
Paddy-Grade A (Rs /qtl)	590	1,310	88	89	106	8	522	1,391	869	166
Dairy (Rs /lit)	12	35	108	88	132	38	1,057	4,634	3,577	338

Source: Kotak Institutional Equities research

The central government's policy of disproportionately rewarding agriculture output (which has, possibly rightly, been criticized to be inflationary) has meaningfully altered the production profile by triggering a massive supply response. Of the 26 million tons increase in food grain production over the 2008–13 period, 19 million tons have come from the *rabi* season, of which 15 million tons is accounted for by wheat alone. The state of Madhya Pradesh has seen more than a doubling of output to 13 million tons from 6 million tons in this period, thereby accounting for around half the increase in wheat production (see Table 5.5). Madhya Pradesh has followed a policy of handsome bonuses over and above the generous MSPs declared by the centre. Across the state (as across the country), farmers have responded by devoting more acreage to wheat and also reinvesting the increased earnings in improving productivity.

Table 5.5: Dramatic improvement in Rabi output has been driven by spectacular rise in wheat production

Output of various foodgrains in the Rabi season, March fiscal year-ends, 2008-13 (mn tons)

	Wheat	Rice	Gram	Others	Total
2008	78.6	13.2	5.7	12.3	109.8
2009	80.7	14.0	7.1	14.6	116.3
2010	80.8	14.3	7.5	11.6	114.2
2011	86.9	13.2	8.2	15.4	123.6
2012	94.9	15.3	7.7	10.1	128.0
2013	93.5	12.5	8.8	14.2	129.1
Change between 2008-13	14.9	(0.7)	3.1	1.9	19.2

Source: CEIC; Kotak Institutional Equities research

Free market price signals

To understand that price works as a reliable messenger to mould economic behaviour of farmers in India, we need to look no further than the case of pulses. When prices of pulses in 2009 shot up to Rs 100 per kg, India was producing 14.5 million tons and was required to import 2–3 million tons. A couple of years later, India's production rose to 18.2 million tons and imports were practically abandoned. Sometimes a knee-jerk reaction when prices rise suddenly and sharply is to throttle price (as, for example, India now routinely does in case of onions and sugar). This distorts the market's natural response. As the palette of India changes (and more on that in the next section), prices will continue to go awry as supply tries to catch up with demand.

Changing demand patterns

While in the case of food grains, government interventions led to a massive supply responses, in the case of horticulture (fruits and vegetables), a very different dynamic worked. A demand surge which was not satiated due to a leaky and creaking supply chain led to sustained inflation. What showed up as food inflation in fruits and vegetables has also signalled to the farmers' increased profitability.

Based on the average wholesale prices that prevailed in 2013, fruits commanded a Rs 1.6 trillion market at farm gate prices and vegetables added up to another Rs 1.7 trillion which compares with the wheat and the rice market (at Rs 1.2 trillion and Rs 1.3 trillion respectively at farm gate prices). Fortunately for India, in fruits and vegetables the productivity compares well with world averages. Farmers have responded by increasing the acreage under horticulture and investing in improving productivity. However, even this needs to radically ramp us as India's plate and palette dramatically alter over the coming decade.

The changing palette of India

We deep-dive into dietary guidelines issued by India's National Institute of Nutrition (NIN) which specifies the calories and various portions of food required by individuals in various age, gender and work categories. Incidentally and for some context, peak calorie requirements in India for men and women (3,490 and 2,850 calories respectively) are 15–20 per cent higher than in the US (3,000; 2,400). Taking the portions of food that every category requires and the data from the Census and NSSO, it is easy to build an annual quantity requirement (see Appendix 3 for details).

We know that not everyone in India gets their recommended dietary allowance. There is significant inequality in the availability of both the quantity and quality of food and calories. However, even if we assume that everyone gets—or over the next few years, will get—the mandated dietary requirements, India's production profile will need to change. India currently produces a lot more of cereals than it needs and much less milk and vegetables.

Surprisingly, India produces almost twice its nutritional requirements of fruits and sugar. Fruits have been a large contributor to food inflation but India seems to grow far more than it needs (exports cannot explain such a large difference). This would underscore concerns about harvests that never reach the table thanks to problems with quality, storage and transportation. It also reflects poorly on the quality of macro-data that is gathered in India. Inability to trace the supply chain of a commodity as important as fruits shows up in the ineffectiveness of any plan that is made to remedy the supply chain. Initiatives like GrapeNet should help reduce wastage and also identify sources of supply.

Historically, governments have found it easy to procure and distribute food grains. The government keeps the support price of cereals high, which makes it remunerative for marginal farmers to produce cereals. From the perspective of a small and marginal farmer, growing cereals is (1) less risky (as there is a guaranteed buyer for the produce) (2) less labour intensive when compared to vegetables and (3) less time (gestation period) and capital intensive than fruits. Similarly, given that India's subsidized public distribution system (PDS) offers mainly cereals by way of food, perforce it becomes the food of choice for low economic groups. India needs to break out of the cereal trap and diversify its agriculture.

As incomes increase, people spend less on food as a proportion of their total expense. We see a trend in the proportion of food expenditure falling consistently across all expenditure deciles in both rural and urban India. More important, cereals as a proportion of total food expenditure fall as incomes rise. As incomes increase diets evolve to include milk, vegetables, fruits, beverages and non-vegetarian products; some of these categories individually become more relevant than cereals.

As we see in Table 5.6, by 2025 India's food requirements will dramatically alter, and in turn will demand a change in its production profile. What is important in any forecast is the trend, the direction of movement and the order of magnitude. Almost invariably, the specific data point will turn out to be wrong. This transition can almost be taken to be preordained as it is driven by (1) the changes in occupation structures as more people move out of physically demanding agriculture and into manufacturing and services and (2) the increasing prosperity of Indians which will make them demand more variety on their plate.

The economics of agriculture

This change may be difficult to come by unless India addresses two fundamental fragmentations: (1) of its landholding structure and (2) its agricultural supply chain. Indian agriculture is very fragmented—119 million cultivators and 144 million agricultural labourers (according to the 2011 Census) put together produce only 4.4 per cent of India's GDP (that is the GDP of agricultural produce at farm gate prices). Large parts of the sector are unorganized and fragmented and the use of technology is low.

Table 5.6: India needs to focus on pulses, milk and vegetables production

Food demand pattern, March fiscal year-ends, 2011-25

	Units	2011	2025E	CAGR
Cereals and millets	mn tons	283.0	181.4	(3.1)
Pulses	mn tons	18.0	38.6	5.6
Milk and milk products	mn tons (1 ton=1,000 l)	121.8	184.7	3.0
Vegetables	mn tons	146.6	229.2	3.2
Fruits	mn tons	74.9	51.1	(2.7)
Sugar	mn tons	24.5	15.1	(3.4)
Fat	mn tons	13.6	15.3	0.9

Note:

(a) The requirement of pulses is also met by non-vegetarian items like egg, meat, chicken and fish.

Source: National Institute of Nutrition (2010); Census 2011; NSSO 68th round; Kotak Institutional Equities research

Landholding in India is increasingly fragmenting. Table 5.7 shows that the number of cultivators increased by 67 million to 138 million over the period 1971–2011. A large part of the increase (56 million) in the number of cultivators came at the marginal farmer level (who own less than 1 hectare), whose ranks swelled from 36 million to 92 million. Over the same period, the small farmer community (that owns between 1 and 2 ha) increased from 13 million to 25 million.

Table 5.7: Land fragmentation continues apace

Holdings of land by number and area, March fiscal year-ends, 1971-2011

Category of Holdings	1971	1981	1991	2001	2011
Marginal (<1 ha)	36	50	63	75	92
Small (1-2 ha)	13	16	20	23	25
Semi-Medium (2-4 ha)	11	12	14	14	14
Medium (4-10 ha)	7.9	8.1	7.6	6.6	6
Large (>10.0 ha)	2.8	2.2	1.7	1.2	1
All holdings	71	89	107	120	138
Average size (ha)	2.3	1.8	1.6	1.3	1.2
Total	162	164	165	159	159

Source: Agricultural Census Division; Kotak Institutional Equities research

Looking at the same equation differently, the land controlled by marginal farmers went up to around 35 million ha. Small (1–2 ha) and semi-medium (2–4 ha) farmers cultivated a cumulative 73 million ha of land. The land in control of medium (4–10 ha) and large (>10 ha) farmers decreased to only around 50 million ha in 2011.

This fragmentation has significant implication on two counts:

a. Typically contiguous land areas grow similar crops as it makes it easier to share knowledge. Also a large catchment area makes it meaningful for some infrastructure to absorb the crop grown. For example, a sugar belt requires a sugar mill, a potato farm requires a cold storage unit or a pulses growing region requires a *dal* mill. Hence, if the cropping pattern of an area has to be changed, it requires the buy-in of a larger number of individuals and also the building of suitable and commensurate infrastructure.

b. Contract farming becomes a challenge as it requires managing a larger number of farmers. Ideally, companies would like to manage a lesser number of farmers as the cost of training and standardization is lower in this. Managing different farmers (with different types of yields and qualities) becomes difficult.

In spite of fragmented landholdings, the price of land has increased significantly (between 2–5 times in many cases) over the last 5–7 years. This has been driven by two factors:

a. Increased prices and realizations: Value of land has risen significantly as the realizations have increased. Realizations themselves have increased both due to the increase in output (yield) and the increase in prices of the output.

b. Increasing urbanization and infrastructure building is leading to increased value of the land as either an industrial or residential plot. Infrastructure projects especially related to roads (like the Pradhan Mantri Gram Sadak Yojana) have created positive externalities by connecting villages to town-markets.

For states where the yields are higher (for example, Punjab and Haryana), or where there have been significant urbanization or industrialization driven developments, many farmers have found it expedient to sell their land and acquire cheaper land in areas which currently have low yields or lesser development. A visit to rural hinterlands in Rajasthan and Madhya

Pradesh clearly shows that many farmers from Punjab and Haryana have come here and acquired larger tracts of land than what they sold off. This also feeds into the increased prices of land seen across the country.

The return from agriculture (especially if a farmer sows staples or commodities) is in low-to-mid single digits if we account for land at market prices. The return on investment that a new farmer can expect (if he were to acquire land at market prices today) is low. Such a farmer who grows two crops and none fail (typically one crop in three years, or six sowings, fails) will be around 7 per cent if he farms in the rural hinterland. As one gets nearer to the cities, the return on investment falls significantly as the land has many competing uses, including those for industry and residence. If one considers land just outside the city, agriculture simply does not make sense.

The reasons why farmers don't shift to cultivation of fruits and vegetables from staples range from their lack of understanding of how to grow these (leading also to a herding mentality of growing what my neighbour is growing, or sticking to what I know best) to the lack of processing, cold storage and logistics facilities. In the case of fruits, the crop cycle is longer (typically more than three years) which requires significant investments of working capital and patience. While the returns are expected to be higher, the overall quantum of loss can be significantly high for a farmer in fruit cultivation in case his crop fails. An integrated system of a fruit processor near the cultivation area can help fruit production increase significantly. All of this can be easily done through well-capitalized corporate entrants in farming.

This significant rise in prices of land means that any new farmer (or a corporate entering farming) will find it infeasible to grow cereals. This means that the focus of a new entrant in farming will be on horticulture: the average realization per ha for fruits is in the range of between Rs 0.1 million and Rs 0.3 million per hectare while the same is between Rs 0.1 million and Rs 0.2 million per ha when vegetables are cultivated. The realization from vegetables is comparable to realization from fields that have the highest productivity in growing staples (say a land in Punjab which will produce 10,000 kg of wheat per ha).

We should assess various aspects of India's agri supply chain to see how poised Indian agriculture is to meet the challenge of change. We look at this from the perspectives of (1) inputs like seeds, finance, fertilizers, soil and water, (2) post-harvest infrastructure like warehousing and institutions like APMC and warehouse receipts and (3) final outputs of agriculture and their processing.

Input prices have remained stable; credit has poured in

The profitability of cultivation from the perspective of a cultivator has increased meaningfully over the last decade. The cost of inputs has remained reasonably stable (relative to the increase in the prices of outputs) and that has created significant profitability for farmers. The cost of inputs typically include (1) seeds (if not saved), (2) fertilizers and pesticides, (3) power and fuel (to run tractors or water pumps) and (4) agri equipment. The cost also includes the imputed cost of family labour and rent. A significant part of the 'reforms' agenda is hence to bring in market pricing for the cost elements of farming.

The estimates of costs are made at an all-India level by the Commission for Agricultural Costs and Prices (CACP), a Government of India body which recommends the price to be set up as the minimum support price (MSP) for any agricultural commodity that will be procured by the government. The profitability is significantly different across regions depending on the yield of the land (which derives from the intrinsic nature of the soil, water availability and the application of fertilizers and pesticides). This happens because while costs across the country are similar (or don't increase proportionately with yields), India sets the same MSPs at a national level (though states are free to add their own bonuses). For states which have high yields like Punjab this leads to significantly higher realization per unit of land than for states with lower yield like Bihar and Madhya Pradesh. A farmer in the northern states also benefits from significant reserves of easily accessible groundwater and in some states, free electricity to pull out the water.

Capital formation in the sector picking up

Profitability in farming has consistently and meaningfully improved over time. However, the profit they make is still a fairly small number in absolute terms for a large majority of farmers as their land size holdings are very small. For larger farmers, agriculture is now becoming economically viable and this is leading to a revival of capital formation in this sector.

From the days of the Green Revolution (1967 to 1979) when the total capital formation in the agriculture sector peaked at 13.1 per cent of its GDP, it fell to 7.9 per cent in 1995. It has recently increased to 18.1 per cent in 2013. To achieve the targeted 4 per cent growth in the agriculture sector, capital formation needs to consistently remain between the range of 16 per cent and 20 per cent of agri GDP as the incremental capital-output ratio is estimated to be between 4–5X (that is, it takes 4–5 units of capital to be invested to generate one unit of growth).

The Government of India has mandated that a certain portion of the banks' advances have to be allocated to the 'priority sector' in which agriculture gets a major share. This has led to significant credit expansion in agriculture over the last decade driven by commercial banks. Banks which are unable to meet these targets are required to make up the shortfall by investing in the Rural Infrastructure Development Fund (RIDF) bonds issued by NABARD, the corpus of which has now grown to Rs 839 billion (as of 31 March 2014). The current practice has resulted in strong growth in agriculture credit but it has still not addressed the needs of the agriculture sector with a large proportion of farmers being deprived of credit.

If we slice the data to see the recipients of credit, the focus on small and marginal farmers becomes clear. While the overall credit to the agriculture sector from commercial banks went up ~10 times between financial years 2001 and 2012, credit to farmers owning less than five acres grew by ~17 times and for those above five acres by ~8 times (Table 5.8). Farmers owning less than five acres had 31 million accounts at the end of financial year 2012, up from 8 million at the end of financial year 2001, clearly showing an increased penetration and financial inclusion. However, this still means that less than a fourth of the marginal and small farmers have access to the banking system.

The banking sector is likely to face challenges in meeting the needs of agriculture credit over the next 8–10 years. We forecast that banks will not be able to achieve the 18 per cent priority sector lending target set by the Reserve Bank of India but will likely stay at the current levels of around 12 per cent. Even at 12 per cent of overall credit, credit/GDP for the agriculture sector will rise sharply to 63 per cent from less than 40 per cent currently as the agri GDP itself grows much slower than the banking deposit/credit growth.

Table 5.8: Credit is increasing to the marginal farmers at a higher pace

Number of accounts and amounts outstanding by land owned by farmer

	<2.5 acres	2.5-5.0 acres	>5 acres	Total
2001				
Number of accounts (mn)	5	4	4	12
Amount outstanding (Rs bn)	72	73	170	315
Average amount/account (Rs)	15,684	19,813	47,712	26,584
2012				
Number of accounts (mn)	16	14	10	41
Amount outstanding (Rs bn)	1,244	1,264	1,406	3,914
Average amount/account (Rs)	75,771	87,504	145,759	96,618
Growth (X)				
Number of accounts	3.6	3.9	2.7	3.4
Amount outstanding	17.2	17.3	8.3	12.4
Average amount/account	4.8	4.4	3.1	3.6

Source: RBI; Kotak Institutional Equities research

This need to lend skews the lending priorities for banks who are also periodically threatened with poor credit culture as politicians announce agriculture loan waivers. Just like in the market of outputs, the government is beginning to realize the importance of letting the price signal work, the pricing of agri-credit should also be made free. Today we have a paradoxical situation where loans for productive assets like tractors are lapped up at upwards of 20 per cent per annum even as the government wants to offer cheap credit.

Cultivation: Sowing the right seeds

Achieving scale and using the right technology can produce significant yield enhancements. Seeds, fertilizer and agri-equipment companies are in the best position to benefit from this trend. Soil and water quality are deteriorating which presents opportunities to seed and sprinkler companies.

Of all the inputs, seeds are at the forefront of significant technological advances. Traditionally, farmers saved the seeds from their crops for cultivation next year (called, not surprisingly, 'saved seeds'). The issue with this is that the species of the seed gets weaker over time as it does not cross-breed making it more susceptible and less resistant to diseases and insect attacks. Seed companies solve this through two different ways: hybridization and genetic modification.

Hybridization requires cross-breeding seeds to get the desired characteristics (more drought-resistant, more pest-resistant, increased yield or quality, etc.). Unfortunately for farmers and thankfully so for the seed companies hybridized seeds do not transfer their qualities from one generation to the next. A farmer cannot save the seeds but has to approach the company again in the next sowing season. The upside for a farmer of course is the potential of a higher yield through better resistance (to droughts, pests, etc.).

In genetically modified (GM) food, the desired changes are brought about by altering the genes of a species—for all practical purposes, the 'natural' process of hybridization is replaced with manual intervention. GM seeds, just like hybridized seeds, need to be purchased every sowing season.

Both hybridization and GM seeds, hence, create a business opportunity in the seeds sector. The global seeds industry is estimated, by the International Seed Federation, to be US$ 45 billion in 2013 while the Indian seed industry's size is only around US$ 2 billion. The argument for paying for seeds revolves around the better yield that a farmer can expect even though apart from the cost of the seeds, overall irrigation and fertilizer costs also typically go up.

A quick word on how the seed business works: seeds move from the germ-plasm stage to the breeder stage. Breeder seeds are then multiplied as foundation seeds which are further multiplied to get certified/quality seeds, which are sold to farmers. Seed companies typically do not own the land for growing the certified seeds (in some cases, foundation seeds also) and hence rely on landowners to grow the seeds for them.

India has taken a liking to hybrid seeds, especially in cash crops like cotton and sunflower. The levels of hybridization in food crops like rice remain low at around 5 per cent. Given the large land area devoted to paddy and the current low hybridization, this can yield a significant bounty for companies which are able to successfully create and market the right products. A similar growth area is the seeds of the various horticultural produce that are fast ramping up production.

Public sector seed distribution companies were set up during the Green Revolution to distribute high quality seeds to farmers but after liberalization of the seeds sector in the late 1980s, a large number of private and foreign companies have come in and now dominate seed sales. Private sector companies have focused primarily on the cash crop sector as (1) the distribution reach required to set up is more compact (cash crops are concentrated in a few areas and typically it is the larger farmer that produce cash crops) and (2) it holds a promise of higher margins as the value per kilogram of the output is typically higher.

Research on staples like rice has not taken off internationally or in India. Research in India is concentrated with the Indian Council of Agricultural Research and the State Agricultural Universities, which have suffered from poor commercialization (the difference between the expected seed output based on that estimated by the research institutes to the actual on-the-ground yield varies significantly). While there has been some breakthrough in Chinese and Japanese varieties of rice, these cannot be used in India as the Indian grain is longer and less starchy.

Over the next few years we should expect to see a very healthy growth for seed companies in staples like rice and wheat, or in higher value items like fruits and vegetables, which are now seeing an increased demand. India has been prevaricating on its decision to introduce GM crops in the food chain. A final decision in this regard (whether yes or no) will help the industry focus both its research and its distribution.

Fertilizers

With the aim of helping small and marginal farmers, the Indian government created policies to keep the prices of fertilizers low. This policy has taken various forms: (1) allowing private companies to earn a fixed returns on their investments (which not surprisingly led to, in some cases, gold-plating of their costs), (2) requiring fertilizer companies to undercharge for some products relative to others (case in point being urea) and (3) government keeping a stranglehold on the prices that the companies could charge farmers (this has led to prices being held in check even though input costs of feedstock is linked to global prices and has moved around significantly over the last decade).

Fertilizers are one of the largest components of input cost for cultivators (others being labour or rent if the land is not owned). This sector is also the most organized one as the making of chemical fertilizers requires large scale units. These characteristics make it both alluring and easy for the government to intervene in this sector. That the interventions themselves have ended up having effects which were not intended has not reduced the desire of the government to continue interfering.

The control of prices which artificially keeps urea cheap relative to other fertilizers has led to its significant overuse. The three main nutrients required in agriculture are nitrogen (N, provided by urea), phosphorous (P, provided typically by di-ammonium phosphate—DAP) and potassium (K, provided by murate of potash—MOP). The typical /recommended ratio of usage between N:P:K is 4:2:1. Given the lower prices of urea (and also for its ability to make a plant look more leafy and green), it has been the favourite fertilizer of Indian farmers, which skewed the ratio to 8.2:3.2:1 in 2013 (Table 5.9).

A better way of providing nitrogen to the soil is to alternate a leguminous crop (like pulses) which can fix nitrogen in the soil as it produces more protein for itself. However, given the risk associated with pulses which cannot take high temperatures or rain variations and lack of marketing support for them (typically requiring *dal* mills nearby), Indian farmers have relied on urea to meet their soil's nitrogen requirements. Given the increasing import dependency of pulses and their increased prices, this change may come by market forces rather than government intervention.

The policy of fixing final selling prices (while allowing the companies to make a fixed return) has led to Indian manufacturing of urea remaining stagnant compared to the increased demand and India is required to import ever larger quantities. A similar story plays out in the DAP segment. Given that India has no potash, it is anyways dependent on imports for MOP. Since the companies have to be paid to make their promised returns, the government continues to foot a large quantum of subsidy. Over the last few financial years (from 2009–14), fertilizer subsidy has ranged between Rs 600 billion to Rs 750 billion annually for the central government.

Table 5.9: Urea consumption remains significantly high as prices are held low due to government subsidy

Consumption of various fertilizers, March fiscal year-ends, 2004-13

	2004	2005	2006	2007	2008	2009	2010	2011	2012	2013
Nitrogenous	11,1	11.7	12.7	13.8	14.4	15.1	15.6	16.6	17.3	16.8
Phosphatic	4.1	4.6	5.2	5.5	5.6	6.5	7.3	8.1	7.9	6.7
Potassic	1.6	2.1	2.4	2.3	2.7	3.3	3.6	3.5	2.7	2.1
Total	**16.8**	**18.3**	**20.3**	**21.7**	**22.6**	**24.9**	**26.5**	**28.1**	**27.9**	**25.5**
Ratio										
Nitrogenous	6.9	5.7	5.3	5.9	5.5	4.6	4.3	4.7	6.5	8.2
Phosphatic	2.6	2.2	2.2	2.4	2.1	2.0	2.0	2.3	3.0	3.2
Potassic	1.0	1.0	1.0	1.0	1.0	1.0	1.0	1.0	1.0	1.0

Source: Indian Fertilizer Scenario, 2013; Kotak Institutional Equities research

For urea the market linkage of prices had not yet been fully established. However, prices of DAP and MOP were decontrolled with effect from 1 April 2010 as part of the Nutrient Based Subsidy Policy, where the subsidy will now be paid on per-nutrient basis (the amount of the subsidy per unit of the nutrient will be fixed and hence the fluctuations in costs will be borne by farmers). This is expected to lead to a more balanced use of nutrients (of course, keeping urea prices under check will mean that urea will continue to remain cheaper, unless DAP and MOP prices fall globally).

Improving the fertilizer mix can also help address (to some extent) the deteriorating soil situation in the country. The other area to look out for in the fertilizer segment is the increasing use of micro-nutrients to replenish the small but essential quantities of iron, zinc, manganese, copper, boron, molybdenum and chlorine.

Soil is deteriorating but there is improvement on the water front

The productivity of land is critically dependant on the quality of the soil. India has a wide variety of soils making it one of the most agriculturally diverse countries. According to the National Bureau of Soil Survey and Land Use Planning, roughly half the Indian soil was degraded as of 2005. Water and wind erosion has degraded more than 100 million ha (primarily deriving from deforestation). India also loses valuable arable land to lack of drainage (water logging) and over-irrigation (which causes salinity/alkalinity) as the dissolved salts come out. According to a report released in 2008 by The National Project on Management of Soil Health and Fertility, India had 517 static soil testing laboratories (STLs) and 134 mobile STLs, which had an annual capacity to test 7 million soil samples. However, most of these were not equipped to check for micro-nutrient deficiency in soil. Even though government subsidizes the setting up of a STL, there is limited private sector play currently though this can change quickly especially as horticulture takes hold.

In order to minimize the dependency of agriculture on monsoons, India has concentrated on bringing an increasing area under irrigation, which grew around three times since independence to 63.6 million ha in 2011. Around two-fifths of India's arable land is now covered with irrigation, providing farmers some fall back in case the monsoons fail. We refer here to the net irrigated area; the gross irrigated area is 89.4 million ha which means that some areas make use of irrigation facilities more than once in a year.

However, India's capacity to store water is a small fraction of what it is in other large countries. As pointed out in the World Bank's 2005 report, 'India's Water Economy—Bracing for a Turbulent Future' India stores only around 200 cubic metre of water per person per year as compared to 2,500 for China and ~6,000 for the US. India has since then hardly created any further storage facilities as large dam creation faces significant opposition both from environmentalists as well as from those who point out that the government typically fails in offering relief and rehabilitation to those who are displaced. This is especially low considering that India receives more than 85 per cent of its precipitation in just four months.

Irrigation in India has hence increasingly become dependent on groundwater as the government's ability to complete large-scale surface projects has waned (due to land acquisition, environmental and relief and rehabilitation issues). This increasing dependence on groundwater has meant that the expenditure on getting the fields irrigated has moved to the farmers themselves and has hence created the perverse incentive to keep diesel and/or electricity prices low so that the water pumps can be operated. Groundwater irrigation has, in some egregious cases, led to water-mining, which is depleting the water-table in some areas of the country and also causing soil salinity.

For a farmer surface water works out be cheaper than pulling water from the ground using a diesel or electricity operated pump. The prices for canal water are fixed per acre and not on the basis of volume used and have not been revised upwards for long periods of time. However, canal water makes a farmer dependent on the local authority's decision of timing the water flow which may not be suitable or effective for different crops. Groundwater pumps have hence grown meaningfully in the country and industry estimates (as gathered from the annual reports of listed companies in this segment) suggest that India now has around 20 million pumps installed. This has also led to one of the favourite promise of politicians to farmers: free or subsidized water.

Indian monsoons pour around 4,000 billion cubic metres (bcm) of water every year. Indian agriculture, which consumes 80 per cent of all water required in India, requires only around 800 bcm of water. India needs to get its surface irrigation back on track so as to obviate the need for expensive power to dig out water. Among other structural changes, this will require India honouring its commitments to previously displaced families and offering—and sticking to—relief and rehabilitation packages.

Increasing wages leading to increasing mechanization

Government policies can have unforeseen and unexpected side effects. While the main effect of the Mahatma Gandhi National Employment Guarantee Scheme (MGNREGS) has been to effectively increase the price of labour in rural India, the side-effect has been its help in increasing mechanization as it becomes more cost effective to hire capital equipment rather than human labour. The minimum wage rate law is now effectively implemented as government stands as a buyer of labour at that price.

Rural wages have risen by double digits over the last few years. An effective implementation of the law has ensured that the wages prevailing in the country are upwards of the minimum wage rate (we can think of

NREGA as the economic cost of enforcing a legal diktat of minimum wages). Wages increase significantly during harvesting time, especially in high yield regions.

These increased wages, especially when compared to the increase in the cost of tractors (adjusted for the larger horse-power that farmers are now buying), represent a significant divergence. We had noted this point in Chapter 2 (Table 2.6, page 40). Taking into account the fact that in its spare time a tractor can be rented out (to other farmers or to infrastructure companies) or can be used as a mode of transport, buying a tractor makes sense for a cultivator. The flow of credit (typically secured against the tractor, which has six-monthly instalments coinciding with the harvesting season) also makes the purchase decision easy. All this is reflected in increased tractor sales. Similar arguments hold for harvesters and tillers, which are also seeing a robust uptick in demand.

Not surprisingly, women, who are less productive when it comes to physical labour than men or machines, have been replaced as a form of human labour. We saw this in greater detail in the chapter on demographics and jobs. India runs short of skilled operators of many agri equipments. Developing these skill-sets can help create more sustainable and higher paying jobs in rural India.

Weather forecasting—still a sore point

In spite of the major investments that India is making on increasing the reach of irrigation in agriculture, almost half the arable land is still dependent on monsoons. One would expect that such large dependency on the monsoon will mean that over the last six decades India would have made significant strides in perfecting the art of forecasting the monsoon. Unfortunately, forecasts by the Indian Meteorological Department (IMD) have seen a 'significant deviation'—more than +/-5 per cent error in difference between the actual and the forecast rains over a large number of recent years. Most recently, this was observed in 2014 where the year ended being classified as a 'drought' (more than 10 per cent lower rains than the long-period average) year even as the forecast was for a 'below normal' monsoon; the actual deficiency was ~13 per cent as compared to the initial forecast of 4 per cent.

What is of bigger concern is that this is an all-India entire period forecast and does not cater to micro-markets or smaller time durations. The space-time distribution of the monsoon is more critical than the overall average number over the four monsoon months. This lack of ability to predict the weather has meant that the weather insurance market has also not picked up, leaving farmers completely at the mercy of the elements. Private companies are now entering the segment of weather forecasting.

GameChangers

Reforming the government interventions

Government initiatives in procuring (to maintain price stability), warehousing (to create buffers against uncertainties) and distributing (to alleviate hunger) are inefficient across the board. While minimum support prices have helped buoy farmer incomes, neither do they cover the entire country nor do they send the correct price or quality signal to a cultivator.

With the lofty aim of de-risking a cultivator, the government has created an elaborate mechanism to procure produce at prices remunerative to farmers. This has involved setting up the Commission on Agricultural Costs and Prices which studies the cost of growing a crop and recommends the price at which the government should buy. The price is also supposed to act as a fiscal nudge: a mechanism whereby the government indicates to the farmers the crops they should sow.

Food Corporation of India (FCI) implements price stability (or at least a pricing floor) by standing as a buyer at the prices indicated by the government as the minimum support price (MSP). MSP is effective for wheat and rice but is ineffective in other commodities (for example, pulses). The government has stepped up the procurement of staples via FCI and now buys around three-tenths of both rice and wheat produced in India. Given the sustained increases in MSP over the course of the last decade, it made economic sense for farmers to grow staples and sell them to the government. It would be better if the government procures at market prices but directly transfers the benefit/compensation to the farmers.

There used to be a very significant geographical skew in FCI's procurement. For example in agricultural marketing year 2009 it procured 42 per cent of its wheat and 25 per cent of all its rice from only one state: Punjab. States demanded and now have the ability to take on the responsibility of procurement on their own. Decentralized procurement now accounts for a fifth or so of FCI's procurement.

In crops where there is no MSP, a farmer gets the price indications based on the market. For example, in spite of no MSP, the fruit and vegetable cultivation area has more than doubled to 16.2 million ha over the last decade as the market prices have risen. Similarly, in pulses for which the government provides little support, India faced a glut in the mid-1990s as the steadily rising prices triggered a huge supply response.

A farmer is required to bring all his produce to APMC *mandis*, of which there are around 7,500, operated through principal markets and sub-yards. Given India's area of 3.3 million sq km, one should expect an average APMC *mandi* to cover an area of 435 sq km, which expressed as a radius of a circle, would be approximately 12 km. This implies that on an average a farmer would need to transport his goods 12 km to reach the *mandi*. However, the average hides significant inter-region variations, ranging from an average of 6 km in Punjab and 12 km in Himachal Pradesh to more than 50 km in the north-eastern states. Carrying the produce over such large distances causes a bulk of the enormous wastage across produce in India. Industry estimates suggest that two-thirds of the wastage happens while the goods are being taken from the farm gate to the *mandi*.

Setting up a new logistics framework

The APMC regime is being reformed across the country. States are now being encouraged to allow private *mandis* to come up which will allow private entities to set up their own yards where trade can take place. This can address the challenge of deepening the penetration of market yards. States are also moving towards modifying APMC acts though a lot remains to be done.

In early independent India, APMCs were set up so that farmers from nearby villages could come to a place monitored by government officials where licensed traders participated in an ascending auction such that farmers could get the best price for their produce rather than selling the produce to the village moneylender to whom the farmer would have been indebted. This seemingly innocent and effective idea met its nemesis in the licensing of traders who then went on to become monopolists or at least, oligopolists in their respective *mandis*.

The Competition Commission of India published a study in October 2012, 'Competitive assessment of onion markets in India', which lay the blame of the onion price spike of 2011 on the oligopolistic tendencies of traders in the *mandis*. The report mentions, among other reasons, the entry barriers in becoming a licensed trader, collusion among them, very low churn in traders and the lack of adequate infrastructure where farmers can bring their produce. The balance of power is tilted against the small scale nature of farmers (a typical landholding of less than 2 ha) and favours the aggregating and financing nature of the trader.

Data seems to suggest that APMC *mandis* anyways account for only between 5 per cent and 60 per cent of the produce across staples, fruits and vegetables in 2013 (see Table 5.10). The law, it appears, is followed significantly in breach as society and markets have found ways to meet the economic needs of connecting buyers and sellers. The reforms now being considered involve removing the requirement on a farmer to bring his fruit and vegetable produce to the APMC market. The idea now is to provide a farmer the flexibility to reach out to the final customer directly whether it is an individual buyer or a retail chain or even by becoming a contract farmer. Various states have now amended their APMC acts in line with the model act, which allows dis-intermediating the APMC market.

As social structures and institutions change (especially in a phase of high economic growth), a review of laws becomes critical. In a democracy, the push to change laws comes in only when the economic consequences of the outdated laws become egregious. In India we have seen such issues emerge most spectacularly in the allocation of natural resources or acquisition of land (its conversion from agriculture to commercial) or taxation (both direct and indirect). A law which requires its own review every few decades will help policymakers fine-tune it before its consequences become unmanageable.

Table 5.10: Only a small proportion of the production ends up in the APMC mandis

Production and APMC arrivals of various commodities, March fiscal year-ends, 2013 (mn tons)

	Production	APMC arrivals	Proportion (%)
Staples			
Paddy	105.2	36.9	35.1
Wheat	93.5	37.1	39.6
Fruits			
Banana	26.5	4.9	18.5
Mango	18.0	1.4	8.0
Papaya	5.4	0.2	4.4
Vegetables			
Potato	45.3	9.4	20.7
Onion	15.8	9.2	58.5
Tomato	18.2	3.0	16.7
Brinjal	13.4	0.8	6.1

Source: CEIC; Ministry of Agriculture; Kotak Institutional Equities research

Private players have started creating *mandis* around their warehouses. A *mandi* is a place for a farmer to bring his produce and the warehouse acts as a place to store it. Unlike the traditional APMC *mandis*, a farmer here can decide to only store the produce and not sell it on the same day. The warehouse operator also typically ties up with a financing company (typically banks seeking to meet their priority sector norms) and provides the farmer financing against the produce in his warehouse. With warehouse receipts becoming negotiable, a farmer need only endorse the receipt to complete the sale of goods whenever he feels the price is right. The sale can be facilitated by the warehousing company which can also act as a 'procurement agent' for a processor.

From the point of view of the private company operating a *mandi*, it can look forward to three sources of income: rental from the warehouse, financing commission and procurement commission. Some are also considering putting up retail outlets to enhance incomes.

Creating the storage

Prior to the Green Revolution, India suffered from acute shortages of food which made it dependent on imports, making it susceptible to political wrangling by countries which exported food. Having achieved self-sufficiency, India wanted to maintain a buffer so as to not be dependent on imports. Indian guidelines stipulate maintaining different buffers depending on the time of the year, ranging from 16 million tons to 27 million tons. Over the last three years given increasing procurements by FCI, India now faces a challenge of storing 60–80 million tons of food grains.

However, the storage space was built based on the expectations of filling up stocks to buffer numbers. Note also that agriculture is a 'state subject' according to the Constitution of India and hence a bulk of the investment in agriculture happens via states. This means that the states have more warehousing capacity than the Centre and some states have more proportionate capacity than the others. While private warehousing capacity exists we discuss only government storage capacity to get a sense of why India faces a peculiar problem of over-flowing granaries (and hence rotting grains) and malnutrition across different parts of the country.

Having a strong infrastructure for cold storage is critical for any country for developing a processed food market. India has looked at the cold storage market from the point of view of primarily one commodity: potatoes. The sectors which demand cold storage facilities range from fruits and vegetables (total annual production more than 250 million tons), dairy (132 million tons), poultry, meat and fishing (15 million tons), flowers (1 million tons) and processed foods.

India's cold storage capacity is concentrated in a few regions and at about 24 million tons, is a small fraction of the requirement. There are various challenges relating to the cold storage industry including unviable economics, lack of power supply and lack of specialized transport that can carry the goods from the warehouse to the consumer. To create favourable economics, the government does extend a subsidy but the other two critical factors (power and specialized transport) are yet to fully evolve.

Adding value by processing

Processing food adds both life and value to it. Given the weak linkages between the field and the final consumer, India did not process its food. Indians have been used to the concept of fresh food eating (whether it is in fruits and vegetables or in meat/poultry/fish or in dairy). Processed food has not been a part of Indian consumer's diet driven both by the lack of supply and the lack of storage capacity at home (fridges). With increasing urbanization, better availability of cold storages at home and lifestyle changes (double income families, nuclearization of families, etc.) the processed food market is evolving rapidly.

An important industry where food processing is beginning to show results is the dairy sector. At the production level of 132 million tons a year in 2013 and at wholesale prices of Rs 30 per kg, the overall value of the raw milk produced at Rs 4 trillion is more than the combined value of wheat and paddy put together. India is unique in its composition of milk consumption: 55 per cent of the milk consumed by Indians is buffalo milk (higher fat content) and around four-tenths is cow milk (equally split between hybrid and non-descript cows), the rest being accounted for by goats, etc. Around a third of the milk is now processed into value-added products like butter, ghee, cheese, etc. which add both life and value to milk.

The productivity of Indian milch animals is significantly below international levels. This stems from the fact that there has been limited research globally on increasing buffalo yields (as they don't account for such a large proportion of milk anywhere else) and the cow-hybrids developed globally have not produced the same results in hot Indian conditions. Note how similar this is to the case of research on rice. India has unique requirements and will need to focus on solving it problems itself. There is no readymade panacea available.

The dairy model relies on the cooperative model of which AMUL has made a great success, which has not necessarily been replicated across other states. Even where private processors are involved, they do not own the milch animals. They source milk from village owners at a price (or proposition) marginally better than what state cooperatives offer. Even though a farmer is not contractually bound to sell his produce to any particular buyer, most cooperatives and private players try to lock in farmers through innovative marketing approaches.

From the perspective of a dairy operator, the higher the proportion of milk that can be processed into value-added products the better will be the realization. Given the lack of storage and processing facilities, India has a significant potential to convert the dairy opportunity into a processed food opportunity and increase the market value of its produce.

Such processing is significantly required in the fruits and vegetables industry. Over the next few years, these sectors will be poised for meaningful growth in volumes and value.

E-WAY: GOVERNING INDIA

Making living easy

INDIA HAS LONG been chastised for its low ranking in various surveys and reports that document how easy or difficult it is to do business in a country. This is also symptomatic of the difficult life that people live in general in India. The 'low-trust' nature of our laws and society means that in India we have created significant friction costs in any interactions between citizens, government and businesses. Digitization of interactions can meaningfully modify—for the better—the way Indians live and do business.

Digital governance is important from several perspectives:

- **Creating, maintaining and upholding various rights:** Indian citizens and consumers are increasingly moving towards digital records of their identities, existence, properties and disputes. A digital existence, which is easier to verify and/or prove, can eliminate the issues of ghost beneficiaries and lost existences. Interaction with enforcing agencies like the judiciary or the police and grievance redress via regulators or consumer courts is improving as people can access these mechanisms with more ease and track their progress without needing intermediaries.

- **Enhancing accountability and transparency:** Digital records are portable across the country and unlike its paper cousin, changes made in digital records can be tracked easily. Authorities responsible for delivery can be accessed, issues escalated and resolutions recorded and later made public, if required. This creates a positive feedback loop of transparency and an audit trail between all the three entities that need to communicate with each other: the government, citizens and businesses.

- **Improving policy making:** Digitization will make it easier to track important changes in the structure and prosperity of the Indian population—its demographics, education, skilling, migration, asset-ownership, taxability and consumption patterns—will be readily available for analysis and policymaking. Drawing correlations between various databases of its citizens will allow the government—and businesses and analysts—to recommend and make better policies and products.

India is creating an impressive digital framework for the government to interact with its citizens and with businesses. Even government-owned businesses now have interfaces that have improved significantly. Over the last decade India has instituted several rights-based legislations, including rights to education, work and food. (1) Reaching the correct and intended beneficiaries of these rights, (2) ensuring the appropriate delivery of benefits and (3) escalation and resolution of grievances is now critical, as the laws give citizens the right to drag their government to court if it fails to deliver. Coupled with the right to information (RTI) and the (right to file) public interest litigations (PILs), Indian citizens are significantly more empowered now.

An important question to ask, though something that we will not delve into as part of this book, is whether the approach of welfare should be 'rights-based' or based on the ability to create employment opportunities so that persons and households can help themselves. In either case, it is imperative to bring in the efficiencies that digitization can make possible.

Changing interactions

Many activities have seen a significant change in government to business (G2B) and government to citizen (G2C) interactions over the past few years. We quickly run through a few of them to get a glimpse of the changes:

- **Tax filing and returns:** Out of the ~40 million people who filed taxes in India in financial year 2014, ~30 million filed these online (see Figure 6.1). Filing a paper-based tax return used to be accompanied by long delays in assessments and refunds. The current process offers an online opportunity to check (1) the tax that has been deducted by various parties on a tax-payer's behalf (Form 26AS) and (2) track the refund status. Typically, for individual assesses filing online, refunds for a financial year ending March usually come by November. It is now mandatory for anyone declaring an income of more than Rs 0.5 million to file taxes electronically. According to the data on the Income Tax Department's e-filing website, it is estimated that there are 6 million people whose incomes are in the Rs 0.5–Rs 2 million range and around 1 million people are above that range.

Figure 6.1: Online tax filers have increased 10X over the last six years

Number of online returns filed, March fiscal year-ends, 2008-13 (mn)

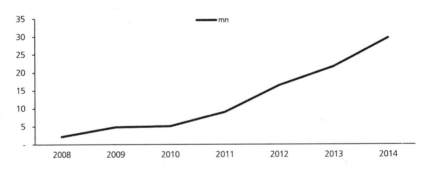

Source: Income tax department; Government of India

- **Voting in general and state elections:** India, the world's largest democracy, runs a very efficient election system. Casting a vote is an electronic affair and hence tabulation of votes and compilation of results takes place quickly and with authenticity. Typical vote counting starts at eight in the morning on the day of counting, it is often complete by the afternoon—quite a feat in a country in which more than 554 million people cast their votes in the 2014 general elections out of a total of 833 million who were eligible.

- **IRCTC or the largest e-commerce portal in India:** The Indian Railways' ticket booking site has wowed many users. In financial year 2014, Indian Railways booked more than 4 times the tickets compared to what it did in financial year 2010: the site booked 158 million tickets amounting to ~Rs 154 billion in financial year 2014 up from 72 million tickets amounting to Rs 80 billion in financial year 2010 (see Table 6.1). To put this in perspective, Flipkart, the current largest private online store, had gross merchandise value sales of Rs 28 billion in financial year 2014—though this is expected to grow many fold in the near future. Ecommerce portals and changing digital modes of payments are helping change the nature of interactions between citizen-consumers and merchants.

Table 6.1: More than 150 mn tickets sold online annually by Indian Railways

Number of tickets booked on Indian Railways' website, March fiscal year-ends, 2006-14

	Tickets (mn)	Growth (%)	Sales (Rs mn)	Average price (Rs)
2006	3		3,170	1,268
2007	7	172	6,780	997
2008	19	178	17,000	899
2009	44	133	38,830	883
2010	72	63	60,110	836
2011	97	35	80,070	826
2012	116	20	94,980	818
2013	140	21	124,190	887
2014	158	13	154,101	975

Source: Annual reports of IRCTC; Kotak Institutional Equities research

- **Getting a gas cylinder:** This has been an item on the 'reforms' list with respect to its pricing. However, booking a gas cylinder in India has never been easier and what is more, the cylinder actually turns up at home in two or three days' time. Besides, the consumer gets updated text messages from the company on the booking and delivery status. And now, anyone can check how many cylinders have been consumed and what subsidy has been provided by the government. Indian Oil, HPCL and BPCL all have their own 'transparency portals' with many details. With these 'transparency portals' in place, it will be easy to implement policy action to cap the cylinder subsidy.

- **Land records:** A portal site of the Department of Land Records, Government of India links to the sites of various state governments (like Rajasthan, Chhattisgarh, Karnataka, Uttar Pradesh and Madhya Pradesh among the larger states) which have digitized land records. From the perspective of industry, this will make way for easier land acquisition (land title is cited to be one of the more important causes of delays) while from the perspective of a landowner, it will make his/her property right more secure and verifiable.

- **Starting a company:** Starting a company, like filing returns or finding information on companies, is now all online. As late as in the 1990s or early 2000s, a trip to the Registrar of Companies was mandatory to look up data filed by companies. Finding a relevant record and then getting it photocopied could take as long as a day. Anyone can now do this online for nominal sums of money and get a PDF document instantly.

These are only some examples of common services for individuals that have markedly improved over the past few years. The key element has been digitizing one or multiple processes. Wherever the interaction, identity or the money aspect has been digitized, it has led to meaningful efficiency gains and better customer experience. The triggers for these changes have been fiscal, economic or, simply, the delivery of better governance.

The troika of digitization

Laying claim to these rights—and government services in general—is progressively being made easier as (1) the digitization of identities of Indians, (2) their online access to service-provider institutions (financial and government agencies) and (3) the spread of internet and mobile phones move apace. Money in India is also turning not just digital but also mobile. Digitalization of money coupled with the digitization of information (such as identities and entitlements) makes for a formidable combination.

E-records of you: It's not just about you...

The first aspect of digitization is the coming online of the Indian identity. The most visible face of this is the unique identity (UID) that is being rolled out across India. Almost all Indians are expected to have their IDs online and biometrically recorded by the end of March 2016. More than 700 million people have already enrolled for Aadhar. Even before UID came into existence, Indians looked up to their government to provide them with documents of identity.

Many states now have their own e-*sewa* (electronic help) portals, which assist residents in availing of various services electronically. Aspects that require interaction between a resident and the state involve those that certify his/her existence (birth, domicile, caste, residency, senior citizenship) or demise; his/her economic status (below the poverty line, ration cards); his/her mode of transport (driving licenses, vehicle registrations, bus and train passes) or lifestyle (drinking permits). Across almost all states, local governments provide basic infrastructure facilities like water and electricity and hence records of such bills indicate not just the amounts due but the existence and residence of a person (private players have also made an entry in this in some specific cases). Across various businesses and professions, citizens and businesses require permanent and periodic licenses with respect to business continuation, local taxation, health, cleanliness and employment.

Typically the department for each of these services sits separately in a state administration set-up. This means that even as some or most of these services are now digitized, they are unable to 'speak' with each other. UID can provide the ability to link the various identities that Indians carry. If the databases of various departments speak with each other, they can create a realistic profile of every Indian.

In many cases, the governments, or government-run enterprises, are withdrawing or are being competed away by strong private players (say, from the fields of telecom, television services or airlines). In many of these 'vacated spaces', private players are deploying technology to both reduce costs and improve revenue. Interactions, which were earlier of the nature of a citizen interacting with the government, are now changing to one where the citizen needs to interact with a business. In many cases, there will be a reduction in interaction between citizens and the government as government organizations withdraw. In cases where interaction with the government is required, 'citizen experience' will improve as the quality of the interaction with the government improves. Reduction in physical contact reduces the chances and quantum of 'speed money'.

...it is also about your properties

Hernando de Soto, an acclaimed Peruvian economist and the author of *The Mystery of Capital* points out that many small entrepreneurs lack legal ownership of their property, making it difficult for them to (1) obtain credit to expand or (2) sell their businesses when either they or their businesses have run the course. The existence of such massive exclusion generates two parallel economies: legal and extra-legal. An elite minority enjoys the economic benefits of law and globalization, while a majority of the entrepreneurs are stuck in poverty, where their assets languish as dead capital. India, with its 120 million small and marginal cultivators and 8.5 million retail (mom-and-pop) outlets requires strong land title records to help these entrepreneurs to prosper and gain benefits of economic growth.

Digitize land records and move to the Torrens system

The Department of Land Records, Ministry of Rural Development, has released a draft version of the Land Titling Bill, 2011 which seeks to provide the establishment, administration and management of a system of conclusive property titles through electronic registration of immovable properties. This will be a 'model law' for consideration by states to implement as land is a state subject. The bill envisages creation of authorities at the local, district, state and national levels. It provides for a mechanism to invite objections and for the resolution of disputes through special tribunals. Currently ~80 per cent of the disputes before the high courts are 'civil' (as opposed to 'criminal') with a large proportion of them having roots in land disputes.

The Torrens system of land records works on three principles:

(1) **The mirror principle**: The register (Certificate of Title) reflects (i.e. mirrors) accurately and completely current facts about a person's title, implying that if a person sells an estate, the new title has to be identical to the old one in terms of description of land, except for the owner's name,

(2) **The curtain principle**: One does not need to go beyond the Certificate of Title as it contains all the information about the title,

(3) **The insurance principle**: This provides for compensation of loss by the state if there are errors made by the Registrar of Titles.

Karnataka's Bhoomi model a success

Bhoomi, Karnataka's digitization initiative, has computerized 20 million records of landownership of 6.7 million farmers in the state. A printed copy of the Record of Rights, Tenancy and Crops (RTC) can be obtained online by providing the name of the owner or plot number at computerized land record kiosks in 177 *taluk* offices, for a fee of Rs 15. A farmer can check the status of a mutation application on touch-screen kiosks, which if not completed within forty-five days can be escalated. Requests are handled strictly on a first-come-first-served basis, eliminating preferential treatment and discretionary powers of civil servants. Operators of the computerized system are made accountable for their decisions and actions by using a bio-login system that authenticates every login through a thumbprint.

An update presentation by the Bhoomi team made in 2013 indicates that 150 million Bhoomi transactions took place where farmers picked up their title deeds and registered changes. The team estimates that annually 5 per cent of the land records mutate (change of ownership either due to sale or inheritance): this corresponds to 1.2 million mutations a year. Many other states have taken on the task of digitizing land records or processes associated with it. Chhattisgarh, Madhya Pradesh, Maharashtra and Uttar Pradesh are among the larger states where land records are available online. In some cases, records also include geo-tagging and photographs of properties (this helps to apply proper valuation frameworks for stamp duty/property tax collections). Many states also capture the plantations made by agriculturalists on their land.

Linking land records with registrations and encumbrances

The current system relies on a wide network of sub-registrar offices (see Table 6.2) which typically work in offline, paper-based environments. The government is working at having all the land records online and ensuring that each encumbrance/right is recorded electronically. There are multiple aspects of digitizing land records including (1) all systems related to land should talk to each other electronically, (2) physical interface with a citizen to be reduced, thereby reducing the importance of middlemen and power-brokers, (3) registration should be possible anywhere in the state (land being a state subject) and (4) all documents creating encumbrance/ right on land need to be compulsorily registered.

Table 6.2: Meaningful progress in registering land records online

Details of computerization of sub-registrar offices, January 2013

Land records and registration offices	
Number of Sub-registrar offices (SROs)	4,407
Computerization	
Total number of SROs computerized	2,915
States/UTs in which computerization completed	24
States/UTs in which computerization partially completed	3
Documents	
Number of documents registered per annum across all SROs (mn)	30
States/UTs in which e-stamping services available at SROs	8
States/UTs in which integration of land records and registration complete	8
States/UTs in which integration of land records and registration under progress	1

Source: Department of Land Resources; Ministry of Rural Development

Linking land records with registration (of both sales and mortgages) will help ensure that the land records remain updated and a city or state does not lose revenue associated with such a sale or mortgage (typically, stamp duties account for a large proportion of a city/state's revenue). States like Gujarat and Delhi, among others, have digitized the registration process.

Process improvements like getting an appointment time are also big wins (anyone who has registered documents will appreciate how helpful getting a time slot is!). Cities like Mumbai and Gurgaon are implementing the e-payment option for stamp duties, registration fees and search fees. Assessments can be generated online and money can, in some cases, be paid online directly into the Government Receipt Accounting System, which then offers proof of payment to the government body, bank and registering individual/business.

Financial assets are being significantly digitized

Financial assets in India have been significantly digitized. Indian stock exchanges and depository participants run one of the largest dematerialized trading platforms in the world. Banks are prioritizing their digital banking through the internet and mobile phones. Insurance companies sell quite a few plans online with internet becoming one of the largest channels for selling 'term' and general (car and travel) insurance products. Mutual funds offer to buy and sell units online without commissions. Even the government-run Employees Provident Fund Organization has a portal, which shows updated balances in accounts of employees.

The gateway to the financial world in India is through a Permanent Account Number (PAN). These asset classes require an investor to be registered with the Income Tax Department and the PAN serves as a unique identifier and record-keeper across transactions. PAN may eventually be linked with UID, which will allow the financially-excluded entry into the financial world.

E-records of your interactions with government

Filing tax returns online

As information and money get digitalized, it is becoming easier to tax the two non-digital entities: (1) people (individuals or corporates) and (2) goods and services. Earlier the activities of economic actors, their tax returns and their money were paper-based. This made it difficult to match economic activities with the money trail. A paper-based trail was, by sheer magnitude of the work involved, available only for sample checking and understanding process-robustness. Digitalization allows comprehensive checking, pattern recognition and more important, leaves a trail of data that can be correlated across entities and over time.

Indians now primarily file their taxes online. Across direct and indirect taxes, there are now unique and electronically linked identities for each taxpayer and there is an elaborate system of matching various transactions by a taxpayer through the course of the year.

Direct taxes require a unique PAN registration with the Income Tax Department. This number serves as a common identification tool across financial institutions (like banks, mutual funds and insurance companies) and helps to reconcile transactions between a deductor and 'deductee' (say an employer for an employee or a customer and a vendor). Tools available on the Income Tax Department's website allow a taxpayer to know the incomes/investments that have been reported against his/her name and the amount of tax deposited on his/her behalf.

The government is working to match the tax records with its databases (see Figure 6.2). Excerpts from two press releases make this clear and provide significant information on the numbers of taxpayers in India and various high-value transactions undertaken by them (both these press releases came from the Ministry of Finance and were hosted by the Press Information Bureau).

Figure 6.2: Profiling of an individual by the tax department now draws from various databases

Various databases in use by government of India in profiling its taxpayers and citizens

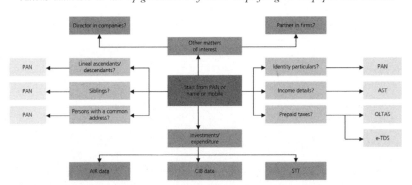

Source: Income tax department

Excerpt of press release #1, 10 December 2012:

A statement made by the Revenue Secretary to the media

In assessment year 2012–13, only 1,462,488 assesses (salaried persons, HUFs, professionals, firms, companies and transporters and retainers) filed their returns disclosing taxable income of over Rs 1 million. Any fair-minded person will agree that this is a gross understatement.

We know that—

- 1,600,746 persons made payments of Rs 0.2 million or more against their credit cards;
- 1,191,037 persons decided to purchase or sell house property worth Rs 3 million or more;
- 5,242,114 persons acquired mutual funds of Rs 0.2 million or more; bonds or debentures of Rs 0.5 million or more; shares issued by a company of Rs 0.1 million or more; bonds issued by RBI of Rs 0.5 million or more;
- 3,383,276 persons made cash deposits aggregating Rs 1 million or more in their savings bank accounts.

Excerpt of press release #2, 11 February 2013:

The Directorate of Systems of the Income Tax Department has undertaken a business intelligence project to identify PAN holders who have not filed Income Tax Return and about whom specific information is available in 148 information codes of Annual Information Return (AIR), Central Information Branch (CIB) data and TDS/TCS Returns. Information in the Cash Transaction Reports (CTRs) of FIU-IND has also been included as part of this data matching exercise. This data analysis has identified target segment of 1,219,832 non-filers linked to more than 47 million information records. Rule based algorithms have been used to identify high priority cases for follow-up and monitoring.

In the first batch, letters are being sent to 35,170 PAN holders by the Directorate of Intelligence and Criminal Investigation. The letter contains the summary of the information of financial transaction(s) along with a customized response sheet and seeks to know whether the person had filed his Income Tax return or not. A Nodal cell has been set up to capture the response and take follow-up action. There will be an online monitoring system to ensure follow-up action and track return filing and tax payment of the target segment.

One of course needs to take into account that the tax structure in India (as elsewhere) is based on income. If someone has cash deposits/ investments of a large amount that may not always mean that the person has earned that income in that particular year. Renewing a fixed deposit, for example, cannot count as income for a particular year.

As the roll-out of the Goods and Service Tax is being planned, significant time and investment have gone into getting the IT infrastructure right. For reasons of simplicity for taxpayers, ease of tax administration and bringing about a national common market, a common PAN-based taxpayer ID, a common return, and a common *challan* for tax payment have been designed.

The basic solution architecture requires that all stakeholders (small and large taxpayers, state and central tax authorities and banks) are on the same platform for four basic activities: (1) registration, (2) payments (called *challans* in India), (3) return-filings and (4) inter-state input tax credits. India has a large, unorganized market and many organized industries face challenges from small businesses that avoid taxes. An electronic filing and recording system will mean that many such businesses will show up on the radar of the government and of industry associations. We expect a meaningful reduction in the activities of the unorganized sector as the GST roll-out progresses. A few years later it will not be surprising if we see similar notices being sent by indirect-tax authorities.

Benefit transfers: UID to the rescue

The system of distributing Indian subsidies has been under fire for two main reasons: (1) price signals get distorted as prices are artificially tampered (reduced in the case of say, diesel and cooking fuels or increased in the case of minimum support prices) and (2) the list of beneficiaries is faulty, which causes large-scale leakages (in the case of PDS).

Taking prices of goods back to 'market' levels (allowing diesel prices to rise or MSPs to fall such that Indian grain becomes competitive again in the world market) will require the government to find a way to 'compensate' people who, in its opinion, require such protection. The UID project allows for unique identification of all Indian residents. It is for government agencies to figure out who needs to get the benefits.

Just like in the tax-collection system, there are three elements here: (1) people who need to receive the benefits, (2) information about the people, their eligibility and bank accounts and (3) the actual transfer of the money. Here too, the last two aspects are being digitized. The number of people who have signed up for UID was 700 million as of end October 2014. However, reports indicate that only a small proportion of people have linked their bank accounts with UID. Only 10 million people may have linked their accounts at the end of April 2013. This data was released as part of the direct benefit transfer MIS, the public dissemination of which seems to have since been discontinued.

As the government starts making it mandatory for each agency to move benefits only through a benefits-transfer mechanism, we may see a sudden and sharp jump in the number of people who link their bank accounts (or open one) with their UID cards. The government's experiment to transfer subsidy on LPG cylinders directly to bank accounts should provide some learning on how the process progresses. In a sense, identifying beneficiaries of LPGs is easy. Anyone who has a connection is a beneficiary but it may be difficult to identify a beneficiary of urea subsidy and determine the amount due to him/her.

Over time, the UID database can link with various other databases (for example, direct taxes databases) such that correlations can be drawn on several issues. The government is starting to roll-out transfer of benefits through the UID system. But even a single item, like scholarship-schemes, encompasses a very wide variety of ministries. For beneficiaries this earlier meant multiple registrations with different authorities and different periodicity and modes of receiving the benefit. While even under the new UID method, each agency will be required to identify the right recipients, the money can be electronically transferred directly into the bank accounts beneficiaries.

As more schemes are added to the direct-benefit transfer model, UID will serve as the identifying link between citizens and schemes. It will be easy not only to remove ghost beneficiaries (either you have a UID or you don't; and one UID gets only one entitlement), this will also allow cross-checking of databases. If someone is benefitting from one scheme, possibly he/she does not need support from other schemes.

Similarly, a holistic profile of a person can be created with the government as it electronically identifies schemes that a particular beneficiary is benefitting from. Understanding the socioeconomic status of a person will be easier as more data is generated with every UID. Identifying 'rich farmers' whose income 'should' be taxed can become easier (from a data perspective, even if not from a political perspective). Conceptually this data can be used as a time-series to see the benefits made available to a person or a family.

The holy grail of a UID-linked direct benefit transfers is for the government to be able to transfer all its 'subsidies' through the direct mechanism. Figure 6.3 shows that the total amount of direct transfers by the government now amounts to more than Rs 3 trillion a year. Being able to send benefits directly can help save meaningfully on leakages (some estimates peg leakages at more than 20 per cent of the government spend, depending on the scheme).

Figure 6.3: Subsidies have mounted to around Rs 3 trillion over the last few years

Break up of major subsidies by type, March fiscal year-ends, 2010-16E (Rs bn)

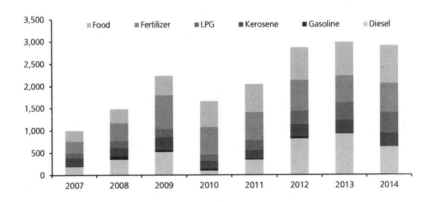

Source: Government of India; Kotak Institutional Equities research

However, this will take a significant amount of time. Banking penetration is low, with around a quarter of the population having bank accounts. Putting everyone on the system will require rethinking the branch-banking model of reaching the final customer. Possibly this will require a more spruced-up version of the business correspondent (BC) model (such that becoming a BC is profitable even at a low number of transactions/float amount) or will require using mobile money as a way to reach the money to the right hands. Given that a large portion of the economy is not banked, a transitory system will be required to provide for the conversion of e-cash to physical cash and vice versa.

Judicial records

Indian courts (especially the Supreme Court of India and the high courts) are significantly getting digitized. This means (1) the filing of cases and basic cross-checking of facts, (2) the 'cause lists' (the schedule of when cases will be heard, in what order and in which court), (3) the status of pending cases and (4) judgments in concluded cases are all now available online.

The process of reaching the court and its proceedings are now online. Linking of various litigants, using a unique ID, is still missing and so are any MIS on the number and type of cases pending and concluded, typical litigants and the average duration of cases. As more data begins to be available on this topic, the common man can better appreciate the working of the judiciary.

E-money on your mobiles

Mobiles enjoy the highest penetration of any communicating device in India: even television and cable & satellite reach only ~165 million and ~145 million homes respectively (as of end 2013). Mobiles, with around 700 million unique mobile subscribers in India, serve as the ideal mechanism to reach out to the vast majority of the Indian populace.

Indian banks have only between 250 and 300 million unique individual bank accounts. The number of ATMs in the country is 166,894 while the number of branches is 117,847 (as of June 2014). This makes mobiles an obvious choice in terms of reaching the unbanked.

The decade ending 2010 saw the emergence of new age banking channels like ATMs and internet banking. These new channels helped reduce costs of reaching customers significantly. They did not however help in reaching out to new or unbanked customers as much as they helped in serving the ones already existing more profitably as the costs of reaching and servicing them came down.

The cost of reaching a customer is low in the case of mobiles as there are no real estate costs (as in the case of branches) and the cost of the instrument is borne by the customer (unlike in the case of ATMs). In the case of branches and ATMs, the reach (or the number of people using them) is determined by the populace that lives within a particular radius. In the case of mobiles, banks or financial services travel with the client.

The real-time two-way communication and the ability to keep an electronic record (audit trail) of the transactions make mobiles an ideal tool for financial services organizations to reach out to customers. The security features in mobile banking are similar to the ones that the financial services organizations have developed for internet banking. The scope of using e-money is pretty wide and we foresee three major uses of e-money.

Channelizing Government of India payments

As the government begins to move towards the payment of subsidies to final recipients (instead of routing them through pricing subsidies, which are accompanied by a black market as the cost differential creates a significant arbitrage potential), many of the current subsidies will begin to flow through bank accounts of recipients.

If one were to look at the large subsidy/government support items, they include MG-NREGS, fuel subsidy, fertilizer subsidy and the PDS subsidy which currently total up to around Rs 3 trillion in financial year 2014. As subsidies begin to reach the final recipients in cash equivalent terms, they may decide to spend it in a manner not intended by the government and some of it could end up as savings and hence, investment. The government started off by paying 2 per cent as service charges for routing the MG-NREGA payments, of which the bank kept 25–50 bps and the BCs, 150–175 bps. However, this has collapsed off late and the retention between a bank and the BC put together is ~75–100 bps.

The internal remittances market

The internal remittances market is estimated variously to be between Rs 400 billion to Rs 600 billion. The internal migrant population is estimated to be around 100 million people. The post office, which is estimated to account for ~20 per cent of the internal remittances market (via money orders), reports that it remitted Rs 102 billion in 2012. This was sent via 69.8 million money transfer instruments, making an average transfer to be Rs 1,450. The commission on the payments via the post office is 4.7 per cent of the amount remitted.

Also, anecdotally many customers have opened no-frills or low balance account in 'urban' areas and have given an ATM card or cheque book to their 'rural' counterparts. As soon as they deposit the cash in the urban branch, they intimate the rural counterpart who promptly presents himself/herself for withdrawal (typically the ATM or the branch could be quite some distance away, especially in unbanked areas).

Enhancing the scope of e-money for merchant transactions

The third, and the biggest, market will be the one where people transfer money to each other (peer-to-peer payments) or to merchants/businesses (peer-to-merchant). The vast retail market where 85–90 per cent of the transactions are settled in cash will be transformed if mobile money can take root. This market has been harder to tackle as many SMEs are still transacting in cash as they do not have the requisite 'acceptance infrastructure' or the cost of such infrastructure makes settling in cash more lucrative. Many countries (for example, Australia and New Zealand) have helped promote measures to move to e-cash by providing specific fiscal benefits.

Deep-diving in the e-money phenomenon

To understand mobile money, we need to understand a few concepts: (1) a store of value, (2) the act of payment and (3) the medium of communication.

A cash note, a bank account or a prepaid card are all stores of value. In some sense, the prepaid talk time that one buys from a telecom company is also a store of value. However, current rules do not allow trading of talk-time to buy goods and hence it is not a store of value from a payments perspective. When this store-of-value changes hands between a payer and a payee, a payment transaction takes place. A payment transaction requires that the payer and payee be authenticated and the transaction is secure. Interestingly, in a cash transaction the transaction is typically not traceable though in a digital media, a record of it will be kept. The medium of communication can practically be anything as long as it can access the store-of-value and securely transfer it to someone else. It can be a cheque, a voice initiated transaction, an internet or mobile initiated transaction or simply a physical movement of cash.

Mobile money serves two important purposes: it links people who are unbanked and for the people who are banked, this can provide quick and handy access to their funds, investments and loans. Transactions over the mobile create an electronic track of payments and hence provide good information on the flow of money in the economy. The key question to be answered is whether the change will be incremental (providing one more way to reach the clients) or transformative (bringing in new clients in the system).

Our estimate of smart phone penetration in India concurs with the BCG-FICCI report which projects 625 million smart phone users by 2020, up from around 160 million at the end of financial year 2014 (see Figure 6.4). Smart phones will have the ability to perform many transactions (both financial and query-related). As cheques and cash get replaced by online transfers, the touch points with customers will change significantly. The BCG-FICCI report expects that digital initiatives can help banks shave off between 100–150 bps in interest rate for customers.

The payment profile of transactions in India remains primarily cash. Retail industry estimates suggest that 85–90 per cent of the total number of transactions in India is settled in cash (even as this is changing at the margin). One of the primary reasons for this is the fragmented nature of India's retail industry which has around 8.5 million outlets which do not have significant scale to make the electronic mode of transfer economical. Given the informal nature of the transactions, many people are still comfortable using cash as a medium of transfer of value, thereby not feeling the need to be a part of the formal banking and payments network. It is not surprising hence that ATMs were used to take out ~Rs 20 trillion in cash in financial year 2014.

Figure 6.4: Smart phones can become the primary banking channel in five years

Number of smart phones, non-smart phones and bank accounts, March fiscal year-ends, 2014-20

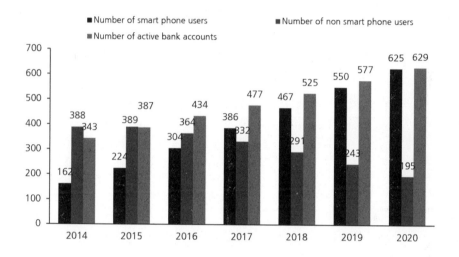

Notes:
(a) Smart phone users: emarketINC; Number of bank account holders; RBI Basic Statistical Returns.
(b) Banakabble population is population with age greater than 18 years.

Source: BCG analysis; Kotak Institutional Equities research

Even in the formal network, Indians have not taken a liking to credit cards in any significant manner. Reserve Bank of India data for financial year 2014 indicates the average ticket size of the credit card transaction in India is around Rs 3,000 and a card is swiped 2.5 times a month. Similarly, debit cards are used primarily as any time money (ATM) cards and not necessarily as payment mechanisms (the average POS swipe is Rs 1,500 and the non–ATM usage a month is once in seven months!). Debit cards are primarily used as ATM cards around 1.5 times a month on average to withdraw on an average, Rs 3,200 per swipe).

Who is working in this segment?

Three sets of companies are approaching this market and in their own unique ways, drawing upon their existing strengths and strategic advantages:

- **Financial services companies:** Banks are creating applications to reach out to their customer base. The cost of transactions via mobiles is significantly lower than through any other mode of interaction. They are creating their own applications which need to be downloaded by a customer to access the organization. In most cases, the application would work on the GPRS network for two reasons: (1) the transactions are too complex to be done over USSD technology and (2) the security requirements typically require a multi-factor authentication.
- **Telecom companies:** Grappling with a large churn, telecom operators are entering the fray to get more 'sticky' customers. Telecom companies see significant value in getting float income on pre-paid cards, commission on transactions done via their cards and possibly a customer who decides to stay on its network due to the facilities provided. They also see an opportunity to provide more value to their retailers (for every top-up sold by the retailer, he gets a small cut).
- **An intermediate option:** Payment service solutions have attracted many entrants: (1) payment apps which make payment to multiple suppliers (like DTH, mobile, utilities, travel, shopping, etc.) much easier and (2) standalone apps which link to specific services that they provide like cabs or restaurants. Companies are incentivizing customers to hold their money in escrow accounts that will be released on their receiving the product or service. Such companies have attracted a large number of customers and significant equity capital.

From the point of view of the companies innovating in this space, one hurdle is that a customer who they are targeting already has access to other modes of e-cash and is transacting via these. For example, the overlap between customers having a GPRS enabled phone and those having an internet connection and a debit or credit card are possibly high. The value-proposition of the offering comes in from the ability to provide the services on-the-go—this is similar to having a mobile email as opposed to an email popping on the office computer. As mobile screens begin to command a greater proportion of time with users, these companies expect to move their offering to suit customers' evolving needs. For many customers who do not fall in the overlap, or who will move on to mobiles directly as their first means of using the internet, this service has its obvious appeal.

Making the inclusion stick

With India scoring low on financial inclusion globally, the government is putting in significant efforts at increasing the level of access to financial products. Financial inclusion refers to the depth, availability and usage of the financial system by the constituents of the economy. Financial inclusion helps create suitable savings opportunities and also allows easier access to credit. The reasons for financial exclusion stem from a variety of sources:

- **Lack of steady income:** As we note elsewhere in the book, around nine-tenths of the labour force works in the informal/ unorganized sector. This means that their incomes are not steady and in most cases, are received in cash. There is hence no compulsion to open a bank account.
- **Not sure how financial inclusion is helpful, products not suitable:** The benefits of being associated with the financial system are not obvious to many. Since their daily needs are met by cash transactions, the need for inclusion is not felt. What gets missed in the process is the financial discipline and avenues of savings and investments. In many cases, the need of an excluded person is a loan, rather than a savings product.
- **Going to bank is costly:** Going to bank takes a toll both on time and money for many. Banks may have unhelpful staff and rigid timings and procedures, which may not gel well with the needs of the financially excluded. In this context, many micro-finance companies have built a model of reaching the excluded (rather than making them come to an office) at times convenient to them (say, prior to start of the working day).

Financial inclusion currently revolves around the concept of reaching out to people who cannot open or have not opened bank accounts. The challenge will be incorporating the habit of savings in people who are being exposed to the system for the first time. As the culture of savings begins to take root, we expect that over time the savings will get channelized into investments. As incomes increase, people who are exposed to the formal banking set-up will be in a better position to start investing, whether in fixed deposits, insurance or mutual funds.

Many of the new savers will be women who till now did not have an avenue to save. Any money saved was liquid (as it was kept as cash) and hence could easily be spent. With the ability to save and withdraw as required (while earning a nominal 4 per cent interest), they will be able to take their financial future in their own hands. As they start getting integrated into the formal system, they will be exposed to life and non-life insurance. For those who are only beginning to save, one medical/accidental emergency or a failed crop can throw them back into the debt quagmire. Access to insurance is hence critical for keeping them on the savings path.

RBI prescribes that banks are required to frame their know-your-client (KYC) policies incorporating the following four key elements: (1) customer acceptance policy; (2) customer identification procedures; (3) monitoring of transactions; and (4) risk management. While a BC can help in the KYC procedure, the final responsibility lies with the bank. From the perspective of a BC, a unique identity can help reduce costs in complying with the KYC requirements, especially with respect to customer identification procedures. In many cases, for a banking-correspondent to get a customer identity involves helping the customer to get one from the government.

Moving from physical cash to e-cash

A country's journey away from cash typically takes place differently at the top and the bottom of the pyramid: (1) pre-paid instruments (PPIs) introduce a consumer to the banking channel at the bottom of the pyramid and (2) debit and credit cards provide convenience at the top. India's top is a small sliver of its population and is over-served and its huge bottom of the pyramid is terribly underserved.

At the end of financial year 2014 as per data released by the Reserve Bank of India, there were 394 million debit cards and 19 million credit cards outstanding and ~160,000 ATMs and a million POS all ready to serve the top end of the market. PPIs, which intend to serve the financially excluded, did only Rs 81 billion of annual transactions. There is hence no doubt on the tremendous potential of PPIs in India. There has been discussion on using PPIs to transfer subsidies in India (like has been the case in Brazil, Indonesia and Mexico) given the difficulty of opening bank accounts and keeping them operational.

ATM and online banking channels are gaining traction and though cheques and cash will not fade away, their importance will shrivel. Savings account transactions are increasingly moving to ATM/digital. Banks are digitizing and mechanizing the transaction processes for current accounts also, for example, by emphasizing on cash deposit machines (CDMs).

The development in mobile banking has come from the 'developing world'. This has happened since the conversion of cash to electronic form has been very successful in the 'developed world'. With credit card and debit card penetration high (and the payment infrastructure put in place already), there is limited incentive for the players in the 'developed world' to create a new payment infrastructure. However, in the developing countries with low banking penetration and high prevalence of cash transactions, the impetus for converting cash into electronic form has come in from the deep penetration of mobiles. We look at a celebrated international example and note that the innovations in mobile banking started in Africa.

M-PESA is one of the most well-known mobile banking stories. Started by a micro-finance company to help collect repayments, it was taken over by Safaricom, a subsidiary of the telecom giant Vodafone, which helped expand its mass-market potential. A subscriber needs to register with Safaricom which provides it with a SIM which has the application loaded on it. The customer needs to create a PIN for the security of his account (typically a four digit number). M-PESA allows cash-in and cash-out via retailers of Safaricom and other associated retailers. The money collected by Safaricom (which it converts to e-cash) is transferred to a 'trust account' (escrow account) with a bank. A typical M-PESA or Airtel

Africa Money customer does a person-to-person transfer of between US$ 20 and US$ 30 and does around 20–25 transactions a quarter.

The money which is loaded on the mobile can be sent to any recipient (not necessarily only other registered M-PESA customers). The final recipient can keep it as a balance on his mobile or can withdraw it as cash from any associated retailer, after paying a sliding-scale commission. The final recipient can be a company or a person selling goods or services. Given the low penetration of the banking sector in the country, the Central Bank of Kenya has been supportive of the growth of M-PESA. M-PESA does not pay any interest on deposits to its account holders, not does it offer any loans. M-PESA, hence, is primarily is a payment mechanism.

Telecom companies with their vast distribution network are natural entities to become payment service providers. They have an inherent ability to convert physical cash into e-cash. The mechanism to load money and to make peer-to-merchant (P2M) transactions from a telecom wallet in India is still riddled with significant costs; peer-to-peer (P2P) transactions for remittances are comparatively more effective in terms of cost, time or convenience. Telecom companies offer payments as a paid service which banks offer 'free' to their current account-savings account (CASA) customers. If telecom companies can get a share float income (i.e. the incomes that banks earn when they lend out or invest the money deposited with them) they will be able to price payment services better. The new payment bank guidelines may prompt the telecom companies to consider becoming payment banks which can help solve the float issue.

In these cases the need for mobile banking emerges from a customer who requires an easier or a safer way to remit money or pay for goods or services. What is clear is that a customer requires the ability to seamlessly pay the final recipient without necessarily requiring the recipient to open a new banking channel or get a new SIM card. The greater the number of entities to which a customer can remit his funds, the larger will be the acceptance of the model: it is important to help create the network effect. This can be done by creating an ecosystem where people find others whom they can identify with and transact with on the same network. This can take place either by creating the remittance ecosystem (such that people find it convenient to transfer from person to person) or developing the merchant ecosystem (such that the payments made to merchants are easily accepted). Some banks in India are experimenting with sending money to mobile phones or Facebook accounts of recipients.

The telecom company led or affiliated model can gain more acceptance given its wider reach and synergies (the large and spread out retail network that sells airtime can double up as the cash-in and cash-out facilitator). Telecom companies can start building-in incentives for recipients to be on their networks without making this an impediment to the process of fund transfers. Regulators are helping facilitate the creation of enabling environments by easing AML and KYC requirements.

Who should get the spoils?

Identifying winners from implementing the mobile banking platform will create meaningful wealth for investors and entrepreneurs. The current regulations, which the RBI has taken the lead in drafting, approach the issue from the point of view of KYC requirements and sanctity of the banking sector. Banks have invested significantly in transaction banking platforms and in debit card and credit card systems which provide stickiness of the banking relationship with the customer. Telecom companies offer reach which is significantly larger than the reach of the banks. Creative new companies are offering to solve the problem of moving money from person to person or person to merchant by offering wallets.

There are two elements in the revenue business model for players:

- The float that will be kept in the system: RBI has maintained that the float needs to be kept by the banking system and any other aggregator of cash/deposits is not allowed to pay any interest on the deposits.
- The commission on transactions: Given the large quantum of transactions and the pricing done as a percentage of the value transmitted, commissions will be a big driver. Ideally, the digital churns of money will be (at least) in high single digits before the conversion of digital cash to physical cash is called for.

How the market shapes up here could determine the winner in the mobile payments space. We believe that the final winner will be one who owns a customer, or one to whom a customer is willing to pay.

GAMECHANGERS

Digitization is no panacea but quite a strong medicine

Digitization is not a panacea to the ills of bureaucracy and red tape in India or anywhere else. It however does provide meaningful advantages. There can still be wilful errors of omission and commission in designing benefit schemes or a restriction of access to relevant auctions. The solutions in many cases will be (1) further digitalization, (2) open access to government services and (3) release of electronic data on transactions/interactions. As people learn the outcomes of repeated interactions with a rule-based system, their behaviour will be moulded accordingly.

Over decades India had become used to the concept of power-brokers who offered to change the system rather than promoting healthy competition while maintaining the design of the system. As interactions within governments get digitized, the need to follow rules and laws will become essential. An example of change in behaviour is the meaningful decline in the number of railway ticket agents who offered to get tickets. The online portal, IRCTC, sold tickets amounting to Rs 154 billion in financial year 2014, which accounted for more than a third of the total passenger fare collected by Indian Railways (Indian Railways' passenger receipts have a large collection of daily ticket sales which are not sold via IRCTC making the proportion even more impressive). The power has moved to a consumer rather than remaining with the intermediary. The average price of tickets sold has been falling, indicating that short-distance travellers are buying their tickets online.

Even as digital literacy remains an area of concern, it is no more debilitating for the common man than the illiteracy he faced when opaque systems prevailed. The increasing spread of education and of access (computers, laptops and most important, mobile phones) means that basic operations can easily be mastered by intermediaries who know how to work the computer system rather than those who know how to work the government system.

There are concerns about the ability, and in some cases, intent of the Indian government (whether as itself or of employees who have access/authority) to handle these large online databases. Privacy concerns have been raised, whether it is when the government wanted to promote a unique ID programme or when the oil companies made data on the number of subsidized cooking gas cylinders used by people. There are portals now where it is possible to see the registered owners of properties or various filings by private companies and partnerships.

An element that should provide comfort, however perversely, is that many of these digitalized systems are still silos with interfaces that work only for a particular function or department that they have been designed for. Over time however many of these systems can, and will, be linked. For example, in the financial services industry PAN (the permanent account number issued by the Income Tax Department) has become a unique identifier. Across other sectors, the UID may serve as the unifying link.

Convergence leading to a network effect

There have been piecemeal developments on both sides of mobile banking: financial inclusion and reaching out to the rich. Person–to–person transfers are being approached from a 'financial inclusion' angle. Given that the quantum of funds that are transacted in cash even in an urban setting, this is a need that has to be met even in already-banked areas or with already-banked customers. The convergence will create the required ecosystem for mobile banking to take off. We expect that the economies of scale will kick-start once there are a large number of players who come on to the mobile banking network.

We are beginning to see various players becoming very active in the space. Companies are beginning to find a niche in which they want to play; everyone is positioning themselves in places which are important to them (financial inclusion or banking to the already banked).

As the various pieces begin to fall in place and more people come on to the e- and mobile-banking network, it will create a virtuous cycle driving a significant portion of financial transactions online. This transition of payment methodology will be similar in magnitude to the transition from gold to paper money making it the next leg of virtualization.

The right policy push

There is significant prodding from the RBI and the government to get banks to work on financial inclusion and on the need for banks to reduce costs. Global examples suggest that the bank-led model for financial inclusion, while having inherent advantages of being prudential do not necessarily take off. Telecom companies in India have a widespread reach (more than 2 million outlets) and the ability to manage micro-payments. The average revenue per user per month in India in less than Rs 200 and recharge vouchers of value as low as Rs 5 are sold by telecom companies which make them ideal players in small value transactions.

Payments and transactions with the mobile banking platform are, on an average, expected to be low ticket items given the objective of financial inclusion. Countries have relaxed the anti-money laundering (AML) and know your client (KYC) regulations to help kick-start the use of the mobile banking channel. Mobile banking helps maintain an electronic record and trail of the transactions.

RBI has allowed telecom companies to operate prepaid payment cards, this will help companies leverage on their reach. RBI has however made it clear that the float from this will not accrue to the company but to the bank, thereby taking away one of the elements of the revenue pool. As the telecom companies possibly move towards the payment bank model, this hindrance will be addressed. An important element of the digital revolution will be the ability of the common man to access it. (1) Hardware availability, (2) bandwidth constraints and (3) user charges remain prominent constraints even as the government—and a healthy dose of private equity money in the wallet companies—has started addressing some of these issues.

India plans to install broadband on an optic fibre network to connect 250,000 gram panchayats as part of the National Optical Fibre Network (NOFN) scheme. Funded by the Universal Service Obligation fund, the scheme will leverage cables already laid by BSNL, RailTel and Power Grid. Industry experts suggest that it might be a better idea to use Ka-band communication satellites rather than expensive ground-based last-mile access; apart from being costly, this requires 'right of way' which suffers from the same set of issues and delays as land acquisition in India. India scores very poorly on broadband availability.

Across several services, however, the online interface, while orderly, disciplined and less prone to corruption, can also be more expensive than the offline world. For example, booking tickets online on the Indian Railways website requires paying the (1) fee to the railways, (2) fee to the banking/financial intermediary and (3) the kiosk operator/agent if the end consumer does not have his own log-in. All this raises the cost of the ticket. Similarly, while banks want to move to electronic clearing mechanisms, cheques are still free for clearing, while the customer is charged for NEFT/RTGS transfers. Such user charges create undue disincentives for customers to switch from offline to online transactions.

Making the customer more demanding

The government has shown its intent by bringing various legislations on speed and digitization of services. A consumer himself needs to get more active in demanding services and more important, information that is generated in providing the services.

For example, knowing how long an officer took to clear a file (quite an antiquated view of the world in the digital age) can help identify the causes of delay. The Right to Information Act allows anyone to get base data from various government agencies. A rigorous analysis of the data can yield insights into bottlenecks.

It is important to note that it is not only for 'paid services' (like, for example, a train ticket) that digitalization and data availability should be made mandatory. In many cases the government spends large sums of money in collecting data or providing services. For example, weather data collected from all reporting stations or the base data generated in all NSSO surveys can be made available (either free or at a nominal charge). Policing and healthcare data, for example, needs to be online so that facts can be verified and the status of crime or health in a particular locality understood.

Getting the data to improve outcomes

An advantage of electronic data is that it can be analysed more easily. Copious quantities of data can be used to reveal patterns and analyses that were either invisible earlier or remained unearthed since the tools to extract such information were not available.

Data needs to be proactively released by government agencies; many countries now have a data.gov site. The open data initiative in UK and the US provide insights into what is possible. UK reports 9,410 datasets across local and central governments, covering a wide variety of fields from hydrology to schools, geology to rural affairs. The US releases 373,029 raw and geospatial datasets and offers 1,209 tools with 172 agencies and sub-agencies contributing (all these numbers as of 13 May 2013).

Increasingly, the idea across the world is to release as much information as is possible on the functioning of government agencies or public utilities. More important, such data is to be presented in machine-readable formats such that analysis is easier and faster.

Get citizens involved

It is critical to get the public to make use of the data by slicing and dicing it. The Executive Order that the US President issued on 9 May 2013 reads:

> Decades ago, the U.S. Government made both weather data and the Global Positioning System freely available. Since that time, American entrepreneurs and innovators have utilized these resources to create navigation systems, weather newscasts and warning systems, location-based applications, precision farming tools, and much more, improving Americans' lives in countless ways and leading to economic growth and job creation. In recent years, thousands of Government data resources across fields such as health and medicine, education, energy, public safety, global development, and finance have been posted in machine-readable form for free public use on Data.gov. Entrepreneurs and innovators have continued to develop a vast range of useful new products and businesses using these public information resources, creating good jobs in the process.

Citizen involvement is now increasingly easier as communication technologies allow people to interact quickly, escalate matters within the service-providing organization and to disseminate the information/ analysis to outsiders. An interesting saying in the world of 'hackers' is that 'information wants to be free'. the typical response of a government on this is 'information costs a fortune'. Using the processing power of the citizenry and sundry analysts, at least the cost of converting data into information can be widely spread.

Addressing privacy concerns

Even as we get excited about the digital revolution, it needs to be borne in mind that privacy of an individual needs to be given due importance. There are instances of many government sites (especially with respect to land records) that are 'open': Anyone can access the dataset therein. Respect for individual privacy will help create a stronger stakeholder support system.

As we noted in the section on UID, the government will have a significant amount of data on an individual, both economic and social. Most of the data possibly still exists with the government even currently but it is in a paper-based format, which makes it difficult to search and cross-refer. However, a determined government can still put together the intelligence on a particular person if so required though finding trends and patterns in the data is currently not possible.

As data starts getting digital, more and more of an individual's data will be 'searchable' and can be used to make a reasonably accurate profile of the person. This will not happen just based on the data collected by the government as part of its taxation or social duty. Most of this data may be voluntarily provided by a citizen or business to open social networks. Putting two and two together will be easier in the new electronic scheme of things.

The upshot of such copious data is that it can be used to see trends and patterns that can be used in many applications—from where to build schools (depending on the birth rate in each area), to where to send medical care (if reports of significant illness outbreaks occur), to where to build infrastructure (as we give away our location or, our travel histories by booking online). It can also help design better fiscal policies: if the cost of education is going up meaningfully, it might be better to provide tax relief on it than on say, leave-travel; or it might make sense to stop subsidized LPG or diesel for particular households or regions.

Depending on how securely the data is kept (or even shared within the bounds of law and privacy), e-governance can help private entrepreneurs and businesses develop new products and services. More available data can help in designing newer business models, for example, knowing when the farmer has come to sell his produce in a *mandi* (at say MSP to FCI) can offer insights to agri-processors who can buy his product and to consumer goods companies that can offer to sell him FMCG goods.

A carrot and stick approach required

The central government should use a carrot and stick approach to get states to implement digitization, just like it did with the Urban Land Ceiling Act (for example, by making the disbursal of JNNURM funds conditional on the repeal of the act). More important, success stories which indicate the potential of revenue generation for the government, will prod this along.

The missing piece, thankfully, is the interaction between various databases which still allows an average Indian some modicum of privacy from the prying eyes of the state. Eventually the various segments of the government will start talking to each other digitally. While that will help to profile Indians better, there are valid concerns regarding the benefits that such profiling may offer. India would do well to first get its multitudes online and get various services and finances online as well.

If we get many of these transitions right, we will potentially get a veritable consumption and savings boom. We explore that in the next chapter.

SPENDING THE DOLLARS

The changing consumption paradigm

IF INDIA IS indeed able to create the million plus employment opportunities every month, decongest its cities, increase productivity in the agricultural value chain and reverse its decline in the quality of output of the public goods through effective governance, it will create meaningful increases in incomes. Such increased incomes will lead to a veritable boom in savings and consumption. India is already one of the largest global markets, but by 2025, we expect it to more than double in real terms. It will also be a vastly different, rich and colourful market as incomes will increase dramatically, and most people will spend more than just to keep body and soul together. Higher incomes will shape far-reaching consumption and saving changes.

We create a RUPEES model, a predictive model that projects Indian consumption patterns. It is no surprise that it anticipates significant transformation by 2025. The affluent will spend more on enhanced lifestyles, less on staples. The poor in today's India will have more money in their pockets and the poorest of the poor category will make a journey towards somewhat more prosperity. The urban market is expected to account for 60 per cent of India's consumption market, from less than 50 per cent today as India's rural areas morph into urban centres.

We do this analysis to get a broad sense of numbers. It is not hard to get a magnitude of the numbers even without building very sophisticated models. The power of compounding works in the favour of the forecaster and as we have noted earlier an economy growing at 7 per cent annually will double in a decade; some sectors will grow faster and some slower. Intuitively, we can look around (or just look at our own spending patterns) and see which sectors will do better and which not so much.

We look at two important aspects critically: (1) the possible rise of inequality in India and what that could mean for its social cohesion and (2) the nature of transition of India's wallet. As we will look at the numbers, we see that Indians will be required to bear the cost of failure of their public goods and services: *bijli, sadak, paani, shiksha, swasthya* and *suraksha* (power, roads, water, education, health and security). Let us hurry to clarify that public goods do not necessarily mean that they need to come from the public sector or from the government: they can come from the private sector. Indeed, in many cases, India has seen marked improvement in the quality of delivery when these goods and services have come from the private sector.

This 'private cost of public failure' has been looked upon by some commentators as an immense market opportunity; we think of this as nothing but irony. It ties down the wallets of Indians to getting basics without leaving enough for them to move up the expenditure curve. Coupled with the potential of rising inequality, the trend of spending significantly on basics means that for the relatively not-so-well-off most of their incomes will be spent in just making ends meet. Improvement in the delivery of public services can free up meaningful time, energy and resources for a large number of Indians and allow them to enjoy a much better life.

Box 7.1: How we put together the RUPEES model

Let us deep-dive to understand how we built our model. We take this journey before talking about the conclusions so that we can grasp some of the terms that we will encounter. More important, we will know the robustness of what we are talking about and what its limitations and constraints are. As with every model trying to predict the future, the idea here is to get a sense of the magnitude and direction; the exactness of the numbers that these pages represent will obviously be missed.

Here are some of the elements that went into building the model:

The primacy of expenditure over income: Statistical agencies like the National Sample Survey Organization (NSSO) find it easier to collect and disseminate data based on consumption patterns and not on income. This is because consumption is more easily visible and people and households are more willing to discuss it, rather than their income. It is typically assumed that a distribution of the consumption pattern reflects the economy's income pattern. This may or may not be true because different households may have different attitudes and priorities with respect to savings and debt (the biggest reason for incomes and consumption to differ).

One reason why income side data is not available in India is also because only around 35–40 million people in India file income taxes (or only 3–4 per cent of India's population). This, of course, is not unexpected. As we will see in our numbers in the model, India still continues to remain a poor country and a very large proportion of its population earns significantly lower than the minimum income chargeable to tax. For example, given the exemption and deduction limits, practically an income of up to Rs 400,000 per year is tax free. Agricultural income (which is what half the population survives on) is tax free. For a country which has a per capita income of around Rs 0.1 million and tax slabs starting from Rs 0.4 million, it is no surprise that more than 90 per cent of the people are not required to file their taxes! This is not to deny that with the citizens who are required to declare their incomes, there remains the scourge of under-declaration.

Unfortunately, meta-data on income tax is not shared by the government which would have given a good handle on how the incomes are distributed among the top 3–4 per cent of India's population. As we will see in our model, the top decile of the population controls and will continue to account for more than half of the consumption market. It will be good to know (both for modelling purposes and for social knowledge) how skewed income distribution is in the top percentile.

The distribution skew: Based on monthly per capita expenditure

(MPCE) data compiled and distributed by NSSO on the deciles-wise distribution of households by income, we construct and project (based on our growth and skew estimates) the distribution of households across deciles over the forecast period. We use multiple NSSO surveys to get a sense of how the deciles have evolved. Our data has been updated to include NSSO's findings in its sixty-eighth round survey.

We also introduce the concept of a skew in our model. Skew refers to the idea that potentially the people who are better off will, at the margin, get higher benefits of the fruits of economic growth. This may be possible because they have better access to health and education and to a better network of jobs. The proportion of skew is a debatable point but it is clear from historical data for the last couple of decades that inequality has worsened in India. The debate on the skew can be on its quantum but not on its existence; it is possible that the skew will either moderate or worsen over time—its evolution is difficult to call.

There is a subtle point about increasing inequality that needs to be noted. Very simplistically, if the richest person was consuming ten units while the poorest was consuming only one unit, the inequality could be described as ten (a more sophisticated version of this concept is the Gini-coefficient). Now if, after a period of time, the richest person consumes twenty-two units while the poorest consumes two units, inequality will have been said to worsen to eleven in our simple calculation. The poorest person is better-off than what he was earlier: however, relative to the richest he has not partaken in the growth proportionately.

Many would derive satisfaction from the fact that the poor person's consumption has moved from one unit to two units; others would look at the ratio moving from ten to eleven and bemoan rising inequality. Some will argue that since there is now more to go around, the poor should now be aspirational to achieve especially since they are now themselves better-off; others will point to the poor quality of life that the poor still live in relative to the rich and to the fact that what matters is relative inequality and not absolute depravation. There is, as is most aspects of life, truth in all these assertions.

Our model shows that reality will be similar to the simple example described earlier. A large section of those who are currently poor in India will reach a stage where they will be materially better-off than their current circumstances but possibly they will not gain as much as their richer brethren will.

Defining the boundaries: We define the boundaries of the categories in the RUPEES framework according to the quantum of consumption. It is typically fashionable to create income pyramids but as we have noted earlier, income data is rarely available in India and hence it is best to create consumption or expenditure pyramids. We divide the Indian households into six categories which we put together into a handy acronym RUPEES: Real-rich, Upper-category, Prospering, Evolving, Emerging and Surviving (see Table 7.1).

Table 7.1: Defining the RUPEES framework

Classifying Indian households in various categories of MPCE, 2012-Rs

	Monthly expenditure		Annual expenditure		Average
	From	To	From	To	
Real-rich	30,000		360,000	–	500,000
Upper-class	20,000	30,000	240,000	360,000	300,000
Prospering	10,000	20,000	120,000	240,000	180,000
Evolving	5,000	10,000	60,000	120,000	90,000
Emerging	2,500	5,000	30,000	60,000	45,000
Surviving	–	2,500	–	30,000	15,000

in PPP USD

	Monthly expenditure		Annual expenditure		Average
	From	To	From	To	
Real-rich	3,000	–	36,000	–	50,000
Upper-class	2,000	3,000	24,000	36,000	30,000
Prospering	1,000	2,000	12,000	24,000	18,000
Evolving	500	1,000	6,000	12,000	9,000
Emerging	250	500	3,000	6,000	4,500
Surviving	–	250	–	3,000	1,500

Source: Kotak Institutional Equities research

To divide India into these economic categories, we needed to define the limits of consumption for each group. We kept the definition of 'Survivors' as a household where the per-person annual consumption is up to Rs 30,000 (or around Rs 80 a day). This is very close to the international definition of the poverty line at US$ 1.25 of consumption a day (or in the case of India, ~Rs 75 a day). Any household in the Survivor category is hence broadly on or below the poverty line. Starting at the lowest consumption category, the Survivors, we typically double consumption limits to obtain the boundary for the next category. For the Upper-category, we do not double the limits, as then the absolute magnitude of the incomes covered would be very large. To get a sense of what a Real-rich household means, the PPP-adjusted per capita consumption of the Real-rich is similar to the average per capita consumption in the US currently.

Reconciling different figures: We faced a very common issue–if one adds together consumption across the various household deciles, one does not reach the consumption figure as tabulated by national accounts, with the NSSO data significantly underestimating overall consumption. We correct this, using two techniques:

(1) NSSO data are available only until about the ninetieth percentile and do not look at the wide observable disparity in the top-10 percentile. We take into account the disparity in this group to arrive at a more granular picture of household distribution.

(2) Even taking this into account does not restore the balance and hence we apply a 'scaling-up' factor to reconcile the NSSO data with national accounts. We expect this scale-up number to gradually reduce.

Tying this up with the population numbers: This exercise is done separately for rural and urban India. From the recent Census of India, we have the number of people in urban and rural India in 2011, and based on technical estimates made by the census team, we have an estimate of India's population of 1.4 billion people by

2025. Using these and an estimate of the number of households, we project the number of households in rural and urban India and the number of their constituents.

We expect the number of households to increase to 329 million by 2025 (194 million rural and 135 million urban) from 249 million in 2011 (169 million rural and 81 million urban). We expect the average household size to shrink to 4.3 and 4.1 for rural and urban respectively by 2025 from the current 4.9 and 4.7. These calculations provide a reasonable break-up of India's 1.4 billion population in 2025, implying 40 per cent urbanization in 2025 from the present 31 per cent.

Rural and urban households: The definition of rural and urban India that we currently use is the same that the census uses. A 'census town' is defined as having (1) a population of more than 5,000, (2) with 75 per cent or more male working population engaged in non-agricultural activities and (3) density of population of at least 400 per sq km. This is urban and places that do not meet these criteria are classified as 'rural'.

With agriculture employing around half the Indian labour force, it typically becomes difficult to have places where three-fourths or more of the male working population has non-agricultural work. This not only creates issues with a more appropriate rural-urban classification but also identifies the point of stress: if more people are not weaned from farming, the ability to connect more people to the growth story may become difficult.

Over the forecast period we expect the overall number of households to increase (as it has done historically) at 2 per cent a year. We expect rural household numbers to grow one per cent a year and hence, urban household numbers to grow at more than twice the overall rate. With (1) declining fertility and (2) an increasing number of nuclear families, the number of people per household is expected to fall significantly.

Maintaining consistency: Once the consumption wallet of a consumer in a given household is defined, aggregating such wallets over the distribution of different households in urban and rural India is easily achieved, which gives us the distribution of the consumption market in a matrix of consumption across different categories of consumers and the categories of consumption. We check to see that the overall ratio of consumption to GDP does not stray from the 62–64 per cent band—indeed we model consumption in a tight band for Indian GDP. The growth we assume in our model is 'real' and hence we do not take into account inflation. This also means that the projected numbers are in terms of the rupee's purchasing power in 2012. Given the impact of inflation, the nominal market size will end up being significantly larger.

It is important here to appreciate the band of 62–64 per cent that we speak of here. GDP is made up of consumption (C) +investments (I) + government expenditure (G) + net exports (exports minus imports, or X–M). In India of late the broad ratios have been such that ~60 per cent of GDP comes from consumption, ~30 per cent from investments and ~12 per cent from government expenditure and the next exports number is a small negative fraction (which reflects that we import more than we export). When countries are relatively poorer, they end up spending a large portion of the GDP on consumption. In the early 1980s India too consumed almost three quarters of its GDP. This proportion has fallen now to around three-fifths. As countries consume less, there is more left to invest and there are economic models which suggest that economic growth is directly linked to the proportion of the GDP that is invested. We expect that the rate of growth of India's consumption will be similar to the rate of growth of its GDP. This means that the proportion that consumption will command in the GDP remains broadly the same over the years.

All of this leads us to our classification of Indian households into the various economic categories: RUPEES (see Table 7.2). In Appendix 4, we detail the rural and urban distribution of the households across the various categories.

Table 7.2: India is expected to see a large uptick in richer households

Distribution of Indian households by consumption expenditure categories, March fiscal year-ends, FY2011-25

	2011	2015	2020	2025
Real-rich	—	—	1	7
Upper-class	—	2	6	10
Prospering	6	15	33	59
Evolving	31	56	86	117
Emerging	89	129	137	124
Surviving	123	67	35	12
Total	**249**	**270**	**298**	**329**

Source: Kotak Institutional Equities research

Making sense of different patterns

We return to NSSO to check how the consumption pattern has been evolving in urban and rural India. We use trend-line data for the past three decades to identify the changes in the shares of the wallet of consumption categories. NSSO goes out to around 150,000 households every five years to understand a wide variety of patterns including consumption and employment. This is one of the largest surveys of its kind in India. Using a long questionnaire, a NSSO interviewer asks the respondents in great detail about many aspects of their consumption and employment.

NSSO data has been consistently showing that the share of food and beverages has been falling across both urban and rural India (see Table 7.3). It is interesting that NSSO's focus on staples has been so high that the food category has been divided into twelve sub-categories even as the share of wallet is now moving to 'Miscellaneous'. Having a detailed understanding of the food category was very relevant when more than half the wallet was being spent on food.

While it is still important to know about food habits and requirements, there is an urgent need to redefine the NSSO questionnaire so that elements of Miscellaneous can be better captured and reported. We highlight that the Miscellaneous category includes, among other things, expenditure on education, medical care, fuel, entertainment, conveyance, rent, consumer durables, household consumer items and household help, financing costs, consumer taxes and cesses.

Table 7.3: India's consumption pattern has been evolving with reduced dependency on food purchases

Consumption expenditure by categories, June year-ends, 1998-2012 (%)

	Rural				Urban			
	1988	2000	2010	2012	1988	2000	2010	2012
Food	64.0	59.5	53.6	48.6	56.4	47.9	40.7	38.6
Pan, tobacco, intoxicants	3.2	2.9	2.2	2.4	2.6	1.9	1.2	1.4
Fuel and light	7.5	7.5	9.5	9.2	6.8	7.8	8.0	7.6
Clothing and bedding	6.7	6.9	4.9	6.3	5.9	6.1	4.7	5.3
Footwear	1.0	1.1	1.0	1.3	1.1	1.2	0.9	1.2
Durable goods	3.1	2.6	4.8	6.1	4.1	3.6	6.7	6.3
Misc goods and services	14.5	19.6	24.0	26.1	23.2	31.3	37.8	39.6

Source: NSSO 68th round report; earlier surveys; Kotak Institutional Equities research

We also juxtapose this with trends from other countries currently with different per capita consumptions (see Table 7.4). It is instructive to see how consumers across the globe with different purchasing powers spend their money. This provides a framework for us when we assign wallet-share to various consumption categories in the Indian market. Since our different categories correspond well to per capita consumption in different countries, it provides us with a good direction guide and a check.

Buying power of a billion plus

What emerges is a long shopping list (see Table 7.5). Some of the big items on that list are (1) housing, education and healthcare, (2) communication and transport and (3) leisure, including hotels, and other new categories, now small enough to be jotted under a Miscellaneous head. This clearly shows two contrasting points: there will emerge a category of people who can spend on leisure and on newer categories of expenditure as they come into more money. However, the largest basket of India's expenditure will still remain staples, even if its proportion falls from current levels. The categories that will see significant growth (in terms of absolute value) will be the ones where there has been failure in providing public goods.

Table 7.4: Global consumption patterns help guide Indian projections

Consumer spending across categories, 2010, for other countries, projections for India 2011-25 (%)

	2010—PPP basis					India		
	Indonesia	China	Korea	Japan	USA	2011	2017	2025
Food and beverages	32.2	22.3	15.0	14.7	6.8	42.8	38.9	33.8
Alcohol and tobacco	5.8	2.3	2.6	2.8	2.1	2.5	2.5	2.4
Clothing and footwear	3.1	7.5	4.1	3.4	3.5	5.3	5.0	4.8
Housing	13.8	14.8	17.3	23.8	19.1	11.1	12.4	13.6
Household goods	5.3	4.7	3.9	3.7	4.2	4.1	4.2	4.4
Healthcare	4.3	6.9	5.4	4.8	20.3	4.4	4.8	5.6
Transport	6.5	6.4	10.8	11.6	9.7	8.3	8.9	9.5
Communications	2.1	4.9	5.7	3.0	2.3	2.5	2.7	2.9
Leisure	1.4	5.3	7.3	10.9	9.3	3.3	3.9	4.5
Education	2.1	4.8	6.3	2.2	2.4	2.6	2.7	2.9
Hotels	13.7	8.4	7.3	7.5	6.2	2.9	3.2	3.7
Miscellaneous	9.8	11.7	14.3	11.4	14.1	10.3	10.9	11.9
Total	100.0	100.0	100.0	100.0	100.0	100.0	100.0	100.0
Per-capita income (PPP, US$)	3,179	4,432	19,068	28,637	43,539			
Expected number of years for India to reach	2	7	28	34	40			

Source: Euromonitor; Kotak Institutional Equities research

Spends might represent payment for capital value. In the housing component, for instance, expenditure can represent paying for capital value or interest on loans or rent. Even if we consider other categories, such as education and car or two-wheeler purchases, finance can play an important role. Therefore, growth in a sector (and its associated sectors, like finance) will be far more meaningful than the indications of consumption numbers. Finance, which is included in the miscellaneous category, will become a larger category of expenditure in India's new scheme of things. A significant proportion of the expenditure will be financial services like banking, investment and insurance.

Table 7.5: The big winners in the Indian consumption story

CAGR and market size of various categories, March fiscal year-ends, 2012-25

	Growth		Market size (Rs bn)		Opportunity
Categories	CAGR (%)	Rank	2012	2025	(Rs bn)
Food and beverages	5.4	12	23,590	46,527	22,937
Alcohol and tobacco	6.9	10	1,403	3,356	1,953
Clothing and footwear	6.6	11	2,904	6,645	3,740
Housing	8.8	4	6,412	19,191	12,778
Household goods	8.0	9	2,282	6,232	3,951
Healthcare	9.4	2	2,482	7,935	5,453
Transport	8.2	8	4,751	13,313	8,562
Communications	8.6	5	1,406	4,122	2,716
Leisure	9.5	1	1,945	6,326	4,382
Education	8.4	6	1,440	4,126	2,686
Hotels	9.2	3	1,661	5,211	3,549
Miscellaneous	8.4	7	5,852	16,758	10,905
Total	**7.3**		**56,129**	**139,741**	**83,612**

Source: Kotak Institutional Equities research

An important point to appreciate is that as households move up the categories, their ability to spend increases significantly in absolute terms (see Appendix 5 for details). Hence, even though proportions fall, the absolute amounts that will be spent on a class of goods can increase. For example, a person in the Survivors category, who spends on average Rs 15,000 a year, spends almost half of his wallet on food and beverages (a spending of around Rs 7,500 a year). As the person and his household moves up the categories, they may spend a smaller proportion of their wallet but the wallet itself increases so significantly that the absolute amount spent on the category increases. For example, a Real–rich person may allocate only 15 per cent of his Rs 500,000 annual wallet to food. However, this will mean s/he spends around Rs 75,000 on food, or more than 10 times what a Survivor does. Segments like food and beverages, alcohol and tobacco and clothing and footwear will grow in their own right, by 5–6 per cent a year, but as they trail overall spending growth, their proportion in the share of the wallet will fall.

It can also so happen that the proportion of the wallet spent on a category will increase even as households move up the expenditure curve. For example, consider this: a household in the Survivors category spends about Rs 600 a year on healthcare (a small proportion of a relatively small wallet) while a Real-rich person spends Rs 45,000 a year, an increase of 75 times over a Survivor. As people graduate into higher categories their approach to well-being may undergo a sea change. They would focus on (1) disease prevention (also captured in the leisure category through health boutiques), (2) chronic diseases and (3) paying more for tests and procedures. In the new scheme of things, Indians are likely to spend more on such categories.

Categories like healthcare, housing, education and transport will grow significantly ahead of the overall consumption market and the growth in GDP. These represent the 'private cost of public failure' market that we have already encountered. One of the simplest ways of making the lives of ordinary Indians easier is for the government to make it easier to provide these services to the common man. India needs to figure out, in specific cases, how it can increase supply meaningfully so that the cost of providing these basic services comes down meaningfully.

On the other hand, categories like leisure, hotels and miscellaneous growing faster than the overall growth rate indicates that there will be a move towards the good life. It will not be surprising to see Indians become one of the largest in-bound and out-bound travellers across the world. The sight of the Japanese or European tourist travelling the world is increasingly being replaced by the Chinese: these numbers suggest that Indians too will be big travellers. Similarly, the local consumption market will evolve to meet the needs to entertainment, education and leisure for Indians—all of these are expected to be high growth areas.

The middle categories evolve beyond survival

India's large and varied population makes it a consumption market that houses a significant number of households across the RUPEES spectrum.

The Indian economy's rapid growth over the last decade (even after accounting for the slow growth over the last couple of years) has produced a big churn. From a low per capita income of US$ 480 in 2003, Indian per capita incomes increased 3 times in USD terms to around US$ 1,500 in 2014. This was not an equally distributed increase and it created a much wider distribution. India moved from having just, what we in our model call, the Survivors and the Real-rich to having reasonable representation in several consumer categories in between, each with their own rising aspirations.

We estimate that India will have around 270 million households in 2015 with 95 million of them in urban India and 175 million in rural India; ~200 million of the 270 million households are currently in the Emerging and Surviving categories. They are either just at the poverty line or are beginning to emerge out of it. There are few households in the Real-rich category.

By 2025, practically all households currently in the Survivors category will have moved up to the Emerging or Evolving categories. By 2025 the Evolving and Emerging categories will comprise about 240 million households out of about 330 million households. The top-three categories (RUP) will have grown more than 4.5 times to 77 million households from an estimated 17 million households today.

The large numbers of Survivor and Emerging households currently form the largest segment by value (almost half) in a Rs 70 trillion Indian consumption market. By 2025, as economic growth, assuming it is reasonably well distributed, increases the number of the Emerging and Evolving category households, they will command almost half the ~Rs 137 trillion market. The top three categories, which account for about 20 per cent of the consumption basket currently, will account for the other half of it by 2025.

As the share of wallet shifts to high-end customers, per capita expenditure in each category will expand creating many sub-categories. We expect to see this categorization and differentiation especially in categories that will lead growth at above-average levels. In the face of such a phenomenal increase in buying power, companies will usher in innovation into premium products and services moving away from lower ticket sizes. With such large parts of the market now catering to high-end customers, there will be significant changes in (1) the types of products and services on offer in each product and service category, (2) the evolution of new sub-categories and (3) the appeal to customers (marketing) and reach (distribution).

When we look at the distribution it becomes clear that the urban part of India has a higher proportion of households in the top-3 categories. This stems from the nature of economic activities in urban India which constitute a bulk of the services sector. Rural India relies significantly (if not primarily) on agriculture which has seen lower growth in their already lower income base. It is hence not a surprise that people want to come over to cities to try their economic fortune.

The risk of lopsided prosperity...and how to mitigate it

India's increasing Gini-coefficient depicts lopsided prosperity rather than well-distributed poverty. We had noted in chapter 2 that a recent UNESCAP report highlighted that India's Gini-coefficient worsened over the last decade to 0.339 from 0.308. Lopsided prosperity has created several categories, each with its own needs. This can take India along the same path as some larger countries/economies with significant income disparity. Brazil's Gini-coefficient was 0.518 in 2010, China's was 0.513 and the US' was 0.471.

Our model assumes growth will be reasonably well spread, though not equally distributed. We take into account a skew in growth distribution. A household in a high consumption category will reap benefits of growth marginally better than a household in a low consumption category.

Two points are important here:

(1) **Big buying power in the top ten percentile:** India has reasonably high income (and hence, expenditure) inequality (see Table 7.6). D9/D1 numbers (which measure the expenditure difference between a person in the ninetieth percentile with one in the tenth percentile) is about three in rural India and five in urban India. However, there is significant buying power in the D9-D10 category (households in the top ten percentile, between the ninetieth and hundredth percentile), which exacerbates lopsided prosperity.

Table 7.6: We project a marginally more in equal society

Estimates of incomes at various deciles in rural and urban India, March fiscal year-ends, FY2011-25

	2011	2015	2020	2025
Rural				
D9	3,798	5,229	6,494	8,064
D1	1,224	1,579	1,884	2,247
D9/D1	3.1	3.3	3.4	3.6
Urban				
D9	8,591	11,152	15,315	21,030
D1	1,705	2,322	3,063	4,041
D9/D1	5.0	4.8	5.0	5.2

Source: Kotak Institutional Equities research

(2) **Increase in the difference between top and bottom percentiles:** When we account for a skew in projected household consumptions, we project a society that will be more unequal by 2025, but not significantly so. The D9/D1 ratio, based on a base-case skew, will move to 3.6 for rural and 5.2 for urban India, not too far from the current levels of 3.3 and 4.8 respectively.

As a reasonably well-distributed growth story unfolds, the Survivor category will emerge to join the large household base of the bulging middle categories. If, however, growth were to be top-heavy, the consumption market may rise in value, but the number of Survivors will not decline as dramatically as projected.

That's a risk that could have unhappy consequences ripping the social fabric. On the other hand a more inclusive development story will make it easier to enhance growth (through hard decisions and reforms). If the benefits of growth are not well shared, political discussion will gravitate towards distribution of the pie rather than its growth.

One way to mitigate this risk is to get more households to take part in the bouquet of opportunities through the creation of jobs. India has spent significant resources on educating its demographic dividend. As the population bulge moves to the working age, it is imperative that an adequate number of jobs be generated.

Change in spending patterns

A more prosperous India's spending on bare necessities (food and clothing) has fallen significantly as a percentage of share-of-wallets. Durables and Miscellaneous goods and services have taken most of the increased spends, especially in urban India. Just how much and what Indians consume, however, have been debated. NSSO surveys show rural and urban India spends 54 per cent and 41 per cent respectively of their wallets on food and beverages (an average of about 50 per cent of the overall Indian consumption basket). On the other hand, Euromonitor estimates this to be about 30 per cent of the Indian consumption pie. Similarly, there is significant difference in the estimation of the pie that transportation commands. Table 7.7 shows how our estimates of rural, urban and overall Indian consumption stand.

Table 7.7: Our analysis has a reasonable resemblance to Indian consumption estimates

Estimates of the break-up of India's consumption basket, March fiscal year-ends, FY2011

	KIE analysis			NSSO		Euromonitor
	Rural	Urban	All-India	Rural	Urban	All India
Food and beverages	45.6	39.9	42.8	48.6	38.6	27.7
Alcohol and tobacco	2.5	2.5	2.5	2.4	1.4	3.2
Clothing and footwear	5.7	5.0	5.3	7.6	6.5	6.4
Housing	10.1	12.1	11.1			14.5
Household goods	4.0	4.1	4.1	6.1	6.3	3.9
Healthcare	4.1	4.7	4.4			4.8
Transport	7.9	8.8	8.3	9.2	7.6	17.7
Communications	2.3	2.6	2.5			2.2
Leisure	2.9	3.8	3.3			1.3
Education	2.5	2.6	2.6			2.4
Hotels	2.5	3.2	2.9			2.9
Miscellaneous	9.9	10.8	10.3	26.1	39.6	13.2
Grand total	100.0	100.0	100.0	100.0	100.0	100.0

Note:

(a) In NSSO terminology, Miscellaneous includes (1) education, (2) medical, (3) rents, (4) taxes, (5) entertainment, (6) goods for personal care and effects, (7) toilet and sundry articles, (8) consumer services (like sweeper, barber, priests, etc.) and (9) conveyance

Source: Euromonitor 'World Consumer Income and Expenditure Patterns', July 2011; NSSO; Kotak Institutional Equities research

We also examine how other economies have evolved by taking consumption patterns of countries with purchasing power parity (PPP)-adjusted per capita income higher than India's. India is nearer to countries like Indonesia and China, and is expected to achieve similar PPP-adjusted per capita income over 2–7 years. India will take 28–40 years to reach the per capita incomes of countries like South Korea, Japan and the US, but comparisons with them help to identify consumption patterns of India's Real-rich, Upper and Prospering categories.

In more advanced countries there is relative dominance of certain categories across consumption patterns. The consistency of the dominant categories strengthens our assumptions that India's growth story could follow a similar plot. We concede that the numbers serve only to highlight a broad trend and the Indian market given its peculiarities could surprise in some categories. The US, for instance, spends a large proportion of its wallet on healthcare, compared with other countries, and South Koreans love their data plans so much that it shows in a higher spend on communications.

We estimate what various Indian categories will spend on several categories, proportionately and in absolute terms, based on (1) the evolution of Indian consumption over time and (2) consumption spends of countries with similar PPP-adjusted per capita incomes.

For necessities, the proportion begins to fall, driven by the fact that there is only so much (in absolute terms) that can be spent on a category. For example, in the food and beverages category, even though the absolute quantum increases across each consuming category, the overall annual spend of a person in the Real-rich category is 'only' 10 times the annual per capita spend of a Survivor, even though the average income differential is 33 times.

For discretionary items, for example leisure, the logic works in reverse. The absolute amount a Real-rich member spends on this category vis-à-vis a Survivor is 100 times, even though the proportion of the wallet a Real-rich person spends is 6 per cent while a Survivor spends 2 per cent.

The quantity of food, for example, that will be consumed per capita does not significantly change or the time spent on leisure will not materially increase, but the emphasis on these segments (as in almost all the others) will be in the quality of goods or services delivered or on the delivery process itself. In food, for example, there is a well-documented trend towards an increased protein-rich diet as opposed to a cereals-heavy diet and in leisure a trend of towards say, plush multiplex cinemas as opposed to stand-alone theatres or foreign jaunts over local family vacations. As a larger proportion of the market moves away from basic necessities, expect a significant rise in premium goods and services.

Beyond our daily bread

The overall tone of the Indian consumption market will move beyond requirements of daily necessities to more materialistic products. Given India's size (number of households) and range of buying power, there will be a meaningful number of customers across the value chain in almost all categories. Hence, it will not be surprising to find the same categories being serviced by price-leaders and very brand-conscious companies.

The relative monetary importance of the top-three categories cannot be overstated. The Real-rich, Upper-category and Prospering categories put together, will by 2025, command almost half the market by value even though they will account for less than one-eighth of the number of households. These categories (with PPP-adjusted per capita incomes equal to the current living standards of OECD countries) will be dominant consumption trend setters. Even though they will number less than one-fourth of the total number of Indian households, their absolute number will be 76 million, which is more than half of all the households in the US currently and significantly more than the number of households in Japan, Germany and the UK.

Meanwhile, the Evolving and Emerging categories (middle categories) will command an almost equal value of market share as the premium end. Companies will need to choose their market or develop differentiated brands to service the entire value chain.

Savings do better in the market than under a mattress

We expect India to be a high savings economy. To achieve 7 per cent a year real growth (our assumption) India will need to have an investment rate of at least 28 per cent of GDP (given India's incremental capital-output ratio of about 4). We have taken India's sustainable growth at only

7 per cent a year, and not 9 per cent, which was commonplace until recently in the light of certain constraints on domestic savings.

For India to be self-reliant in funding growth (even as it liberalizes its FDI and FII norms), it will need to channelize its high savings into productive investments.

The current structure of India's savings leaves a lot to be desired:

(1) Around two-thirds of household savings (14.8 per cent of 21.9 per cent of GDP in financial year 2013) go into real estate (buying of gold is not considered a saving in Indian accounts). Such savings are either dead-weight losses or illiquid and do not create adequate incremental output. India needs to move its savings into financial assets so that it can improve productivity of savings.

(2) The government and its enterprises have been less than exemplary savers. With the government's fiscal deficit requiring constant financing, it (a) crowds out private investment and (b) keeps interest rates high. A fundamental shift in the profile of borrowers (with the government being less of a borrower) can be a significant growth driver.

With savings being the focus of an Indian citizen (prodded by the government), we do not expect consumption as a proportion of GDP to grow meaningfully. We expect consumption to be in a 62–64 per cent band and hence our estimates do not take into account that meaningful uptick is possible if Indian saving-consumption habits were to change.

Financing consumption

There are two ways to spend on a category that can expand: (1) a large proportion of current income can be diverted to the category or (2) through financing (i.e. taking loans to consumer), if the category is amenable to it. In the case of diverting current income into the category, growth will be limited by new consumers or old consumers' increasing spends on the category. The amenability of a category to finance can give a greater impetus to the growth of a category. Categories like housing including housing goods, transport, education, and to some extent leisure, can see a disproportionate rise due to financing (some part of this is captured in the Miscellaneous line, which includes banking and financial services).

However, financing, especially of consumer products, can help boost consumption spends if the expectation of (nominal) growth in the consumer's income is more than the (nominal) cost of debt. This means that over time a consumer will have much better ability to pay for current consumption, making it sustainable. However, increased financing, not backed by an ability to repay, can create significant fluctuations in the growth patterns of these categories.

Serving up cities, with a capital C

A transformed economic fabric will translate into a shift to urban buying power. Urban consumption will grow to be marginally higher than rural consumption as more households emerge in urban India due to (1) more families turning nuclear in urban India, (2) households moving to urban from rural areas and (3) more rural areas qualifying to be classified as urban as population growth makes towns/villages larger agglomeration units.

The story of India's consumption market metamorphosis is not just about the concentration of urban growth but is about per capita income growth. This will come from (1) increased movement of labour from agriculture to the manufacturing and services sectors, which will tend to be in urban areas, or an urban sprawl around a zone of economic activity or (2) a big increase in agricultural productivity (not just in terms of fertility of land but in per capita terms). Agricultural per capita income will grow mainly because people will move away from farming. In short, urban India will continue to offer better opportunities for income expansion.

A new creature that will emerge from this societal reorganization will have a wing-span that will straddle a considerable geographic area. Rural hubs will bulge at the seams and burst on to urban city spaces. Tier-2 and tier-1 towns will morph into larger metropolitan cities. For companies that means a larger number of differentiated markets with their own needs and preferences.

India's urbanization, as we have noted earlier, will be incremental in nature. Over the past 40 years, India has urbanized slowly. The 2011 Census highlighted that India was urbanizing at the margins. Census 2011 defines a town (regarded as an urban area) as a demarcated area whose population exceeds 5,000, among other criteria. About four-fifths of India's rural population lives in towns smaller than this according to the 2001 Census, (data for the 2011 Census are unavailable). A statutory town is, in effect, a census town whose status has been recognized by the local state government and a municipality, corporation, cantonment board or whose town area committee has been notified. There has hardly been an increase in the number of villages in India.

The increase in census towns indicates a more spread out growth of India's tardy rate of urbanization. The process is being driven by the nature of growth of the economy. The economy is becoming increasingly dependent on services as its engine of growth and on agriculture as its largest employer. Unless there is a definite thrust towards a manufacturing-led economy, we do not expect the rate of India's urbanization process to change.

GameChanger: A growing pie is easier to share

Throughout the metamorphosis there are two big assumptions: (1) sustainable long-term growth of the Indian economy and (2) reasonable distribution of the fruits of that growth.

The projections should be achievable as we have assumed (1) a savings rate of only about 28 per cent, which is significantly lower than the recent performance of Indian savers and (2) no meaningful improvement in capital-output ratio. Growth in internal consumption, government spending and increased exports should help the economy to grow. However, if the economy does not grow, it will create a stagnant pie of which more people will want to get a share. It is easier to share a growing pie and hence the focus must remain on economic growth.

The perceived and actual equality of the division of the pie is important to (1) continue fostering aspirations and (2) keep in check social unrest. The significant disconnect in the average per capita income (and consumption) in rural and urban India highlights the need for inclusive growth. There are two ways to narrow this gap: (1) by transferring resources from a section of society that is doing well (tax the rich and give the poor) or (2) by creating sustainable income streams for those who have not benefited, or integrated, with market-oriented reforms over the past two decades.

India has experimented with the former strategy over its history and will require significant effort at the grassroots level to push for the latter. This will require that the Indian economy creates enough employment opportunities in the manufacturing and services sectors so that people pull out of the less productive agriculture sector. Creating these opportunities will require an efficient (1) land acquisition framework, (2) ease-of-business policies, (3) skill development and (4) employment-matching mechanisms. One of the concerns that India will have to address is increased consumption of raw material and energy. India will need to work towards an environmentally sustainable way to satisfy its consumption upswing from the perspectives of an improved global environment and to avoid the price rise that raw material and energy could see due to increased demand from India.

The narrative that India will need to communicate and nurture is one of hope and aspiration. It should give confidence and ability to its poor and deprived that they can indeed move up the curve of a better material life. This links back to the point of Indians being provided with reasonable quality public goods so that they can spend their time, energy and money on pursuing their dreams and happiness.

CONCLUSION

IN THE JOURNEY of a country there is no end state, there is no final destination that it needs to reach. The progress of this journey may be measured by the milestones that the country and its citizens want to achieve in their journey. What a country wants to achieve is shaped by its context: (1) wanting to become an independent sovereign (for example, during the independence movement and also when India launched the Green Revolution to wean itself away from imported food); (2) wanting to increase the material prosperity of its citizens (for example, when India started focusing on economic growth); and (3) wanting to reduce the inequalities that economic growth either brings along with itself or perpetuates (for example, the large redistributive policies of the last decade).

In chapter after chapter in the book, we have seen how India is changing: its jobs, industries, consumption, urbanization, agriculture and governance are all changing. For every transition we have noted the pivots of change, the aspects of social and economic life that are changing and that may need some hand-holding either from policymakers or from people themselves. The touchstone of our analysis and recommendations is whether the government is able to take itself out from its inherent tendency of vitiating prices. If left to themselves, without letting them run riot due to the tendencies of both the government and the corporations, prices have the ability to both balance out the aspirations of the stakeholders and to provide the correct incentives for right actions. The ability of the government to play a neutral facilitator without being an arbiter of prices is a key reform that India needs. We list down some specific areas of focus and change for India.

Building resilient and flexible institutions

There is no right path or direction that a nation can or needs to take; there is no ideal that a country and its citizens need to reach and then go no further. Since there is no destination, the definitions of milestones continue to change and hence a country and its citizenry continuously remain in a state of a churn. A churn means that there are competing worldviews of what can and needs to win. Each set of characters in the churn hopes and works hard to ensure that their perspective wins. To simplify, owners of capital would want rules that make their returns safer and higher, labour would want that their jobs remain protected and salaries growing and owners of land and resources would want continued participation in any progress. The churn can hence continue till a winner emerges, or what is more realistic in any social setting, a compromise emerges that puts into equilibrium the various competing worldviews (even if the equilibrium itself remains temporary).

If societies and citizens will always continue to remain in various transitions, what we need are institutions that will synthesize and distil the various perspectives to help create consensus and then implement such consensus into action and achievement. This remains easier said than done. There is no simple template which identifies what institutions are required; more important, the nature and scope of institutions does not remain etched in time making the process of institution formation very context and evolution dependent. Institutions are required so that society lives harmoniously which requires balancing conflicting objectives well. The art of creating balance is the essence of running a country. Listening to the needs of the people but still guiding the citizenry to a thought-through path is key to a nation's orderly prosperity.

One of the most important institutions in any society is the upholding of trust between the members. As circumstances of the various participants change, the ability to maintain trust between them that they have not been short-changed is critical. Typically, the onus of this falls on the social and legal rules the societies frame for themselves. India has seen a general corroding of the fear of law: in some cases because justice in India can get meaningfully delayed or in some cases, because the laws themselves are suddenly made to change, sometimes retrospectively. Building resilient institutions requires instilling confidence in the members of the society that the rules are well thought through and will be implemented without fear or favour.

Managing expectations during transitions

Indian mythology talks of the various positives and negatives that come about when society is in churn. The negatives need to be handled with caution and care and require the fierce but unselfish persona of Shiva. The positives are easy to celebrate. However, one must remember that the big fight between the 'gods' and the 'demons' took place not during the churning but afterwards on the topic of distribution of nectar. As India's society celebrates many of its wins, it needs to keep an eye on the distribution of its wins: that alone will create sustainable prosperity.

A churn means that we will have to battle both the romanticism of the ways of the old and the fear of the new. No one says this will be easy. People will need to be made to understand the force of the changes and will need to be prepared for the changes. They will need to be co-opted into the changes that will come about. Sometimes the changes can be anticipated but sometimes they will come about suddenly. For example, it was a slam dunk decision to send your kid to study to become an engineer in the early 2000s; by the turn of the next decade, it did not remain an obvious career choice. The type of work will change, the nature of activities itself will change and this will require constant retooling of our lives and aspirations.

There will be much to celebrate in the transitions. As Indians study more and get battle-ready for newer jobs that will come with economic growth, they will make old shackles irrelevant. These jobs may be in the field of manufacturing or in services but they will surely not be in agriculture. The nature of jobs in agriculture will also undergo dramatic changes—a tractor operator is already replacing manual labour; eventually, harvesting, sorting and warehousing, etc. will all get significantly mechanized. However, given that a large majority will fear such change, it is important to hand hold them during these transitions. The easiest way is to make the other options lucrative and easily accessible.

Newer jobs will mean that people will move to cities where they should benefit from the economies of scale in providing them basic public utilities. It is only when Indians get access to these basic utilities that they will spend their monies not just on the basics of life but on pursuits of leisure, which could mean more days off or higher education on topics of interest. It will not be easy to do simply because it is not clear currently how cities will price this creation of infrastructure and hence where they will find the funds to do the same. The trade-off that collectively paying higher for utilities now will eventually bring costs down for all needs to be well communicated and explained.

Discarding the old ways and experimenting with the new

What is important to note is that certainties, dogmatisms and ideologies don't work. What will work is creating a balance between conflicting objectives. For example, sometimes the solution will require whole-hearted market reforms, sometimes it will require the government to step in; sometimes we will need to give 'rights' to the citizens, sometimes we will need to enable them to afford the basics; sometimes it will require that the public sector works to achieve transparency and accountability, sometimes, the private sector will need to be drafted in. How society chooses to answer these questions will determine the direction that it will move along.

In many cases there will be iterations in reaching solutions but the fear of revision (and indeed, retracement) should not hold us back from taking the first step. Two good examples of how the country has been learning come from recent heated debates on the auction of natural resources and the legislation on land acquisition. In both the cases, we have arrived at a solution which is vastly different from what we practiced for many decades. Are the new solutions final and forever binding? No. They will change with time as they develop their new incongruities and inconsistencies. However, being aware and agile in response is key to avoid them into blowing up into big issues later. Let us quickly see what we learnt and where we are in the two situations.

Suddenly, after the 3G auctions, the country realized that there is significant value in what was in effect air. Around the same time, the national accountant and auditor pointed out that the process of 'allocating' resources like coal have led to immense loss of value for the country. Both these jolts have created the ground for auctioning of natural resources. We have hence moved from 'allocating' the resources to 'auctioning' them. Is this the end state? No. A couple of decades down the line, we will, as a country, realize that the resources are now getting concentrated in the hands of only those who can participate in the auctions. Invariably, that will mean that the incumbents in the industry, foreign or Indian companies and promoters with deep pockets alone can participate in these auctions. We will then possibly want to figure out a better way of encouraging new entrepreneurs and sharing the wealth around. However, the current crisis demands a current and context-relevant solution and that is what we are currently working to put in place.

On land acquisitions, the government and its functionaries had become key intermediaries in acquiring land using the state's power of eminent domain. These land parcels were then passed on to the public or private sector for further development. The land could be one which was rich in natural resources and hence valuable for mining or it could be relevant to industry or real estate players as a convenient place for their construction. This led to the creation of extra-legal elements which helped acquire land and there were many instances of forcible acquisitions leading all the way to murder. From such a position where the state could use its unfettered right to take away anyone's property, we have now moved to a situation where land acquisition requires individual consent and in case of public projects, consent by a large super-majority. This is now being criticized as being too harsh on those who want to acquire land (and states have started changing the new law and bringing back the old one). Is this hence a closed chapter? No. We will need to design many changes to achieve equilibrium between competing interests. The process of conversion of land from agricultural to non-agricultural remains mired in ways which are openly corrupt. All of this will indeed need to change.

Fixing the broken link between education, skill development and jobs

India has invested massively in its education system. A large number of children enter the education system but few continue to finish off their secondary education and even fewer go on and graduate. As the investment of time and resources spent on this aspect of labour supply continues to increase, the number of years that students will stay in school will increase. We have been seeing a trend of higher enrolment ratios and lower drop-out rates across the board over the last many years. What remains a challenge for India is the poor quality of education that public schools offer. Education being a public good, the failing state has passed on the onus and cost of this to private individuals. Parents are increasingly sending their children to private schools.

Irrespective of whether the children study in private or public schools, one reality that they will need to face is that the education system is not speaking with and hence is not geared to solve the needs of the industries that will eventually hire them. Education has remained a silo with which the job market has had limited interaction. Two examples will suffice to show how broken the system is at different levels: (1) when the engineering boom started in India in the late 1990s and the early 2000s, there came a massive supply response by colleges which created far more seats than the number of engineers required by India's IT or other industries and (2) the industry continues to demand semi-skilled and skilled labour but few are available. India ended up training a whole bunch of engineers (many of them quite poorly) when what was needed were people who brought some specific skills to the work-table.

The reality of job markets changes quickly and we are only now beginning to talk about flexibility in the labour market. As the economy doubles every decade, it is but certain that the nature and scope of jobs will change. New industries will require new types of skills and as old industries expand, they will need to dip into a well-trained talent pool. The key here is to link vocational training to industries. Post the primary school education, there needs to open up a parallel opportunity for children to learn a couple of vocations of their choice eventually allowing them to choose whatever they think suits them best either due to interest or remuneration.

Many industries are wary of investing in the skill development of the people that they employ. This travesty arises because companies, not being allowed to determine the size of its own workforce (both hiring and firing in a manufacturing unit are difficult), take a large proportion of them on 'contract'. By keeping the cost of firing so high, India has basically made its businessmen choose a short cut. If the cost was made more manageable (like a reasonable severance pay for employee when firing) the outcome could be quite different and companies will start taking the training of their employees more seriously. It should come as no surprise that IT companies have built large campuses for training their newly hired employees but few manufacturing firms do so.

Creating an export base in India

In order to build foreign exchange reserves, a country either needs to export more than it imports or it needs to attract more foreign capital than it invests in other countries. India's account with the external world balances more via its capital account than its current account. This means that on a running basis of annual exports and imports, India is not able to generate enough foreign exchange to add to its reserves. This keeps India reliant on foreigners investing their dollars in India.

Economists have historically looked at the net flow of manufactured goods (trade surplus/deficit). This works best for countries that are export powerhouses for goods, something that the East Asian countries did over the second half of the last century. A country like India which does not have a big manufacturing base has relied on its services sector (IT sector) and the remittances from its diaspora (both IT and non-IT). In order to appreciate the quantum of the foreign exchange that the IT sector brings in (~US$ 67 billion in financial year 2014) and the diaspora sends in (~US$ 65 billion in financial year 2014), we compare their total with the oil imports of India (~US$ 168 billion in financial year 2014). India's IT industry has come as a saviour in its quest to mitigate its energy deficiency. Instead of just looking at trade surplus/deficit, India needs to keep a tab on its current account surplus/deficit.

Even a small single digit current account deficit requires that India relies on foreign capital to shore up its reserves. It should hence come as no surprise that some of the largest companies in India are now more than majority owned by foreigners; indeed almost a fifth of all the listed companies in India are owned by foreigners. This is without taking into account the unlisted foreign companies that do meaningful business in India (for example, in consumer and staple goods, electronics, mobiles and telecom).

India had earlier (in the 1980s) mooted the idea of requiring foreign firms doing business in India to list here. That rule has been quietly done away with to make it easier for foreigners to do business here. Foreign investments do indeed bring in superior technology or new ways of thinking of how to organize a business. However, a country cannot continue to have a current account deficit financed by capital account flows. It will rather quickly (over a generation or two), find that many of its iconic companies that it does business with do not belong to the locals. The government may have foreign exchange coffers to show by allowing increased foreign ownership but increasingly it may end up finding that the businesses are not controlled from within its jurisdiction.

This requires a two pronged response: (1) Instead of just importing goods, India needs to facilitate the setting up of the foreign companies' production units in India (especially in consumer goods, electronic goods, mobiles and telecommunication equipment). India must convert the outflow of its import dollars into inward investments, (2) India must channelize its own local savings into investment. Indians have, over the last 5–7 years shifted meaningfully to investing in physical assets like property. India needs to work on reviving financial savings and linking them to the financing needs of the industry.

India needs to facilitate the creation of an export hub. It is somewhat secondary whether what India exports are goods or services. Creating delivery centres to serve world demand is critical for generating employment for its demographic dividend. More important, India has seen that an exposure to and links with the external world bring in significant incomes, growth and improvement in the lives of its citizens (look no further than the IT industry).

Managing the increasing inequality in the distribution of income and wealth

The boost in consumption and savings in India is critically dependent on its ability to create enough employment opportunities and to spread the fruits of economic growth reasonably equitably. We have spoken about how employment can and needs to be generated. India starts off from a meaningful inequality in the distribution of both income and wealth. The progress of the nation will be smooth if everyone has an opportunity to partake in the fruits of economic growth. The opportunity to enter the workforce to get a rightful share of the pie depends on good health, reasonable education, decent pay and low cost of living.

In the chapter on consumption, we saw that a large portion of growth of the Indian consumption wallet will come from Indians spending on the necessities of life: what we have called through the book *bijli, sadak, paani, shiksha, swasthya* and *suraksha* (power, roads, water, education, health and security). This stems from the failure of the government to offer these goods and services that are of good quality and at reasonable prices to its citizens. India has unfortunately priced these utilities so poorly that in most cases they have been run down. Indians have hence had to resort to private provisioning of these basic utilities. This imposes a burden on the poorer section of society since a disproportionately larger portion of their wallet is spent on ensuring these basic goods and services. We also saw in the chapter on urbanization that India needs to invest between Rs 120 trillion and Rs 150 trillion on meeting the infrastructural demands of its urbanization. However, if the pricing of the infrastructure is not right, we may not see many of these infrastructure projects come up.

The argument for keeping the prices of basic utilities in India low is similar to the one made earlier for keeping the price of natural resources low. Indians will not be able to afford 'market prices' for these. The dominant thinking is now evolving to say that it is not a question of whether Indians will be in a position to afford the final prices or not but the natural resources need to be allocated transparently and objectively and at a price. A similar change in thought needs to come in the field of public utilities. By definition, public goods mean that access to the goods cannot be cut off because one cannot pay for them. India needs a smarter way to develop the ability to pay in its people rather than offering these services at highly uneconomic prices. That smart way is to transfer money to the people who cannot afford the service. India has witnessed its citizens moving away from the public distribution system for their food requirements and from government schools and hospitals for their education and health requirement as they have grown richer. Similarly, the diesel deregulation which increased prices of diesel by more than 50 per cent over the last couple of years has been absorbed quietly by the people. If quality services are offered, Indians will be happy to pay, for example, toll roads and power in cities.

If Indians get credible and consistent access to good quality public goods, it increases their chances of being able to join the workforce as healthy, well-educated or appropriately skilled persons. As governments and policymakers, the focus can only be on providing equality of opportunity and not of outcomes. What a person makes out of that opportunity will depend on his/her skill, effort, luck and a host of extraneous factors. An important way to spread material prosperity to households will be for women to find productive employment opportunities. We have seen how poor the female workforce participation ratio in India is. This takes us back to the question of being able to create enough jobs in the economy to absorb both men and women who become eligible to enter the workforce.

The inherent inequality of wealth distribution can be tackled in two ways: (1) tax the old wealth either during its existence (wealth tax) or at the death of the owner (inheritance tax) or (2) help create new wealth. India has given up on inheritance tax and collects paltry sums of monies via wealth tax. It needs to focus on creating new avenues of wealth rather than spending energies in trying to run down the old wealth. For example, billionaire owners of tech, pharma, banking and other sectors over the last generation did not come by taxing old wealth.

It must however be noted that India's laws (at least on the fiscal side) are far friendlier for owners of capital than for providers of labour. Income from labour is taxed at the marginal rate while income from capital carries many exemptions. For example, dividend and long-term capital gains are tax-free and there are many incentives for investing in capital equipment (like accelerated depreciation or buying second homes). India would do well to reflect on the objectives of its fiscal policies. As we have noted across the book, there is no right answer but only a judicious balance that needs to be achieved at various points in time.

Clear title to property and the ease and ability to transfer it

When discussing both agriculture and urbanization, we came across a similar point: citizens need to have enforceable titles to their land. Hernando de Soto, in his seminal book, *The Mystery of Capital* noted that it is not that the poor do not have capital—it is that they do not have enough or proper title to the capital to make it a collateral. India's agriculture and its urbanization both suffer from the fact that their titles to land are not clear. It is pertinent to remind readers that even in the most optimistic scenario of 550 million people living in urban India by say 2025 (or 40 per cent of India's then population), urban India will occupy only around 5–6 per cent of the land area of the country. Urbanization is no significant threat to agriculture or food security in India.

Landholdings in India are fragmenting as people continue to have legal entitlements to their land long after they have left it to find work in cities. Increasingly, these landholdings are being recorded in a digital format. Digitization of land records currently means that the registration process of new transactions on land (mortgage, rental, sale, partition, etc.) are recorded digitally and can be made available for searchers to see. However, few states have completed the task of digitizing the cadastral land records such that it becomes visually clear who owns which property. Once that is completed, ideally, the records will work similar to how the demat registries work in the equity and debt markets. Not only will the land records will be held online, so will their transfer and partition. The government has mooted that eventually India should move to a similar system (called the Torrens system). However, significant detailed work remains to be done on this.

Even as the land record digitization continues apace, another reform required is in the ability of an owner to sell his land and convert its land use. The process of converting land which is currently designated as agricultural to non-agricultural requires multiple sign-offs. Given that the value of land zooms dramatically when it gets converted, there are high rents to be paid when getting such sign-offs. The power to designate the use of the land needs to lie in the hands of the owner of the land. There is genuine concern that town planners have on the haphazard use of land. However, this needs to be addressed by having a robust and dynamic town planning process. If the owner of land can decide the end use of for his land, s/he can partake significantly in the upside that emerges as cities and industries expand.

Land remains one of the last and largest bastions of hiding black money. Digitization of land records and recording of transactions online will facilitate analytics on the identities of both the buyer and the seller and also on the price. The reason land remains a safe place to hide/invest black money is because the government records of the value of land (on which registration charges like stamp duties are paid) are hopelessly out of line with reality. In some cases the difference between the market price of land and the government recorded price can be as high as 5–10 times. This allows for registering the transaction at a fraction of the actual price in cheque and the rest in cash (with attendant implications for government revenue). Better analytics on the prices at which land is changing hands can not only help curb the menace of black money in land but also provide a boost to government coffers.

Digitization of identity, interaction and money

In many of these discussions, we touched upon the idea of using technology to reach people. In the chapter on e-governance we discussed that this is indeed a significant work in progress. All three aspects (1) identity of people, (2) their money and (3) their interactions (with the government, its agencies or others) need to be digitized and they should be in a position to speak with each other. With the roll-out of UID or Aadhar, India has given a digital and biometric identity to more than 700 million people. The government is engaged in making many of its services to citizens digital. RBI and the government have been taking steps to ensure that money becomes both digital and mobile though there still continues to be some fascination for bank accounts as opposed to mobile accounts to ensure financial inclusion.

Once all the three pieces fall in place, India can leapfrog across a wide variety of its failings. The focus of India's policymakers and its economic analysts when talking about the advantages of digitization is only on the subsidies that the government needs to cut. Subsidies in the field of food, fuel and fertilizers amount to between 2 per cent and 3 per cent of the GDP of the country each year. No doubt there will be marked improvement in the delivery of these subsidies via better targeting and there will potentially be large savings due to stoppage of leakages. More important, as the subsidies get delivered directly to beneficiaries, market prices will prevail for these which will have their own important impact on influencing or shaping demand.

A primary failing of the Indian state has been its inability to offer *bijli, sadak, paani, shiksha, swasthya* and *suraksha* (power, roads, water, education, health and security) to its citizens. In many of these sectors, the subsidy is not explicitly identified because there is no international price benchmark. In the case of oil and fertilizers, it is easy to calculate subsidies because we import a very large portion of our requirements. Similarly, when grains are purchased at high minimum support prices and sold at low single digit rates, there will inevitably be a subsidy left in the books of accounts. In the case of public goods, there is no accounting entry of a subsidy but only a sustained poor quality of the service.

What the use of technology can do is identify the beneficiaries and help in making conditional transfers. A small consumer of electricity or water can be given payments in lieu of his paying the market price. If a child is going to school (which can be electronically tracked), payments come into the accounts of the parents or the child. If someone has fallen ill, digital identity and access to insurance can offer cash-less check-ups and for security in old-age or in deprived conditions, direct transfers are possible. The opening of bank accounts will allow the creation of credit histories and the ability to cross sell investment and insurance products. More important, technology can assist in imparting education, skill development and healthcare to the people.

Technology can only solve the problems of identification, communication and financial transfers, physical infrastructure of a school or a health clinic will still be required and indeed required to be run well. This will not be easy. There are many vested interests that benefit significantly from the current state of affairs. If any of the aspects represents the mantra of churning, the digitization initiative is their epitome. Managing this transition will require creating a completely new vista and vision for India. The old ways have got to be made irrelevant in such a comprehensive manner that they cease to remain relevant.

A call for action

The transitions that we have discussed in this book are social, political, economic and demographic. Many of these transitions are sweeping through India without there being adequate data and fact-based debate on how to tackle the challenges thrown open by this vigorous change. Tackling these challenges holistically requires an understanding of their inter-linkages and their orders of magnitude and this requires having a sound grounding in facts and data.

These transitions will throw up a lot of opportunities to re-create India and will threaten various entrenched interests. This will open up many calls for 'reforms' and also for maintaining 'status quo'. When any stakeholder seeks 'reforms', the perspective of asking for change remains narrow and in some cases, short-sighted. Governance is the art of balancing conflicting perspectives and interests and that is the touchstone on which we will have to measure our government.

One mechanism to balance the aspirations of varied stakeholders is to foster functioning markets which help evolve right 'prices'. In India, this onus of balancing has historically been taken over by the government through its rather visible hand. Getting the government out from its inherent tendency of vitiating prices will be a key change that we in India should aim for. If left to themselves, without letting them run riot due to the tendencies of both the government and the corporations, prices have the ability to both balance out the aspirations of the stakeholders and to provide the correct incentives for right actions. The ability of the government to play a neutral facilitator without being an arbiter of price is a key reform that India needs.

A high growth rate makes many of the old certainties disappear rather quickly and this can be both unnerving as well as liberating. There will be many faceless people who will benefit from this transition, just as there will be quite a few who will struggle to make sense of the new

India. Those who can find their way in these times of great change will find themselves commanding great wealth and recognition. Identifying such people and the business opportunities that they pursue will bring reflected glory to both employees and investors. This book will have served its purpose if it has given you a bird's eye view of where to begin your journey.

APPENDICES

Appendix 1: 330 mn employment opportunities can be generated over the next 15 years

Proportion and number of skilled workforce requirement between FY2008-22

Industry/service	Proportion (%)				Numbers (mn)				
	Level 1	Level 2	Level 3	Level 4	Level 1	Level 2	Level 3	Level 4	Total
Automobiles and automobile components	50	25	20	5	17.5	8.8	7.0	1.8	35.0
Banking, financial services and insurance	20	40	30	10	0.9	1.7	1.3	0.4	4.3
Building, construction and real estate	81	15	4	2	39.2	7.1	1.7	0.7	48.7
Chemicals and pharmaceuticals	23	28	45	6	0.4	0.5	0.8	0.1	1.9
Education and skill development	20	30	45	5	1.7	2.6	3.9	0.4	8.7
Electronics and IT hardware	20	26	50	5	0.6	0.8	1.6	0.1	3.2
Food processing	81	10	9	2	7.5	0.9	0.8	0.1	9.3
Furniture and furnishings	80	12	7	1	2.7	0.4	0.2	0.0	3.4
Gems and jewelry	75	5	19	2	3.4	0.2	0.9	0.1	4.6
IT and ITES industry	—	50	40	10	—	2.7	2.1	0.5	5.3
Leather	89	4	6	1	4.1	0.2	0.3	0.0	4.6

Media and entertainment	20	30	45	5	0.6	0.9	1.3	0.1	3.0
Organized retail	52	13	32	5	8.9	2.2	5.5	0.8	17.3
Others (including healthcare)	60	20	15	5	10.1	3.4	2.5	0.8	16.8
Textiles and spinning	86	11	3	1	3.1	0.4	0.1	0.0	3.6
Tourism	40	30	20	10	7.1	5.3	3.5	1.8	17.7
Transport, logistics, warehousing and packaging	20	40	25	15	8.2	16.4	10.3	6.2	41.1
Unorganized sector	90	5	3	2	91.8	5.1	3.1	2.0	102.0
Total/average	**63**	**18**	**14**	**5**	**207.9**	**59.5**	**46.9**	**16.2**	**330.5**
"Annual numbers"					13.9	4.0	3.1	1.1	22.0

Note:

(a) Skill Levels:

Level 1: Skills that can be acquired with short/modular and focused intervention, enhancing employability of those with minimal education.

Level 2: Skills that require technical training, knowledge of complex operations and machinery, skills of supervision.

Level 3: Skills that require long drawn out preparation as demonstrated by acquisition of degrees and that involve highly technical or commercial operations.

Level 4: Skills that are highly specialized, involving research and design.

Source: National Skill Development Corporation; Kotak Institutional Equities research

Appendix 2: Those in the unorganized labour force are condemned to low incomes and very limited wealth accumulation

Calculations showing the financial evolution of two labourers: one in organized sector and the other in unorganized sector

	2010	2015	2020	2025	2030	2035
GDP (US$ bn)	1,366	1,984	2,743	3,848	4,911	6,267
GDP growth—real (%)		5.6	7.0	7.0	5.0	5.0
Total labour force (mn)	484	534	584	634	684	734
Organized sector share in GDP (%)	65.0	66.3	67.5	68.8	70.0	71.3
Unorganized sector share in GDP (%)	35.0	33.8	32.5	31.3	30.0	28.8
Organized sector share in employment (%)	10.5	10.5	10.5	10.5	10.5	10.5
Unorganized sector share in employment (%)	89.5	89.5	89.5	89.5	89.5	89.5
Organized market						
Portion of GDP (US$ bn)	888	1,314	1,852	2,645	3,437	4,465
Labour in organized market (mn)	51	56	61	67	72	77
Per-capita value add (US$)	17,476	23,438	30,197	39,735	47,861	57,940
Per-capita wages paid (US$)	6,117	8,203	10,569	13,907	16,751	20,279
Savings (US$)	1,529	2,051	2,642	3,477	4,188	5,070
Wealth—beginning (US$)		10,538	27,673	56,279	94,394	146,010
Return on wealth (US$)		648	2,030	4,061	4,824	7,427
Wealth—ending (US$)		13,236	32,345	63,817	103,407	158,507
Unorganized market						
Portion of GDP (US$ bn)	478	669	892	1,202	1,473	1,802
Labour in unorganized market (mn)	433	478	523	567	612	657
Per-capita value add (US$)	1,104	1,401	1,706	2,119	2,406	2,743
Per-capita wages paid (US$)	331	420	512	636	722	823
Savings (US$)	33	42	51	64	72	82
Wealth-beginning (US$)		223	571	1,132	1,851	2,792
Return on wealth (US$)		14	42	81	94	142
Wealth-ending (US$)		279	664	1,277	2,018	3,016
Share of labour						
Organized sector (%)	35					
Unorganized sector (%)	30					
Savings rate						
Organized sector (%)	25					
Unorganized sector (%)	10					

Source: Kotak Institutional Equities research

Appendix 3: The dietary requirement of India's 1.2 bn people is very varied

Food requirement over various age, gender and work categories, March fiscal year-ends, 2011

	Units	Total	Infants	1-3	4-6	7-9	10-12		13-15		16-18		Sedentary		Moderate		Heavy		Seniors/non-workers	
							Girls	Boys	Girls	Boys	Girls	Boys	Men	Women	Men	Women	Men	Women	Men	Women
Cereals and millets	mn tons	153.7	0.1	1.5	3.3	4.9	3.5	4.8	4.3	6.0	4.1	6.5	15.3	2.4	15.1	3.3	32.4	14.2	4.7	27.2
Pulses	mn tons	32.8	0.1	0.8	0.8	1.6	0.9	1.0	0.8	1.1	0.9	1.3	3.1	0.5	3.0	0.7	6.5	2.7	0.9	6.2
Milk and milk products (1 ton = 1,000 l)	mn tons	166.3	3.0	12.6	13.8	13.7	7.2	8.0	6.6	7.2	6.3	7.2	12.3	2.6	10.1	3.0	16.2	8.9	3.1	24.7
Roots and tubers	mn tons	72.9	0.4	1.3	2.8	2.7	1.4	1.6	1.3	2.2	2.5	2.9	8.2	1.8	6.7	2.0	10.8	5.9	2.1	16.5
Green leafy vegetables	mn tons	41.0	0.2	1.3	1.4	2.7	1.4	1.6	1.3	1.4	1.3	1.4	4.1	0.9	3.4	1.0	5.4	3.0	1.0	8.2
Other vegetables	mn tons	77.8	0.2	1.3	2.8	2.7	2.9	3.2	2.6	2.9	2.5	2.9	8.2	1.8	6.7	2.0	10.8	5.9	2.1	16.5
Fruits	mn tons	44.2	0.7	2.5	2.8	2.7	1.4	1.6	1.3	1.4	1.3	1.4	4.1	0.9	3.4	1.0	5.4	3.0	1.0	8.2
Sugar	mn tons	13.2	0.1	0.4	0.6	0.5	0.4	0.5	0.3	0.3	0.3	0.4	0.8	0.2	1.0	0.3	3.0	1.3	0.3	2.5
Fat	mn tons	13.6	0.1	0.6	0.7	0.8	0.5	0.6	0.5	0.6	0.4	0.7	1.0	0.2	1.0	0.2	2.2	0.9	0.3	2.1
Number of people	mn	1,210.6	20.3	68.8	75.4	75.2	39.5	43.7	36.0	39.5	34.4	39.4	112.0	24.0	92.0	27.0	148.0	81.0	28.8	225.8

Notes:

(a) We assume that people employed in agriculture, industry and services correspond directly to heavy, moderate and sedentary life-styles.

(b) Senior citizens and non-working people in general are assumed to require the diet of a moderate activity person.

Source: NIN; Census 2011; NSSO 68th round; Kotak Institutional Equities research

Appendix 4: India is expected to see a massive uptick in richer households

Distribution of Indian households by consumption expenditure, March fiscal year-ends, FY2012-25E

	2011	2012	2013	2014	2015E	2016E	2017E	2018E	2019E	2020E	2021E	2022E	2023E	2024E	2025E
Rural households (mn)															
Real-rich	–	–	–	–	–	–	–	–	–	–	–	–	–	–	–
Upper-class	–	–	–	–	–	–	–	–	–	–	–	–	–	–	–
Prospering	–	–	1	2	3	4	5	6	7	8	9	10	12	13	14
Evolving	11	18	18	18	21	23	26	29	31	34	38	43	47.1	51	57
Emerging	51	70	77	84	88	91	96	100	104	107	109	110	111	112	111
Surviving	106	82	77	71	64	58	52	46	40	35	30	25	20	16	12
Total	**169**	**170**	**172**	**174**	**175**	**177**	**179**	**181**	**183**	**184**	**186**	**188**	**190**	**192**	**194**
Urban households (mn)															
Real-rich	–	–	–	–	–	–	–	–	0	1	2	4	5	6	7
Upper-class	–	–	1	1	2	3	4	5	6	6	6	6	8	8	10
Prospering	6	9	9	10	12	14	16	18	21	25	29	33	36	41	45
Evolving	20	25	29	33	36	39	43	47	50	52	54	57	58	59	59
Emerging	38	40	41	41	41	41	39	35	32	29	26	23	19	16	13
Surviving	17	10	8	5	3	1	–	–	–	–	–	–	–	–	–
Total	**81**	**84**	**88**	**91**	**95**	**98**	**102**	**106**	**110**	**114**	**118**	**122**	**126**	**131**	**135**

Source: Kotak Institutional Equities research

Appendix 5: Understanding the RUPEES wallet

Proportion of annual expenditure-wallet spent on various categories on a per-capita basis

Proportion (%)	Real-rich	Upper-class	Prospering	Evolving	Emerging	Surviving
Food and beverages	15.0	20.0	30.0	40.0	45.0	50.0
Alcohol and tobacco	2.0	2.0	2.5	2.5	2.5	2.5
Clothing and footwear	4.5	4.5	4.5	5.0	5.0	7.0
Housing	17.0	17.0	15.0	12.0	11.0	7.5
Household goods	6.0	5.0	4.5	4.0	4.0	4.0
Healthcare	9.0	8.0	6.0	4.5	4.0	4.0
Transport	11.0	11.0	10.0	9.0	8.0	7.0
Communications	4.0	4.0	3.0	2.5	2.5	2.0
Leisure	6.0	6.0	5.0	4.0	3.0	2.0
Education	4.0	4.0	3.0	2.5	2.5	2.5
Hotels	5.0	4.5	4.0	3.5	2.5	2.0
Miscellaneous	16.5	14.0	12.5	10.5	10.0	9.5
Total	**100.0**	**100.0**	**100.0**	**100.0**	**100.0**	**100.0**
Average expenditure	*500,000*	*300,000*	*180,000*	*90,000*	*45,000*	*15,000*
In Rupees						
Food and beverages	75,000	60,000	54,000	36,000	20,250	7,500
Alcohol and tobacco	10,000	6,000	4,500	2,250	1,125	375
Clothing and footwear	22,500	13,500	8,100	4,500	2,250	1,050
Housing	85,000	51,000	27,000	10,800	4,950	1,125
Household goods	30,000	15,000	8,100	3,600	1,800	600
Healthcare	45,000	24,000	10,800	4,050	1,800	600
Transport	55,000	33,000	18,000	8,100	3,600	1,050
Communications	20,000	12,000	5,400	2,250	1,125	300
Leisure	30,000	18,000	9,000	3,600	1,350	300
Education	20,000	12,000	5,400	2,250	1,125	375
Hotels	25,000	13,500	7,200	3,150	1,125	300
Miscellaneous	82,500	42,000	22,500	9,450	4,500	1,425
Total	**500,000**	**300,000**	**180,000**	**90,000**	**45,000**	**15,000**

Source: Kotak Institutional Equities research

REFERENCES

OVER THE LAST five years that I have written the various pieces that have gone into making this book, I must have read hundreds of different papers, met with a large number of subject experts and ravaged through untold number of links on the vast expanse of the internet. The references that I mention here hence can only be illustrative as a large part of my learning and hence my writing is based on assimilating and absorbing a huge variety of information. Given that this book presents abridged but updated versions of the reports and articles that I have written there are many places in the book where the references that I mention below may not directly be relevant but have helped me think through the issue or explore it in greater detail.

I club references to a few sources up front as these have been the building blocks of my stories, reports and articles. These organizations, listed alphabetically, helped aggregate or create the data that is available on India:

1. 'Agricultural Statistics At a Glance'. Various editions of this report have been useful in getting data on Indian agriculture and its trends. Reports on this portal are a treasure trove of data (http://eands.dacnet. nic.in/latest_2006.htm, last accessed on 13 January 2015). Coupled with this, the other significant source of granular data on Indian agriculture is the Agricultural Census of India which is done once every five years. The latest version of 2011 can be accessed at http:// agcensus.nic.in/agcen201011.html (last accessed on 13 January 2015). The data, analysis and reports on the portal of the Commission on Agricultural Costs and Prices (CACP, http://cacp.dacnet.nic.in/

Last accessed on 13 January 2015) are also very helpful. The Food Corporation of India website (http://fciweb.nic.in/, last accessed on 13 January 2015) has readily accessible and frequently updated data on, among a variety of things, India's food stocks.

2. Bloomberg and CEIC. These are paid datasets that we use at Kotak and I have, in a few cases, taken data from these sources.

3. Census of India. I have extensively used data from the 2011 Census which is available at http://censusindia.gov.in/ (last accessed on 13 January 2015). Data from the 2001 Census is also available online at this portal. The Census data was helpful in collecting not just data on the numbers of our fellow-citizens but on their material well-being, their age distribution, their educational achievements, etc. The Census portal has enough data to keep a researcher awake and excited many a night.

4. Ministry of Finance's budget documents. Most of the government expenditure and tax collection data is collected from budget documents. Expenditure on education and on subsidies is calculated from the documents found at the portal http://indiabudget.nic.in/ last accessed on 13 January 2015). I have also referred to a couple of press releases from the Ministry of Finance.

5. The National Sample Survey Organization (NSSO) survey reports. I refer to various survey reports in this book: sixty-first, sixty-sixth, sixty-eighth and sixty-ninth feature most prominently as they refer to some of the latest and the most pertinent rounds for the purposes of this book. Even as I quibble about the quality of data that is available because of the low frequency of this data, the NSSO surveys remain one of the most detailed surveys conducted in India on various issues like employment, unemployment, consumption habits and quality of housing.

6. Planning Commission. The reports that Planning Commission, well, commissions, bring out are detailed and data-oriented. I have learnt significantly from the reports that have been kept on the portal at http://planningcommission.nic.in/ Last accessed on 13 January 2015). The portal also serves as a good place to pull out long-term trend line data.

7. Kotak Institutional Equities. My fellow colleagues produce outstanding

research which has consistently been rated as being amongst the best in India on, as we call it, the (Dalal) Street. Many of my datasets and a large component of my learnings come from discussions and debates with my colleagues.

8. Reserve Bank of India (RBI). The various long-term trend line series and data points released by RBI have been used across the various chapters where I look at India's or its states' GDP breakup, banking sector penetration, agricultural outputs, etc. RBI's (1) Database on Indian Economy and (2) Handbook of Statistics on Indian Economy have been the first ports of call on any data related to the Indian economy. These datasets are available online at RBI's website (www.rbi.org.in) and are frequently updated.

I now list some of the specific reports, articles and websites that have been helpful in my writing of this book:

All India Council for Technical Education, Report on intake by institutes. Available at: http://www.aicte-india.org/stinstitutes.php, last accessed on 14 December 2014.

All India School Education Survey (2008), *Eighth AISES*. Ministry of Human Resources Development. Available at: http://aises.nic.in/surveyoutputs, last accessed on 14 December 2014.

Angel, Shlomo, with Jason Parent, Daniel L. Civco and Alejandro M. Blei (2011), Making Room for a Planet of Cities (Policy Focus Report). Available at: http://www.lincolninst.edu/pubs/1880_Making-Room-for-a-Planet-of-Cities-urban-expansion, last accessed on 14 December 2014.

Annual Report of the Ministry of Labour and Employment in India (2014). Available at: http://labour.nic.in/content/reports/annual-report.php, last accessed on 14 December 2014.

Annual Report of the Ministry of Micro, Small and Medium Enterprises (2014). Available at: http://msme.gov.in/Web/Portal/AnnualReport-Msme.aspx, last accessed on 14 December 2014.

Annual Status of Education Report, 2013 (2014), ASER Center, all their reports are accessed from http://www.asercentre.org/Keywords/p/205.html, last accessed on 14 December 2014.

BCG-FICCI (2014), 'Indian Banking 2020: Making the Decade's Promise Come True'. Available at: http://www.iba.org.in/events/FICCI-Sep10.pdf, last accessed on 14 December 2014.

Bloom, David E., David Canning, Günther Fink and Jocelyn E. Finlay (2007), *Fertility, Female Labor Force Participation, and the Demographic Dividend*, Working Paper 13583, National Bureau of Economic Research Working Paper Series.

Built-Up Urban Areas or World Agglomerations (10th Annual Edition May 2014 Revision); Demographia World Urban Areas. Available at: http://www.demographia.com/db-worldua.pdf, last accessed on 14 December 2014.

Central Electricity Authority (2013), 'Report on Eighteenth Electric Power Survey of India'. Available at: www.cea.nic.in/reports/planning/dmlf/eps_mega.pdf, last accessed on 14 December 2014.

Central Pollution Control Board (2009), 'Status of Water Supply, Wastewater Generation and Treatment in Class-I Cities & Class-II Towns of India'. Available at: www.cpcb.nic.in/upload/NewItems/NewItem_153_Foreword.pdf, last accessed on 14 December 2014.

Cho, Man (2013), 'Managing Housing Market Volatility: Korean Case', Frontiers in Development Policy: Workshop on Innovative Development Case Studies, Presented at the World Bank Institute and KDI School Conference, Seoul, Korea, 21–22 November. Available at: https://www.kdevelopedia.org/resource/view/04201311140129002.do, last accessed on 14 December 2014.

Competition Commission of India (2012), 'Competitive assessment of onion markets in India'. Available at: http://www.cci.gov.in/images/media/completed/AO.pdf.

Export performances (2014), SEZ India. Available at: http://www.sezindia.nic.in/about-ep.asp, last accessed on 14 December 2014.

Ghani, Ejaz, Arti Grover Goswami and William R. Kerr (2012), 'Is India's Manufacturing Sector Moving Away from Cities?', World Bank report policy research working paper. Available at: http://documents.worldbank.org/curated/en/2012/11/17039474/indias-manufacturing-sector-moving-away-cities, last accessed on 14 December 2014.

ICRIER, working paper #286, 'Creating Jobs in India's Organised Manufacturing Sector,' by Radhicka Kapoor, September 2014.

Ministry of Chemicals and Fertilizers (2013), 'Indian Fertilizer Scenario', Department of Fertilizers. Available at: fert.nic.in/sites/default/files/Indian%20Fertilizer%20SCENARIO-2014.pdf, last accessed on 14 December 2014.

Indian Railway Catering and Tourism Corporation Limited, Annual reports, A Government of India enterprise. Available at: http://www.irctc.com/annual_report.html, last accessed on 14 December 2014.

Labour Bureau reports on wage rates in rural India. Available at: http://

labourbureau.nic.in/schemes.html, last accessed on 14 December 2014.

Mahatma Gandhi National Rural Employment Guarantee Act portal for NREGA MIS. Available at: http://www.nrega.nic.in/netnrega/home.aspx, last accessed on 14 December 2014.

McKinsey Global Institute (2010). *India's urban awakening: Building inclusive cities, sustaining economic growth.* Available at: http://www.mckinsey.com/insights/ urbanization/urban_awakening_in_india, last accessed on 14 December 2014.

Ministry of Housing and Poverty Alleviation (2012), 'Taskforce on promoting affordable housing'. Available at: mhupa.gov.in/W_new/AHTF%20 REPORT%2008_07_2013.pdf, last accessed on 14 December 2014.

Ministry of Road Transport and Highways (2011–12), Offices of State Transport Commissioners UT Administrations, 'Basic Road Statistics of India'. Available at: http://morth.nic.in/index2.asp?slid=314&sublinkid=142&lang=1, last accessed on 14 December 2014.

Ministry of Urban Development, 'Minimum set of standard performance parameters'. Available at: http://moud.gov.in/servicelevel, last accessed on 14 December 2014.

Mohanty, P.K. (2014), *Urbanisation in India: Challenges, Opportunities and the Way Forward* (see chapter on 'A Municipal Financing Framework'). Sage Publications.

Morris, Eric (2007), *From Horse Power to Horsepower.* University of California Transport Center. Available at: http://www.uctc.net/access/30/Access%20 30%20-%2002%20-%20Horse%20Power.pdf, last accessed on 14 December 2014.

National Bureau of Soil Survey and Land Use Planning (2005), Available at: http:// www.agricoop.nic.in/Nrm/STATNRM.pdf, last accessed on 14 December 2014.

National Institute of Nutrition (2010), *Dietary Guidelines for Indians: A manual.* Available at: ninindia.org/DietaryguidelinesforIndians-Finaldraft.pdf, last accessed on 14 December 2014.

National Skills Development Corporation reports on skill gaps in various industries. Available at: http://www.nsdcindia.org/nsdcreports, last accessed on 14 December 2014.

National Water Policy (2012), Ministry of Water Resources, Government of India. Available at: http://wrmin.nic.in/writereaddata/NationalWaterPolicy/ NWP2012Eng6495132651.pdf, last accessed on 14 December 2014.

New Zealand Quality Control Association (NZQA) portal at http://www.nzqa. govt.nz/, last accessed on 14 December 2014.

Planning Commission in India, 'Understanding Skill Development and Training in China: Lessons for India', Institute of Applied Manpower and Research in April 2014. Available at: http://planningcommission.gov.in/reports/genrep/rep_devch1104.pdf, last accessed on 14 December 2014.

Revision of the World Urbanization Prospects (2014). United Nations Department of Economic and Social Affairs (DESA). Available at: http://www.un.org/en/development/desa/publications/2014-revision-world-urbanization-prospects.html.

Ruiz-Mier, Fernando, Meike van Ginneken (2005), 'India's Water Economy—Bracing for a Turbulent Future'. Available at: http://documents.worldbank.org/curated/en/2008/06/16784682/indias-water-economy-bracing-turbulent-future, last accessed on 14 December 2014.

Sinha, Abraham and Vohra (2008), 'India's Demographic Dilemma, Talent Challenges for the Services Sector', a report by The Boston Consulting Group (BCG) and Confederation of Indian Industries (CII).

Soto, Hernando de (2000), *The mystery of capital: why capitalism triumphs in the West and fails everywhere else*. New York: Basic Books.

Statistical Yearbook for Asia and the Pacific (2013), The United Nations Economic and Social Commission for Asia and the Pacific (ESCAP). Available at: http://www.unescap.org/sites/default/files/D.1-Income-poverty-and-inequality.pdf, last accessed on 14 December 2014.

Statistics on India's income-tax e-filing are accessed under 'e-filing statistics' tab. Available at: https://incometaxindiaefiling.gov.in/, last accessed on 14 December 2014.

Sud, Surinder (2009), *The Changing Profile of Indian Agriculture*, Business Standard Books.

Telecom Regulatory Authority of India, Consultation Paper on 'Encouraging Telecom Equipment Manufacturing in India', 28 December 2010. Available at: http://www.trai.gov.in/WriteReaddata/ConsultationPaper/Document/consultaionpapertdradiv28dec10.pdf, last accessed on 14 December 2014.

Vocational and professional education and training in Switzerland—facts and figures (2014). Available at: http://www.berufsbildungplus.ch/de/startseite/international.html, last accessed on 14 December 2014.

Wilbur Smith Associates, Ministry of Urban Development (2008), *Study on Traffic and Transportation Policies and Strategies in Urban Areas in India*. Available at: https://casi.sas.upenn.edu/sites/casi.sas.upenn.edu/files/iit/GOI%202008%20Traffic%20Study.pdf, last accessed on 14 December 2014.

ACKNOWLEDGEMENTS

The book that you now see has evolved over the course of the last five years: a period of time when Kotak Institutional Equities (KIE) decided to invest its time and resources in someone who had been a consultant, a financial analyst and an entrepreneur to become an observer of India. The idea of having on board a thematic analyst was to give to our clients an overall macro view of what is happening in India and more important, given the trends that we were observing, to formulate our thoughts on what could happen. In the list of people who need to be acknowledged first, it has be the senior management team of Ravi Iyer and Sanjeev Prasad that believed in the product and nurtured the GameChanger product as we called it.

The Kotak group was more than forthcoming in championing and pushing forth with the idea that our learnings and knowledge gained over the last half-a-decade be penned into a book. Uday Kotak and C Jayaram owned the idea of making this book possible and Karthi Marshan and his entire marketing team took it upon themselves to make it a success. I would hazard to think that this commitment by the senior-most team at Kotak is what gave Kapish Mehra of Rupa and his team the comfort of taking on the risk of working with a first-time author. I must mention here the generous help that my friend Raghavendra Singh has continued to offer since we first met four years ago—no door remains closed when Raghu knocks on it.

The GameChanger product would have remained another research idea and not turned into the brand that it has if it were not for Merle

Almeida who took it upon herself to make the product look very appealing both on the language and visual fronts. Her amazing ability to convert what an analyst says to what a creative person would understand would make for such fascinating covers of the report that the audience would be compelled to pick it up and at least glance at it. The many designers of the GameChanger covers, I must attribute a large part of the credit of why the GameChanger series were read to you.

My colleagues have been very helpful in providing insights into their sectors and industries. My knowledge and understanding of the various facets of India's corporate sector and policymaking came from my varied and constant interactions with them over the course of many cups of cutting-chai and joint-reports. In no particular order, I would like to thank Kawaljeet Saluja, Sandeep Bhatia, Lokesh Garg, Rohit Chordia, MB Mahesh, Nischint Chawate and Suvodeep Rakshit for all their ideas and insights.

One of the joys of working at KIE is that one interacts with some of the best brains in the investment industry as our clients. Their ability to look at the analysis presented to them and distil it into ideas that would make their ultimate investor's money has kept the excitement and pressure on all of us to perform. I am also thankful to them that they have patiently listened to—and encouraged—the long-term nature of work that GameChanger offered to them. The other set of people who deserve heart-felt gratitude are promoters and senior executives at the various companies that I would harangue to understand their sectors and companies. For someone who would one quarter look at companies in the water sector and work on mobile money in the next, the incredible help and support that I received from them is simply unparalleled. For sake of propriety, I will desist from naming anyone specific here.

Many of my friends and well-wishers have suffered reading the initial manuscript and offered very constructive suggestions on it. There are many aspects of this book that have benefitted from the wise and practical suggestions made by them. In no particular order, I would like to thank Ireena Vittal, Sanjay Pugalia, Vivek Kaul, Ankita Srivastava, Amar Choudhary, Abhijeet Awasthi and Vijay Dhanuka. Their varied and diverse perspectives helped give this book substance, making it become a story and a narrative rather than just a compilation of an analyst's reports.

I must also commend here my heart-felt gratitude to my previous employer, The Boston Consulting Group. They instilled in me the critical thinking and the big-picture view that I am now able to bring to the table. Specifically, I would like to thank Abheek Singhi who took time out to explain to me the nuances of book publishing and marketing. My countless teachers across some of the best schools that India has to offer helped me reach where I am today—a big thank you to you all.

Last but not the least, I cannot but not thank my family. I have gone job-hopping and career-hopping and exploring various nooks and crannies of what I like doing and what I don't and I can always count on my parents, Mohanlal and Sushila, my parents-in laws, Girdhar and Shobha and wife Nikita to be there to back me up. Having written research over so many years, I assumed writing a book will be as easy as cutting and pasting the earlier reports. As the reality of the book as a project dawned on me, they steadfastly remained committed to my late nights and working weekends at office. My six-year-old daughter Kanak has been patiently waiting for those weekends to come back when we went swimming together. I do hope when she reads this book a few years later, she finds that I have helped her make some sense of the various tumults that our generation is going through. I also hope that makes up for the time that we could not spend together.

INDEX

Green Revolution, 68, 125–126, 134,
137, 147, 206, *see also* agriculture
gross value added (GVA), 20, 37
groundwater irrigation, 141
Gujarat International Finance Tec-City
(GIFT), 95

hackers, 180
high-density urban phenomenon, 91
'high value engineering', 71
higher education, 27, 35–36, 41, 209
hire-and-fire rules, 38, 49, *see also*
temporary labour
housing capacity, development of,
119–120
hybridization, 136–137
hypocrisy, 5

illiteracy, 13, 176
imports, 4, 52, 54–62, 67–71, 78, 127,
138, 147, 190, 212
inclusive development story, 198
income distribution, inequality of,
185–186, 214–216
India Millennium Deposits, 54
Indian Council of Agricultural Research,
137
Indian Institute of Management, 36
Indian Meteorological Department
(IMD), 142
industrialization, 15–16, 56, 131
infant mortalities, 24
inflation, 9, 11, 36, 57, 67, 127–128, 190
inflow and outflow of dollars, 58–60
internal remittances market, 167
internet banking, 166
IRCTC, 153, 176
IT revolution, 57
IT services industry, 54, 68
ITI, 42, 44, 47–49

Jawaharlal Nehru Urban Renewal
Mission (JNNURM), 115, 182

job growth, 23
jobless growth, 34
judicial records, 165

Karnataka's Bhoomi model, 157–158
know-your-client (KYC), 172, 175, 178

Labour Bureau, 34
labour-dependent rural jobs, 41
labour force
elasticity, 30
participants, 25
participation by women, 24
participation rate (LFPR), 31
productivity, 39
rise in, 22
labour intensity
manufacturing, 75
production, 40
labour-intensive employment, 32, 66
labour-intensive industry, 66
labour market, 18, 21, 24, 30, 32, 34–35,
38, 41, 46, 211
labour protection, 74
land acquisition, 15, 64, 72, 102–103,
140, 154, 178, 205, 210
land auctions, 116
land fragmentation, 121, 130
land record, 154, 158–159, 216
Land Titling Bill, 156
landholding, 130
life expectancy, 17, 24–26, 110
low-cost housing, 99, 120
low-end skill development, 42
LPG gas cylinder, 153–154
subsidy on, 163

Mahatma Gandhi National Employment
Guarantee Scheme (MGNREGS),
141
manufacture hub, 4
marginalized farmers, 10
market-oriented reforms, 204